and GOD created MaNChESTeR

SARAH CHAMPION

Photography
IAN T TILTON

WORDSMITH

British Library Cataloguing in Publication Data
Champion, Sarah
    And God Created Manchester
       1. Greater Manchester (Metropolitan County),
         Manchester. Rock Music
    I. Title II. Tilton, Ian
    781.660942733

ISBN 1-873205-01-5

First published 1990
WORDSMITH, Progress House, Charlton Place,
Ardwick Green, Manchester M12 6HS.

Design and production: **WORDS**MITH.

Cover design: Tandem Design & Illustration,
23 New Mount Street, Manchester M4 4DE.
Cover illustration: Robin Whyler.

Print: H Shanley (Printers) Ltd,
16 Belvoir Street, Tonge Fold, Bolton BL2 6BA.

©Sarah Champion, 1990
©Ian T Tilton, 1985-1990

All rights reserved. No part of this publication may be
reproduced, stored in a retrieval system, or
transmitted, in any form or by any means, electronic,
mechanical, photocopying, recording or otherwise,
without the prior permission of the publishers.

For Mum, Dad, Phil

For loyalty, inspiration, patience:
Jon Ronson, Mike West, Paul Robinson, Paula Greenwood, Ian Runacres, Ian T Tilton.

AcknowledGements

Thanks for help, ideas, breaks, time:
Alison Martin, Steve Barker, Dave Haslam, Greg Wilson, John Robb, Mandi James, Phil Jones, Tim Chambers, Guy Lovelady, Steve Harrison & The Charlatans, Gareth Evans & the Roses, Graham Massey, Tony Michaelides, Dean Johnson, Bruce Mitchell, Martine & James, Andy McQueen, Kenny, Eastern Bloc, Leo at Identity, Dave Booth, Colin Sinclair, Chad Jackson, Tib Street Barber, Gina Morris, Mike Shaft, Andy Spinoza, World Of Twist, Bob Dickinson, Steve Redhead ...
and Niall Allsop and Freya Rodger of **WORDS**MITH.

In the BeGinninG ...   9

Contents

1. WhY Manchester   11
All routes lead to the capital of The North

2. Last Exit to Manchester   13
A guided tour to musical Manchester.

3. Smithsmania   21
The cult legend of The Smiths.

4. DoomsdaY PaY-Off   27
The Fall, longest surviving, most prolific Manc band.

5. KinGs of the Slums   33
Inspiration for many, inner-city Hulme.

6. WhistlinG in the Dark   41
Indie music's DIY dream.

7. Manchester La La La   47
Pale-faced pop bands for pale-faced pop-kids.

8. Wheels of Steel   53
Manchester's electro/breakdance scene.

9. On the Groove Train   61
Rap and house - descendants of Northern Soul.

10. Move over TonY ...   67
The blossoming of Manchester's indie/media scene.

11. SPiral Bound   79
Inspiral Carpets, Transit-vanners made good.

12. A VillaGe HYmn   97
James, intelligent pop amid brain-dead scallidom.

13. ParlY PeoPle   105
Happy Mondays, mad-cap crazies that myths are made of.

14. Acid to EcstacY   111
A cultural revolution of hedonistic partying and illegal raves.

15. SomethinG's BurninG   121
Stone Roses, what the world is waiting for?

16 ScallYdelia   131
A fashion concept that grew from the underground.

17. Into the 90s   137
The next Big Thing.

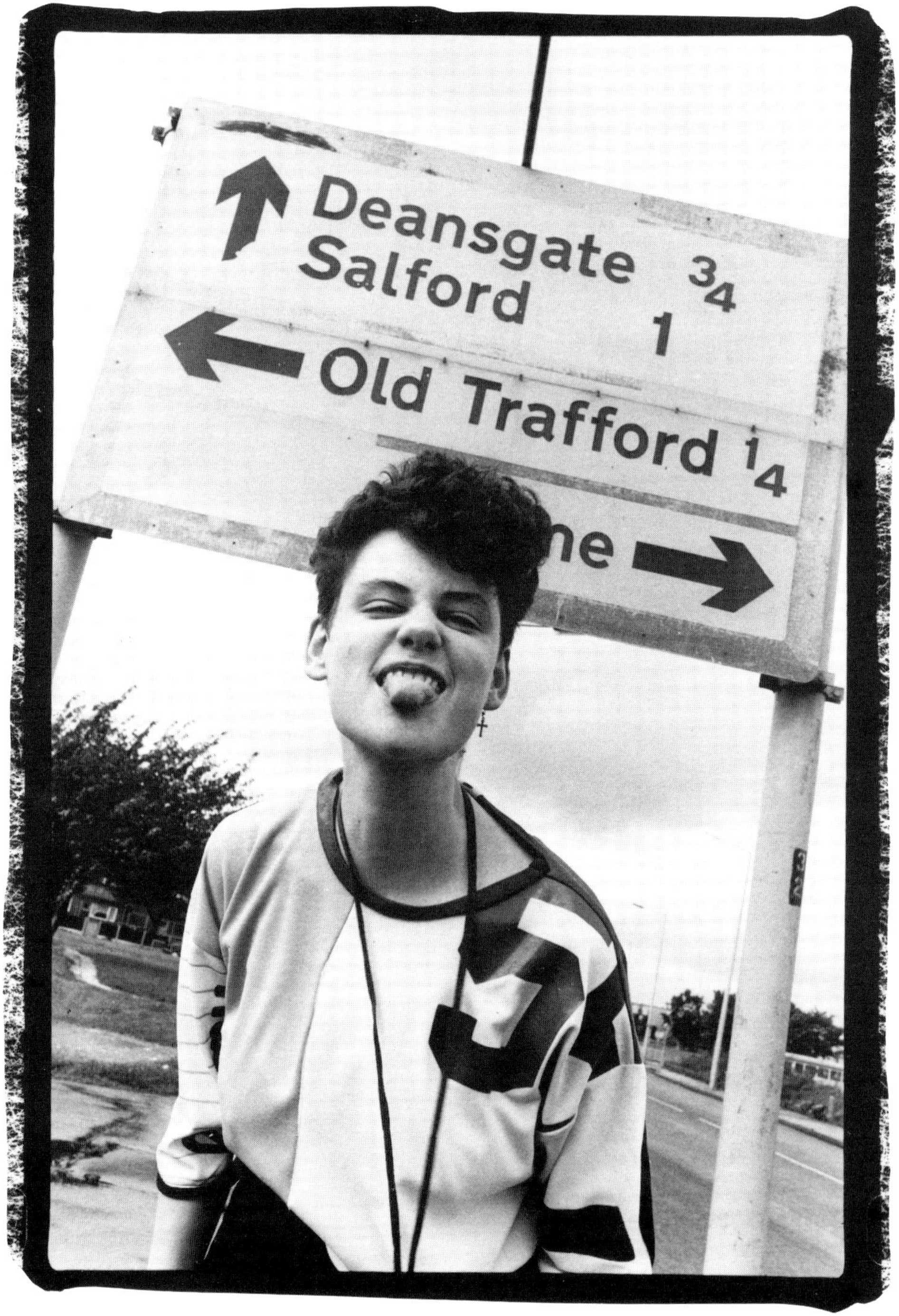
Deansgate 3/4
Salford 1
Old Trafford 1/4

In the 60s the first multi-coloured, day-glo hippie bus started a magical mystery tour across America packed with the original acid-heads. Its destination plate read 'Further'. By the 70s the hippie dream had turned into The Great Rock 'n' Roll Swindle and the only buses out of conformity-city were going 'Nowhere'. At the end of the 80s the world's youth was looking in only one direction, 'MANCHESTER'. The *only* place to be!

In the BeGinninG ...

And God Created Manchester

Welcome to the land of rain. Get your hair cut, form a band, buy some flares, ride the hype, drive borrowed cars at a crazy hundred miles-an-hour. Hooded-tops, house raves, rap crews, football, guitar bands, scallydelia, Morrissey clones, fanzines, indie labels, gay clubs, Ecstasy, pub-rock, street poetry, Victorian architecture.

This is Manchester, homeland of some mad, mad, mad fuckers, have *you* got the stamina to survive?

From the terraces to the nightclubs, Mancunians love their city. The slogans start here. 'Born In The North, Return To The North, Die In The North', a favourite T-shirt worn by Mancunians whenever they're in The South. A slogan that says all that's good and bad about Manchester pride. Northern Pride. British pride. Patriotism. Flag waving. Chanting. Football. This book. *Singing Rule Britannia As The Walls Cave In* (as The Chameleons put it). Positive thinking or just brain-dead behaviour?

The rainy city ruled by *Coronation Street* and The Haçienda. So go the clichés. Built in an industrial revolution; painted grey by Joy Division, red by Mick Hucknall and blue by Man City. Morrissey opened up a misery dictionary, while Happy Mondays nick-named it *Madchester*.

At the end of the 80s Manchester's scruffy off-spring became national pop stars. Truth and hype became rapidly confused, so that soon even the city's kids lost track of reality. Suddenly, it was not just Mancunians themselves hyping their home town, but music mags, Sunday supplements and tabloid trash!

OPPOSITE
Sarah Champion, St Georges, Hulme, September, 1990.

Yet all the hype told only ten per cent of the story. Many veterans of the scene were left behind like unlucky prospectors after The Gold Rush. What the hell was there they could do about it?
This is the reality.
There is more to Manchester clubland than The Haçienda. Dry 201 is not the only place to buy a drink. Happy Mondays used to be really unhip. Stone Roses used to be crap. 808 State are a bedroom band. Factory is only one of 20 Manchester record labels. So there? Tell it as you might, the media really wouldn't listen, happy sucking-off Tony Wilson.
This book tells more of the story, or as much of it as can be written in 50,000 words. It's about the people who made the scene, the people left behind and the people who will never be forgotten.

And God Created Manchester is about Manchester, but not about Joy Division, The Electric Circus, John Cooper Clarke, The Distractions, The Smirks, Jilted John, Buzzcocks, Jon The Postman, Slaughter And The Dogs or The Worst!!! Another volume maybe. Neither is it about 10CC, Herman's Hermits, Freddie And The Dreamers, Wayne Fontana, The Hollies. No, this book starts around 85. It's about the 80s one-way trip, when kids, who'd never even heard of punk, pushed a new, hedonistic self-destruct button.

And God Created Manchester is a pretty Biblical title, but this is the most Holy of places. Make the Pilgrimage now!
This book is for those who've lived here through good and bad; for the day-trippers who have been, seen and gone away again; for those who will visit in the future; and also for those who may never have the opportunity.
Inevitably, books about Manchester music have told a story that is black and white: facts and figures, dates, releases, chart entries. But pop music is *more* than names and numbers. It's emotional, inspirational, spiritual, crazy.

And God Created Manchester is bright, multi-coloured, kaleidoscopic. It fucks facts in search of more lurid, wilder, dafter glimpses of what music is *really* about!

And God Created Manchester is not parochial for, when the lights go up, the music stops, your head caves in and you're alone in your room, a record collection and a sense of place may be all you have left to cling to.

Manchester sounds, clubs and fashions are a vision to live and die for. Almost a religion. This book catalogues fragments of the dream.
Rave on! Rave on!

Sarah Champion
Manchester, August 1990

Why? Why? Why? Why? All these journalists storming in and out of Manchester asking 'Why?': *Newsbeat*, *New York Times*, *The Sun*, *Daily Mail*, *The Observer*, Radio Four, BBC World Service, Soviet National TV. All of them trying to catch the swing; trying to figure out what they're missing. Can't they see? Can't they taste? Can't they feel it? It's in the air, the water and the architecture!

061 WhY Manchester?

1   And God Created Manchester

Why Manchester? 'Cos cool kids from across the globe move here year after year to start bands. 'Cos it's the Capital of The North, sucking up talent from Merseyside, Lancashire and Cheshire. 'Cos of venues, like The Boardwalk, unafraid to showcase new 'local' acts; 'cos local newspapers document future heros; 'cos Manc entrepreneurs risk cash putting out 'unknown' bands.

Why Manchester? Simply because there are hundreds of people out there doing their own thing. Clubs, venues, pluggers, labels, radio shows, record shops, T-shirt printers, clothes designers, rehearsal rooms, fanzines ... Manchester's success is borne of years of graft, thousands of bands, tens of indie record companies, hundreds of failures. Think of it this way. It took Stone Roses, Happy Mondays, James and Inspiral Carpets a collective 160 years in the music biz before their first Top 40 hits. Overnight sensations? Applications to Manchester's University and Polytechnic rose by around 30% at the beginning of 1990. The Manchester myth. Leave home, go North, get your hair cut, get some flares, form a band, get rich. Then worry about the music! A myth that's very 'punk' in its ideals. Kids moved to Manchester to wear raincoats, to be punks, to read Oscar Wilde, to dance at raves. The words and tunes came last.

Teenage angst. Teenage dreams. Teenage bands. Hip kids, intellectual kids, brainy kids, stupid kids, musical kids. Leaving home. Leaving jobs. Leaving parents. Leaving girlfriends and boyfriends. Leaving school. Teenage runaways with their hearts set on

Manchester where the streets are paved with rock 'n' roll. A land of possibilities where forming a band can bring instant fame.
79-84: Miserable young men in raincoats worshipping Joy Division from bedsit hell.
84-87: Camp kids with quiffs, Oscar Wilde books under their arms.
88-91: Clubs smiling with drugs, shops full of hooded-tops, psychedelic guitar pop. A continual cycle of new faces, fresh vibes, eager pop consumers.
Pack your rucksack, leave a goodbye note and head to The North.
Looking back to 78: "When I was 18, I packed in my job and moved to Manchester for life on the dole because I was into Buzzcocks' SPIRAL SCRATCH EP and Birmingham was full of glam rock. Within weeks I was starting a band ..." Ian Runacres, who joined Dislocation Dance, a soul/jazz band favoured by Morrissey.
Looking back to when there was no Affleck's, no Eastern Bloc. Nothing but Virgin Records where youthful Mick Hucknall, Johnny Marr et al would pin up band ads to entice new arrivals: " I auditioned Mike Joyce," says Ian, "His record collection was out of its sleeves all over the floor and he had Elvis all over his wall. He was crap!"
Looking back to 85: Manc pop no-man's land. Punk with attitude, John Robb left his home town, Blackpool, for Manchester. "Where else was there? Only Liverpool where you get hassled if you have a funny accent and students and locals don't mix ..."
Looking back to 86: When the shamble-pop, jangly la-la-la scene had a grip of NME, Mike West of The Man From Delmonte. "At the age of 22 I'd never been to a nightclub and had only seen four live bands, John Miles, Girlschool. I'd never heard of New Order, but then I saw Tony Wilson on TV being interviewed in the bath ..." He packed in art school and moved immediately, an itinerant scruff-bag, born on the move between Australia, Italy and New York.
Looking back to 87: Not from The North or The South ... even further afield the Manc influence was shaping people's lives. From small-minded, small-town New England USA, Muffin of The Exuberants flew in to Ringway to form a band. She was only 19.
"Where else could I go? There's nowhere in the world. All the bands I liked best came from Manchester. James, Buzzcocks, The Fall. From the age of 14 I read Melody Maker. I'm surprised I wasn't disappointed, having spent years and years of high school, thinking, 'My God, I've got to get to Manchester!' Everything I thought was good about being in a band has been ..."

Looking forward to 91: Pack this book in your rucksack and take The Last Exit To Manchester. It could be the decision of your life.

So much to answer for. Day-trippers, sightseers, tourists, ravers, rovers, adventurers, scallys, pop-kids, fugitives; all pouring into town. Manchester.

Last Exit to Manchester

And God Created Manchester

Madchester. Mcr. Capital of The North. Where do you begin? For all the A-Zs, street plans, tourist guidebooks, visitors' maps, none point out musical landmarks. There's no signpost outside Piccadilly Station saying 'Manchester Scene: This Way'. No guided tours, no easy route in. Your guided tour starts here. Savour the vibes!

"I love it all, music, fashion, everything," says Manc Leo Stanley of Identity. "A guy was saying to me, he'd driven up from Newark to see Inspirals at G-Mex. Driving up the motorway, he said that as soon as they hit Princess Parkway they could *feel* the buzz! It was really uncanny. As for Identity, I just wanted to take money away from London. The South have politically and financially raped the North of England."

Some Manchester folklore. A cultural, social and financial line divides North and South. The North is a wasteland. Skint. Poor. Unruly. Dirty. Problem families. Scruffy kids. Badly educated. Politically stupid. Pig ignorant. As for The South. It's posh. Arty. Intellectual. Nice. Clean. Respectable.

Nah, we're not talking about Britain's over-hyped North-South Divide here. More the invisible barrier cutting-up Manchester. One side studenty: the other scummy. Traditionally, the Southside has got rich, while Salford and the Northside has remained a wasteland of naff estates peopled by dole-kids, junkies and production-line workers. So goes the myth. The myth that inspired the band Northside!

"Well, there's Manchester, and there's South Manchester," Shaun Ryder of Happy Mondays once pointed out, comparing old Salford haunts to his new, 'posher' Didsbury residence.

"North and South Manchester are like different countries, different worlds," smirked teenage indie-DJ, Tin Tin, in his Blackley high-rise. "Living well in

North Manchester is 'ard. You have to make friends with the right people."

Pop-wise, the divide was always just as sharp. Like London rules Britain, Manchester music is governed by The Southside. The few square miles of Rusholme, Whalley Range, Didsbury, Hulme and Chorlton are home for most of the students, journos, record labels, managers, people in power. The Northside begets only odd, ugly, uncouth and totally working-class divs like The Fall or John Cooper Clarke. A state of imbalance in the 80s; right up till the rise of scally pop when the scum-side image of Mondays, Northside and Paris Angels was romanticised.

Happy Mondays' second LP, *BUMMED*, slouches into life with *Country Song*. 'I'm a simple city boy, with simple country tastes/Smoking wild-grown mari-jo-ana keeps that smile on my face/Depending on my mood, mood, mood, mood, mood/Listening to my system, just the other night/Watching my TV with the sound turned down/checking out the late, late, late, late night Fight Night ...' As much a document of North Manc lifestyle, as *This Charming Man* was to South Manchester.

Salford roots is a legacy the Mondays share with Tony Wilson, Albert Finney, Graham Nash, Alistair Cooke, Mark E Smith and John Cooper Clarke. Salford, forgotten city. In 88, *NME* photographer, Kevin Cummins, had an exhibition, *Salfordians,* at the Viewpoint Gallery featuring the above. "In Salford," he told *City Life*, "People have an attitude where people will say, 'You're from Manchester,' and they'll say 'No, I'm from Salford,' and are quite proud of the fact they're from there. But a lot of people are also proud to get out of what is is quite solidly a working-class area with not very attractive housing. Why should you live somewhere all your life, just because you were born there?"

Kevin photographed Hilda Ogden, fictional Salfordian. "I met Jean Alexander at Granada reception dressed as Hilda and drove her here. It was wonderful because she'd never be seen in the streets dressed like that. And when we got out these three blokes working on the site over there did a double take. They couldn't believe it - Hilda Ogden got out! It's almost like a cartoon character coming to life."

Shaun Ryder told Merseyside fanzine *Get Out*, "We had to move out of Salford and down to South Manchester. Go with the trendiest. But it's a nice, easier way of life, it's more peaceful. You go out and feel like a student, you know. We kept annoying shopkeepers at first 'cos they talk to you a bit like a dick, you know, you're a stewdie. Got nowt against stewdies, but I don't like being classed as one."

"All our mates now say like, 'Let's get moving Southside.'" sniggered Bez.

To experience South Manchester, take a forty-something bus outta town down Oxford Road. For every hundred feet you burn, a thousand rock 'n' roll tales. Everyone from New Order to The Fall must have spewed up here sometime or other. Walk the pavement. Feel those vibes! Burning up through your sneakers like hydrochloric acid. Kiss the concrete, 'cos you've just found *home*!

Coming from St Peter's Square, on your left The Tropicana where Chad Jackson mixed and many a hip-hop jam was held. A few feet further on Jilly's Rock Club, formerly Rafters, where Buzzcocks, Costello, Bauhaus, Magazine performed in 78 and Granada TV filmed *So It Goes*. Easterhouse, Happy Mondays and The Weeds all squeezed in for old-time's sake during The Festival Of The Tenth Summer 86. Next door, Fagins, ex-venue which saw the Some Bizzare Tour with Depêche Mode and Soft Cell in 80. Now used only for comedy events, stag parties and girls-nights-out, all 'tashes and white shoes. Still on your left, the Palace Theatre, heavily trashed by Smiths' fanatics in 85.

Cornerhouse, at the crossroads of Oxford Road and Whitworth Street, is a kind of ICA-MCR. Trendy cinemas, trendy bookshop, trendy café, trendy bar and, ironically, of least importance, trendy galleries. Until Dry 201 opened, the trendiest bar in town.

On down Oxford Road, past the Refuge Building, past the BBC, now well into studentville: the Poly Union; veggie café, On The Eighth Day; Johnny Roadhouse's second-hand instrument shop; A1 Music; Pandemonium Records; the Royal Northern College Of Music. Punky-poet, John Cooper Clarke, had a poem about Oxford Road, rhymed it with 'commode'! Clarke had a rant for every street in town, notably *Beasley Street*, the rubbish bin of Gorton, East Manchester, homeland of Roses' Reni.

OPPOSITE
Haçienda queue, 1985.

OPPOSITE
Hulme, September, 1990;
Salford, August 1990;
G-Mex, July 1986.

Further on, the University Union where 'stewdies' rioted in 85, protesting against Leon Brittan. Later, stewdie Steven Shaw (and others) claimed to have been beaten up and burgled by Manc cops, hence the book *With Extreme Prejudice*.

Rusholme is next, fave with Smiths devotees due to *Rusholme Ruffians*. A golden mile of Indian shops and restaurants, with some of the most volcanic curries in The North. Trendy music-biz-types eat at the Tandoori Kitchen where Asian scally/house act, Social Kaos, wait on tables.

Rusholme's Dickenson Road has plenty of pop history. In 64, a converted church became *Top Of The Pops*' first studio. Roses' Mani lived in the area, to be close to the International Club which, guided by veteran Roger Eagle, opened on April 23, 85. His claims-to-fame: promoting The Twisted Wheel and the 60s 'happening', Magic Village; staging Bunnymen, Wah and Holly Johnson at Liverpool's Erics in the 70s.

Eagle was (and always has been) a huge fan of blues/world music. He often guests on Radio Lancashire, Piccadilly and KFM as 'Jukebox Johnson', spinning rare R&B. He was intent on creating a pub-style 'old' venue. "There are lots of people of 40 who like music. Why should they be excluded because they haven't got enough hair to have the right hair-styles," he told *City Life*. The concept? Pub prices, cheap door prices and an early finish to lure people with kids/day jobs. "I hate all this pretentious drivel, bands seem to have forgotten they're here to entertain. I want people to come here instead of going to the pictures."

Eventually The International was run by Matthew Cummins and Gareth Evans who gave their band, Stone Roses, regular Friday night slots. Sister hell-hole, International 2 (formerly the Carousel Club on Plymouth Grove), led to even more classic gigs. Duran Duran in November 88; the Stone Roses/James anti-Clause 28 Benefit; Public Enemy. In 1990 it dropped its reggae shows after a drugs shoot-out and both clubs were sold to local money-man, Paul Coombes.

Back on the main road (now Wilmslow Road). On the right Platt Fields where Morrissey had his photo taken as a kid. It later appeared on the cover of *Last Of The Famous International Playboys*. Platt Fields was the site for historic free gigs in 85 and 87, paid for by the council. The first featured *everyone*: Simply Red, James, ACR, Jazz Defektors, Kalima, The Creepers, Yargo, Big Flame, Easterhouse, Laugh. Two years later a youthful Happy Mondays, Dub Sex and The Man From Delmonte were swept away in a storm with just a handful of ardent followers.

Wilmslow Road eventually hits Withington and Didsbury, the epitome of South Manchester. Birthplace of the Factory Empire which set up in a bedroom on Palatine Road. Tim Booth of James and their manager, Martine, lived just across the landing. Bruce Mitchell, Vini Reilly, Tony Wilson and various Fac minions all live within a few yards of each other to this day. *This* is respectable Manchester!

"I've been everywhere and lived everywhere, but I still ended up buying a house a quarter of a mile from where I was born," laughs Bruce. "Factory's caretaker looks after my garden."

The Didsbury Set. Horrid notion at the heart of things in the early 80s. Coffee-tables, jazz, polo-necks. Grown-up, sophisticated 'acts' like Kalima. Charity shops. Veggie cafés. Herbal medicine. Burton Road with its hippie boutiques like Gazebo selling silk scarves, CND earrings, pot plants. Diluted alternative culture. The 60s' hippies, grew up, went to teacher training college, became Guardian-reader clichés. Then came Green-living/Yuppies/Thirtysomething and a whole new generation bought the same old crap. Revolution never meant more than incense, wicker baskets and piles of ethnic nicknacks.

Three-plus miles away in Chorlton, you could visit Keppel Road where (snigger) The Bee Gees grew up. Pop sightseers should pop into Safeways hypermarket on Wilbraham Road. It's a well known fact that *all* the stars shop here. Everybody from *Coronation Street* celebs to Man Utd players. Mick Hucknall spent most of 85-87 waiting to be recognised near the vegetable counter. The Stone Roses have been regulars here, especially Ian Brown who lives a two minute stroll away.

Safeways is about half-a-mile from Cosgrove Hall, headquarters of the animation company for whom John Squire used to work. Their blockbusters have included *Dangermouse*, *Wind In The Willows* and the trippy *Chorlton And The Wheelies*! Chorlton is crammed with Roses' connections. Reni used to be

a 'female' kissagram for Livewires on Stockton Road. Just 100 yards away, they recorded an 8-track demo at Adventure Studios in 87 on which their debut album was based.

The Smiths, Easterhouse, Carmel and The Colourfield all used rehearsal rooms behind a second-hand TV warehouse on Barlow Moor Road. Not very far from The Oaks pub, notorious punk venue that saw the likes of The Banshees. Heading back to town, Whalley Range, bedsit-land vital in The Smiths' formative years. Manchester's feeble attempt at a Red Light district. No sex shops, strip-joints, just a few scummy business execs prowling the roadside. On to Moss Side. Home to MC Tunes, Yargo and A Guy Called Gerald. Burnt by riots in 81, a drug war rages and it has the scuzziest shopping precinct in town ... home to smart reggae shop/sound-system, Baron, and new 'community' recording studio, Fourbeat. A lively reggae scene brought bands like Exodus, Harlem Spirit and T-Dynamix, kicking around venues like the West Indian Sports & Social Club and Band On The Wall, going overground for the annual Moss Side Carnival in Alexandra Park.

Cue a Yargo song full of inner-city clichés. 'Pub crawlers and kerb crawlers, out on the street/Drug pushers and ponces, fugitives from the heat/Hustlers and scufflers and junkies and jakes/And muggers and burglars and posers and fakes/And each of them hoping, they'll get the breaks ...' *Another Moss Side Night* on Yargo's *BODYBEAT* album was a poem by local Kevin Qtoo, first published in the arty Chorlton fanzine *Fly*.

Weirder, blacker, freakier was Barry Adamson's *MOSS SIDE STORY* (Mute) released in 89. After a decade playing bass with Magazine and then Nick Cave And The Bad Seeds, Barry was returning to his Moss Side roots for some pretentious self-indulgence. A movie on record, *MOSS SIDE STORY* was the moody, atmospheric soundtrack to a film existing only in Barry's head! A 'provocative', instrumental thriller, subtitled, 'In a black and white world, murder brings a touch of colour ...' Glimpsing frames of 60s' Moss, back-to-back houses and sinister strangers. *Snub TV* shot a five-minute version.

Suburban South Manchester. Trekking further. Out beyond the city limits ... leafy Cheshire.

Rural apathy, wealthy commuters, big posh houses, would-be Sloanes. The Cheshire Set. Slagged off by The Creepers on their album *ROCK 'N' ROLL LIQUORICE FLAVOUR* (Intape). Wilmslow, Alderley Edge, Whaley Bridge, Knutsford ... could this be the Home Counties? It's the setting for Granada TV's *Neighbours*-style 90s' soap, *Families*. Struggling to be trendy, the show's younger characters sported MADCHESTER shirts and purple hooded-tops and all trooped off to see Happy Mondays at G-Mex!

Stockport is the capital of Cheshire. Chainstore city! Shopping malls, bland, bland, bland. Lots of people called Craig. Home of Strawberry Studios, created by 10CC in 68: used by everyone from Paul McCartney to Joy Division. Stockport, home of KFM pirate, now legal, radio. Also The Cheaters, What?Noise, Rig, Cut Deep Records and a second-hand bookshop in Upperbank, owned by journo Paul Morley and then Joe Moss, The Smiths' first manager. Frankie Vaughan, high-kicking 60s' idol, once lost a bet and recorded *Stockport! Stockport!* (That's Entertainment Records), a version of Sinatra's *New York! New York!*

Stockport was a joke, Manchester even more so. People laughed when it was proposed that Manchester bid for the Olympics! Cotton mills, factories, tumble-down textile warehouses, Manchester always had that *grey* image. Fuelled by miserabilists, rain, raincoats, doomy Victorian architecture, Joy Division and The Smiths.

A city that inspired Karl Marx; where Dalton and Rutherford discovered atomic energy; where the Trade Union Congress was formed; where the world's first passenger railway was built; where 11 Mancs were killed at Peterloo in 1819, demonstrating for the right to vote. Manchester, a political, left-wing, historical, industrial, grey, grey, grey, grey town.

Yet, in the 80s the world was in motion. Manchester prospered not just in its musical notoriety, but as a 'redevelopment' boom-town. Urban greyness was bought up, knocked down, refurbished and turned into something credible, a city with a future. The bleak, abandoned Manchester Ship Canal was reincarnated as Salford Quays, a Docklands-style yuppie-verse with a ten-screen Cannon cinema and skywardly-priced flats.

Shaun Ryder in *Get Out*: "Salford's like the East End

at the moment. It's like real yuppieville, you know what I mean? All the flats and everything that used to be old flats, well they're knocking them down and building swimming pools ... "

In the 80s, warehouses, abandoned old shells utilised for groovy all-night parties, became new office blocks and de-luxe apartments for upwardly-mobile Northerners. Whitworth Street/Piccadilly rave-zones were 'redeveloped' into Granby Village and Piccadilly Village! Out past The Haçienda, the old City Road gasworks is next on the list ... with a new name, Grand Island.

"I'm sure everyone in Manchester lives in the same house," John Peel once sniggered. By the end of the 80s it was almost a fact! Everyone moved to India House. Two minutes from Cornerhouse; three from arty venue, The Green Room; five from indie club, The Venue; and seven from The Haçienda.

India House, a vast Victorian edifice, was 'redeveloped' into posh flats for city workers; a Hall of Residence for the Manc Pop University; rest home for musicians, NME journos, Haç employees, burglars and one slightly looney arsonist! Not quite as 'exclusive' as Cromwell Court, centrally-heated maisonettes with lawns, gardens, balconies ... surreally located atop the Arndale!

In 89 everyone was moving up, up, up. Factory bought up a ruin on Upper Brook Street, behind the BBC, and turned it into a 3D ad for Happy Mondays. From pavement to roof, they plastered their embryonic HQ with lurid BUMMED posters; 300 larger-than-life Shaun Ryder likenesses, freaking out commuters like the coming of Big Brother aka Our Kid.

Just a quarter mile towards town, 48 Princess Street is the heart of Manc music bizness. In adjoining offices are Simply Red, Playtime Records, Happy Mondays, Playhard Records, Revenge and more.

A mile across town, 23 New Mount Street has captured Manchester's enterprise culture. Community radio station Sunset, Inspiral Carpets, James, Great Leap Forward, Ruthless Rap Assassins, Bop Cassettes, Red Alert Pluggers all occupy the same building! Crazy Manc cottage-industry, making business trips to London redundant.

Are you bored with all these facts and figures? Suit yourself. Skip this chapter!

Manc musical tourists should also check out the Lesser Free Trade Hall on Peter Street. The North's equivalent to the 100 Club, where the Sex Pistols played in 76. Only a handful of kids caught the reckless set ... but thousands more say they did. Just like Collyhurst's Electric Circus, where *So It Goes* filmed the Pistols, Clash, Boomtown Rats, Ramones, Talking Heads; Virgin released the album, *SHORT CIRCUIT: LIVE AT THE ELECTRIC CIRCUS*.

That was *then*. That was in Manchester's *old* days. Punk? It was a joke wasn't it? Even at its height, it was still a minority thing. Hardly sold *any* records. Didn't really change anything either. After punk came Joy Division, Manchester's next biggest export. Yet even at their peak, even all over the cover of *NME* and hyped-to-death by writers like Paul Morley, it was *nothing* compared to the 90s' Manc boom.

Even The Smiths were small-time compared to scally-insanity. In 86 Factory organised The Festival Of The Tenth Summer to celebrate a decade of Manc dominance since the Sex Pistols played the Lesser Free Trade Hall. After a week of city-wide events, it culminated in G-Mex's day-long rave, The Tenth Event. The Smiths, New Order, The Fall, Pete Shelley, Jonn Cale, OMD, John Cooper Clarke, ACR, Sandi Shaw performed, yet it didn't even sell out! Times move on. The Manchester bands of the 90s could sell out G-Mex 20 times over.

"Not only is Manchester a hotbed of musical talent, it's now being touted as Britain's top holiday centre! Yes! Tourists the world over are flocking to enjoy the colourful sights and sounds of the rainy city ..." joked *Smash Hits* in June 90, with Stone Roses on the cover and pin-ups (!) of Inspiral Carpets, MC Tunes and The Charlatans!

Manchester, a cultural theme-park. Stroll down *Coronation Street*, sup real ale at the Rovers Return and buy souvenir cloth caps, fireplace ducks and jars of Betty Turpin's Red Cabbage. Beats Buckingham Palace, Disneyland or New York, hey? Take the Last Exit To Manchester. Kiss the concrete. Walk the pavement. Feel those vibes!

Knock! Knock! Who's there? Morrissey? Morrissey who? In the second age of Aquarius, no-one gave a fuck about Morrissey. Last of the famous international camp playboys. His reign as Queen of Manchester's empire had lasted seven years: it came to an end in just 30 minutes.

Smithsmania

3 And God Created Manchester

While East Europeans had been preparing to rise up, a Manchester cultural revolution had been discussed in hushed whispers for two years. In November 89, the night Stone Roses and Happy Mondays were on *Top Of The Pops*, dictator Morrissey was overthrown. He ceased to be of importance. Until that moment his every word, action, social scam was documented in the national music press. By the following day, he might as well never have existed! A cruel circus.

It's a familiar cycle. Remember Boy George? And Marilyn? Both took the tabloid press for all the glamour they could snatch, Queens of the lig-scene. When they hit hard times, the press followed, burning them to the bone on a human barbecue. Tales of junkies and beach-bum lifestyles. But what did they expect? Can't have it both ways.

After two years of sycophantic Mozzer nipple-licking, building his reputation out of all sensible proportion, *NME* dumped him overnight. "Morrissey being trampled on is a fact of pop life," said Mandi James. "If the Beatles had carried on they'd have been dumped. If Elvis was still alive, he would have been forgotten. That's the way it goes."

Morrissey's genius had actually died just prior to *STRANGEWAYS HERE WE COME*. From then on, he became a bad parody of himself. However, for want of something fresh to hype, the music press clung on to him.

There's a movie to be made. You've seen *Paris, Texas*. Now check '*Manchester, England*'. It's about all the angry, tortured young men. Confused outsiders. Misfits. Boys with quiffs, walking alone through moody monochrome side streets. *Look Back In Anger*

OPPOSITE
Morrissey's shirt, The Festival of the Tenth Summer, G-Mex, July 1986.

translated to a Whalley Range bedsit, the *Billy Liar* of the early 80s. Where *Paris, Texas* loops a twangy cactus riff from start to finish, '*Manchester, England*' samples and repeats that mournful Marr guitar of *How Soon Is Now*.

In the 80s Britain was turned Arndale-bland by everyone from Duran Duran to Stock Aitken and Waterman. Like punk never happened! In the 90s Britain was swept by a clubbing-hippie culture, a tide of happiness. Like The Smiths never existed.

But the fact remains, The Smiths are one of the greatest rock bands of all time.

The Smiths did *not* revolutionise the pop industry, change the world or even establish a significant new musical genre (there have always been guitar bands). Rather, they were one last great stand against the values of commercialism, image, capitalism and consumerism. Last bastions of The Old World. In the 19th century Luddites took up their pick-axes and smashed mill machinery, yet they could not stop the Industrial Revolution. So what hope had four Mancs taking on the whole multi-national music industry? As they say, you can't stop progress!

The Smiths were never a part of any kind of scene. So they created their own! Morrissey was a social outcast, outsider, freak in the corner; so he exploited his handicap to an extreme. He was the vicar at the pop tea-party, acting out a comedy of manners, *double-entendres* and Sunday-afternoon camp.

In an age when punk-chic was purchasable in chainstores when kids, spinning on their heads, sold Weetabix and even grannies rinsed their hair purple, Morrissey was a new kind of rebel. Since time began (around 1956) rebellion was about teenagers, broken windows, fast cars, fast food, fast sex and drugs for even more speed. Yet, here was a rebel in his late 20s. A rebel who didn't smoke, drink, eat meat, swear, hurt animals or have sex. Shocking! The ultimate of scandals!

Go on Morrissey, you can tell us. It was all just a gimmick wasn't it? Really, when you get home you sniff a line of coke, dye your hair green and shag ten groupies, like *normal* people ... don't you?

"Morrissey's a big acid-head. You can tell by his words. His lyrics do have a trippy edge to them! Standing outside Salford Lads' Club sounds like the kind of thing you'd do when you're tripping," says *Sounds*' John Robb, with the most preposterous Morrissey theory yet, obviously a load of bollocks!

"Morrissey's problem is he doesn't go out enough," rants journo, Andy Spinoza. "It mystifies me why he needs to be a recluse. If he loosened up, had a good time, swanned round The Haç, like Hucknall, people would get used to him and not give him any hassle." Apart from extreme paranoia, a good reason for Morrissey staying home, was the fact that it elevated him to 'untouchable' status. Only topping himself, like Ian Curtis, could have ensured a greater degree of mystique. A contrast to the Mondays and Roses, men of the people who you'll meet in The Haçienda, on a street corner, at a party. "You meet people and they get a bit hysterical," says Ian Brown. "So I try and talk to them ordinary-like, calm them down, make them realise I'm normal."

Morrissey was permanently out-of-sync. That was the point. Hated reggae, despised dance music, never prepared to listen harder. 'Says nothing to me about my life' ... but how do you know, if you don't listen? After The Smiths split Marr kept a silence, broken only when he agreed to do an interview with *Debris*. His interpretation of The Smiths' split was not what anyone expected. "We'd got ourselves down a musical cul-de-sac. Anything that sounded remotely Sly Stone or Fatback just wouldn't have been allowed. In fact, at certain times on some of the tours, if the fans had known what I was listening to they would have gone mad."

Unless Morrissey opened his mind and ears, the war between himself and Marr would never end. However, in July 88, ridiculous rumours circulated that The Smiths were to reform. The truth of this false alert has never been properly explained. Basically, it was a scam created by Gareth Evans, manager of the then-unknown Stone Roses!

In order to butter-up a local hack, Gareth gave them the 'exclusive' tip-off that he'd spotted Johnny Marr in Omega Records, Northwich (later significant as The Charlatans' homeland). Apparently, Marr had been on his way to a reunion with Moz. Naturally, this meeting had never actually taken place! But the hack told a friend who told John Peel who, in turn, broadcast it on-air. Within the week *The Sun* had claimed that its

OPPOSITE
Morrissey, G-Mex, July 1986;
The Smiths, G-Mex, July 1986.

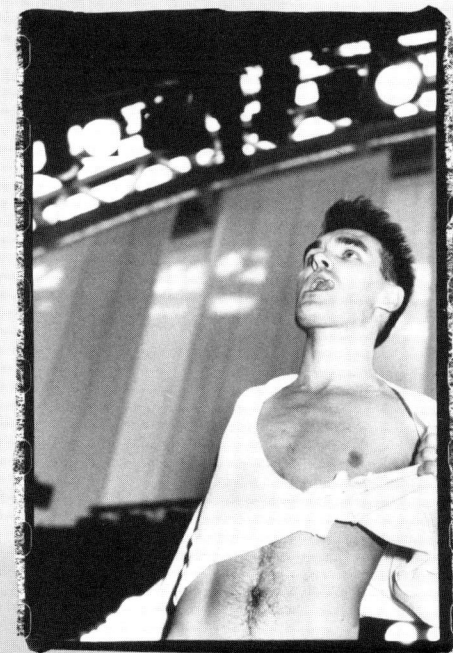

Free Trade Hall, Peter St, Manchester

Phil McIntyre presents—

The Smiths + Support

Thursday, 30th October, 1986

Evening   Doors Open 7.00

SIDE CIRCLE

£6.50 (£4.50 UB40 + I.D) inc VAT

---

sources exclusively revealed a re-formation, while NME's front cover blared, 'Smiths To Reform'. Desperate, hey?

It was also NME who revealed, 'Morrissey Is Married!', another story later usurped by the tabloids. He had tied the knot and was living in Little Hulton with a wife and two kids. OK, not the Morrissey, but a Morrissey! Stephen Morrissey and wife Julie, lived on Mondays' estate where call-boxes were permanently out of order, the buses never turned up and the only entertainment was the Spa pub (where Stephen played pool).

When the Morrissey family got a phone in 86, their name 'Morrissey S' appeared in the directory, the only 'Morrissey S' in all of Manchester. While Steve was at work, Julie began to receive calls, "from giggling schoolies who wanted to know if Morrissey was in." She'd never heard of The Smiths, so was pretty freaked out! "I think she was beginning to get funny ideas about me!" said Steve.

"The people who called seemed to think I was this Morrissey's mother," said Julie. "I'd ask them which Morrissey they wanted, 'cos I didn't understand what was going on. One girl asked if I could get her a pair of the guitarists' underpants. Someone else, a bloke, wanted to know if my son really did sleep naked on a big mirror!"

Once, a girl phoned Steve at one in the morning threatening to kill herself. "I said I couldn't do 'owt. Told her I wasn't the Morrissey, but she wouldn't stop." Someone else asked for a reverse-charge phone call from LA, while one girl proposed marriage. He told her he had a wife. She hung up in shock!

Smithsmania did not die the day the band split. It lived on with new fans who missed them play the Free Trade Hall 87, G-Mex 86, the Palace 85 or Free Trade Hall 84; who'd never seen them live.

In the summer of 88, the first Smiths Convention was held at Manchester University's Student Union building. It defined the direction Smithsmania would take from then on. Every year, this annual event becomes more extreme, Smiths devotees become dafter parodies of themselves and the original Smiths vibe becomes more distant, hazed by romantics, day-dreamers and time.

Red and yellow gladioli hanging out of back-pockets, a queue of disciples flaunting an infinite variety of tour T-shirts snaked up the staircase. Excitable, chattery as school-kids in a dinner queue, they hugged close their duffle bags, clutched George Orwell books. Girls indulged in mannered giggling, while boys ran fingers self-consciously through lovingly-cultivated quiffs. Both sexes peered through National Health spectacles ... despite having perfect vision.

For many, it was the highlight of 88 ... the highlight of their lives ... save, of course, for Morrissey at Wolverhampton Civic Hall.

From all over the globe, teenagers had come to pay homage to the most important anti-pop pop group ever. From Spain, France, Holland, Glasgow, Nottingham, Leeds, Southend they'd travelled to take pictures of Whalley Range, kiss the concrete, make sense of the songs.

Grey, grey, grey Manchester, romantic holiday top-spot for manic depressives. Rain, rain and more rain. A coach tour of 'Landmarks of Smithdom'. "It's wonderful! The depressing, drizzily atmosphere Morrissey goes on about ... I didn't know it was really like this!" Of course, it never rains in Manchester ... unless there's a test match or a Royal visit.

Strangeways here we come. "Morrissey ... Morrissey ... he once stood here?" exclaims a boy staring up at the 'Stephen Street' nameplate in awe ... only yards from a 'Strangeways' road sign and opposite the entrance to HM Prison Strangeways itself.

"It does not look the same!" exclaimed a Finnish radio reporter disappointedly. The Strangeways road sign was photographed by Steve Wright at the request of Rough Trade, for The Smiths' parting album, *STRANGEWAYS HERE WE COME*. Steve had skirted the Northern edge of town, photographing a folio of 12 or more different signs. By the time Rough Trade selected one, he couldn't even remember which location it was taken at! Smart tourists figured it out and had the foresight to bring their own step-ladders and chisel!

Next stop, Salford Lads' Club, off Regent Road, which appeared on the cover of *THE QUEEN IS DEAD*. As the coach arrived four pre-teen authentic Salford lads were huddled in the doorway with their bulldog. They posed for photos, perhaps expecting tips like the fake-punks in London. Snidey. Makes no

music paper

By Ray King

MEMBERS of Manchester's controversial group The Smiths issued a writ against Manchester music azine. Their record, nger Morrissey and arist John Marr claim Little Children, at Moors Murders, were libelled by an protest for in the encouraged by th azine, have offered benefit concerts Muze's defence. Morrissey a Smiths have court cal headlines almo they started.

---

sense to them, this interest in their slummy, scummy home territory. They'd seen many Smiths fanatics stop off at this shrine. Sneered, shouted insults, mugged them, begged for cash.

"They're round here everyday, the Americans and that," says one 'lad', rubbing his nose on his sleeve like the old street-urchin cliché. "Stoooopid! The Smiffs ... It's bobbins!"

As for the club's owners, pop fame was not a compliment. More a disgrace, nuisance, outrage, with devotees queuing up to scratch their messages on the famous door. Anyone who phoned was told, "We hate The Smiths. We're going to sue them!" Their threats never came to anything, but the caretaker took pleasure in hosing down all who came close, shouting obscenities through the letterbox at all who tried to take photos, night or day.

Despite towerblocks, docklands, yuppieville, Salford retains some of that pre-60s, back-to-back-houses, working-class magic. The real Coronation Street is just yards from Salford Lads' Club, making it double-double appealing to tourists with misty-eyed visions of northern England.

Salfordian to the end, May Edward's Off Licence provided a touch of that surreality. Famed simply because the Smiffs had once had their photo taken outside. Coachloads descended, asking a confused May if they could take her photo. "Ooooh! I'm not dressed for it ..." She proclaimed, scurrying upstairs to slap on make-up, change her dress.

"I've never heard The Smiths, you know" she said. "I was in hospital at the time the photo was taken. It was only when I came home that the kids came in and said my shop was famous ..."

On the other side of town, in a street of semi-detached houses, as ordinary as any, was the one-time home of Morrissey himself, still lived in by his father. Kings Road, where Morrissey once took *Oxford Road Show*'s TV cameras. Mr Morrissey was at home, but ignored frantic knocking by a tactless reporter who shouted through the letter-box, "What's it like having people constantly disturb your privacy?"

Back on the bus, one girl bragged how she sneaked into the back garden and actually saw "Morrissey's toilet!" Since, contrary to popular belief, Manchester houses no longer *have* outside loos ... she must have been telling fibs. As the man in the nearby sweet shop gloated, "Yes, Stephen used to come in here *every* morning on his way to school and buy sweets from the penny tray ..."

After gobbling up cola-bottles and chewies, young Stephen would then cross the railway footbridge to St Joseph's Junior School. Yes, *the* iron bridge which Morrissey would later refer to in his lyrics. Round the corner is Morrissey's Catholic secondary school, St Mary's, supposedly attended by a whole collection of Manc pop-stars including Marc Riley.

The final shrine was Southern Cemetery where Morrissey wandered ... gathering future lyric material. The authorities had banned the day-trippers from wandering inside but photographing *the* Cemetery Gates was thrill enough. Captivated by the morose graveyard spectacle, the party narrowly escaped being mown down by a hearse and cavalcade of mourners! Such a beautiful irony ... Morrissey might have staged it himself. I can hear the song now, "What a beautiful way to die/run down by a hearse/could have been worse ..."

On through Whalley Range and Rusholme, the handsome young devils returned to the University, opposite the Holy Name church, immortalised in *Vicar In A Tutu*. Instead of nicking lead from the roof, this earnest bunch laid down their wilted gladioli in respect ... as if Morrissey himself were dead and this were his annual memorial service. All very odd, considering he was alive, well and living in Altrincham. Inevitably, fucked-up teenagers left behind by the 90s' scally-mobile cling to *HATFUL OF HOLLOW, THE SMITHS, MEAT IS MURDER, THE QUEEN IS DEAD, STRANGEWAYS HERE WE COME, LOUDER THAN BOMBS* and *RANK*. Rubber rings to keep them afloat. For as long as there are lonely kids, The Smiffs will live on, fashionable or not. The Smiths both saved and ruined many adolescent lives. Yet, in so many ways, the Roses and others have done better by these youngsters: encouraging self-belief, not self-pity; fun, not misery; optimism, not negativity.

'Listening to The Smiths' has become as much a social embarrassment as the reasons for doing so. Knock. Knock.

Four minutes. Four minutes to live! 240 seconds! What would you do? Kiss goodbye, blow your brains out, call your mum, dance in the street, do a conga through The Arndale, hide under a table, boil an egg? Nuclear obsessions peaked around 85, having escalated since the 60s ban-the-bomb era. School projects involved choosing the élite guest-list for your city's bunker. Who would you exclude and why? Apocalypse *now*. Protect and survive.

DoomsdaY PaY-Off

4   *And God Created Manchester*

War Games? Push the wrong button and the world would end. On May 11, 85, South Manchester was nearly wiped out. The end of the universe as we knew it. At 8pm, in eight urban zones, The Four Minute Warning sounded. Chorlton, Whalley Range, Moss Side ... like 1000 fire alarms triggered simultaneously ... just as it sounded on Frankie Goes To Hollywood's *Two Tribes*.

Four minutes and counting. Bewildered Mancs out on the streets, frozen like icicles, indexing regrets of things they'd-always-meant-to, but never-had-time-for. What to do? Four minutes to live? What would *you* do? Four minutes ticked to five, five to six, six to seven, and we were all still alive. Some hours later the alarm halted, but the ringing in the ears continued, like when you've stood too close to the speakers at a gig. Only a, "British Telecom fault," reassured a local paper. Uh-huh?

Three minutes, 50 seconds. Three weeks after this 'false-alarm', the last of the mohicans, anarchos, freakies, alternatives, punks with hair dyed every shade of purple, piled on to bumpy buses. Thousands of weirdos headed for Clitheroe Castle bandstand, for a free gig fashioned by Radio Lancashire's *On The Wire* and broadcast live. For sleepy-town Sunday-afternoon Lancashire, *this* was the holocaust. *These* punks, scorched and ragged as cartoon characters caught in a Bugs Bunny bomb-blast, going green with radiation sickness.

Three minutes, 40 seconds. Onstage The Fall, the

OPPOSITE
Mark E Smith, October 1988

OPPOSITE
Brix E Smith, April 1987;
Craig Scanlon, Mark E Smith, March 1990;
The Fall, October 1988.

only Manc band who could survive a nuclear strike. Long after The Haç has been rubbled to an asbestos and alabaster turd, The Fall will be seen covering Kylie down The Holocaust Memorial Hall for 'lucky' survivors. After all, they've lasted 14 years and 15 plus albums. In a city with enough has-beens, would-bes, may-bes and never-weres, The Fall are Manchester's longest running punk act.

Three minutes, 30 seconds. Mark 'E-for-Edward' Smith, who ends every word with 'ah', may be the only remaining memb-ah, but he has kept ahead of the biz, ahead of his time, never dragged back into nostalg-ah.

Unlike Buzzcocks who burnt-out far, far too fast. Tattered survivors of 77's rebel era, bygones, living punk memorabli-ah, all various memb-ahs, struggled for life in the 80s. Howard Devoto's dull Luxuria, misunderstood and misplaced in time; Steve Diggle's Flag of Convenience and their rockist album *NORTH WEST SKYLINE*; Pete Shelley's failed band, Zip.

"Everybody's scared," commented Diggle. "They'll come out and say they're gay; they'll say that they support animal rights; but no-one will admit they are into rock music."

Three minutes, 20 seconds. Going nowhere fast, FOC became Buzzcocks FOC, with Springsteen-ish single *Tomorrow's Sunset*, featuring Andy Couzens, Chris Goodwin and Gary Hamer who eventually kicked out Steve to form The High. Fellow Buzzcock Pete Shelley in 89, "I feel sorry for Steve. He has obviously hit hard times. You can bet 'FOC' is in really small print. It'll confuse people and anything which confuses people is sure to rip them off."

Steve, bitterly, "I wrote *Promises* and *Harmony In My Head*, two of Buzzcocks' four Top 20 hits. Surely that entitles me to use the name as much as anyone else? Loads of songs that jointly credit me and Pete, I actually wrote and he added a few words. I don't resent Pete, but I do resent journalists perpetuating the myth that he created the Buzzcocks single-handedly."

Pete, meanwhile, was also accused of cashing-in, his 81 hit *Homosapien*, re-recorded techno-style with boys-town beats and high-camp vocals. "Saying '*Homosapien II* is a cash-in', is like seeing the works of Mother Theresa as a publicity stunt."

Three minutes, 10 seconds. Despite bitching, the Buzzcocks reformed for a US/UK tour 89, while EMI released a Buzzcocks boxed-set *PRODUCT*. Almost nine years after they'd split up, Pete Shelley and Steve Diggle, joined by Steve Garvey and John Maher, were back together. But times had changed. "The new-wave, punk thing came through, and I knew we could do better than that," Mark E Smith told *Manchester Magazine* in 86. "I remember watching Slaughter And The Dogs and the Buzzcocks and thinking how lousy they were and thinking we're much better when we're messing around."

Three minutes and counting. Arrogance or inspiration? Following The Fall is like tracking somebody's life, watching them grow from a baby to middle age. The Fall were born in the mid 70s when Mark was working his way through endless dead-end jobs. Salford Docks, Urmston Containers. Tony Friel, Karl Burns, Martin Bramah and Una Baines joined Mark, and they stepped-out in May 77, supporting the likes of The Worst and The Drones, playing hip Ranch Club, appearing on Virgin compilation, *LIVE AT THE ELECTRIC CIRCUS*.

Seven years, 15 singles into their career and The Fall were still toddlers. They'd been on Step Forward for early albums *LIVE AT THE WITCH TRIALS* and *DRAGNET*; moved to Rough Trade for *TOTALE'S TURNS* (live), *GROTESQUE*, *SLATES* and *PERVETED BY LANGUAGE*; and two releases on Kamera, *HEX ENDUCTION HOUR* and *ROOM TO LIVE*. Things were just *beginning*.

Two minutes, 50 seconds. Clitheroe Castle came midway between ninth and tenth albums *WONDERFUL AND FRIGHTENING WORLD* and *THIS NATION'S SAVING GRACE*, both for Beggars Banquet. Suddenly, their garage-groove was crossing into 'real' pop-music ... attracting new fans like a sinister pied-piper leading school kids through opium fields. After the gig, a 14-year-old hip-kid, who'd been slumped in a shop doorway waiting for a bus home, jumped in front of their van, begging a ride to Manchester. They agreed, feeding her with apples, chocolates, coke all the way home. Yeah, yours truly! Two minutes 40 seconds. You see, The Fall had sympathy with precocious teenagers. They'd been just 19 when they started playing; Karl Burns had

been drumming in metal acts since he was 13 and bassist/guitarist Marc Riley who, at just 16, would join soon after they formed!

If Mark was the Robin Hood of alternative pop, his (now-ex) wife, Brix E Smith, was Maid Marion. Brix, daughter of wealthy US shrink and mate of The Bangles, escaped a life as an all-American robotic Stepford Wife by running away to rock 'n' roll. She was carried to England on the back of The Fall's white horse in 83 after she met Mark at a Chicago gig. They were married, she got a job in the band, and they lived happily ever after ... for a while anyway.

Two minutes, 30 seconds. Brix was inspired completely by her mother, a 60s model who worked with the Kennedys, produced *CBS News* and became head of Motion Pictures for the State of Illinois (we're told). "She was a smart business women," Brix told *NME*. "A wonderful woman and mother and my total inspiration. I came from a background where a woman could be beautiful and strong and do this. I saw that and I knew I could do that as well."

Like an old lady buying up fake sequined glamour from Oxfam, Northern dour-guys, The Fall, embraced Brix's show-biz style. "The Fall are probably the most unpopular group among women *ever*. We've never had a good review [until now!] from a woman journalist ever in the whole world," said Mark in 86. "Brix has heightened the sexiness of the band. Or so a lot of people tell me."

Two minutes, 20 seconds. In *Melody Maker*, Brix said, "When I came into The Fall, it was like an already painted canvas, so I just added light and shadow where I could." In Ocotber 86, the eleventh album, *BEND SINISTER* was so raw, it proved Brix wasn't softening them too much, however. Everything from the obscure *Bournemouth Runner*, about a fan who stole their backdrop, to *US 80s 90s*, adopted by punk-ballerina Michael Clark ... and *Terry Waite Sez*, a ridiculous rhyme that became especially significant when Terry was kidnapped only months later!

Two minutes, 10 seconds. "Sounds like it was recorded in a couple of hours in someone's bathroom," wrote Robin Denselow in *The Guardian*, *very* sussed guy! Two minutes and counting. *Mr Pharmacist*, was their wonderfully unacceptable single choice after a Just-Say-No anti-smack phase had kept the back pages of 'youth' mags booked up for months. 'Hey! Mr Pharmacist! Won't you give me some energy.' Speed-freaks, racing, racing, racing, accelerating from sachet-to-sachet, feeling like the headcase in *The Scream* cartoon ... Mr Pharmacist was a cover of Texan garage band, The Other Half, but speed/barb addiction was a fave Mark E Smith topic.

One minute, 50 seconds. *Rowche Rumble*, Fall's third single circa 79, was more real-life hedonism. Back when Mark worked down the docks, he once took charge of a 40-ton consignment of barbituates from the Swiss firm, Roche Chemical Company ... naturally, by the time it reached its destination, both Mark and the container were several cartons short of a full load! The Man Whose Head Expanded.

One minute, 40 seconds. "If someone wants to smoke or drink themselves to death on whisky, jump out of windows or whatever then it's their basic right," Smith told *NME*. "I always thought that was what Britain was all about."

One minute, 30 seconds. The Fall were pop's peasant outlaws, out on their own, John Peel's fave band *ever*. If you want to wind Peelie up, just tell him your band is better than "The Mighty Fall"! Mark E Smith, wearer of wild Crimplene blouses, train-spotter tank-tops, gold lurex shirts. A court jester at his own mediæval banquet, his rant influenced by everyone from sci-fi Stephen King and freaky Philip K Dick, to trashy tabloid journalese and Lanc colloquialisms. Nonsensical logic, ranted as surreal as 60s' Captain Beefheart or dub-master Lee Perry.

One minute, 20 seconds. The Fall, like Joy Division, became faves with wierdo record collectors in some of the globe's most unlikely low-spots. Like tortured French kids still murmuring their daily mantra, '???' (the day Ian Curtis committed suicide), you'll find European punks who know Fall lyrics by heart. They were even professionally translated into German!

One minute, 10 seconds. The Fall, bigger abroad than in Manchester it often seems. "Most Mancs don't appreciate what's on their own doorstep," Mark told *City Life* in 86. "Or they don't until it appears in the *Evening News* and all that. It's real then. And they don't appreciate the fact we've stuck around here, living here."

One minute and counting. Meanwhile, Brix had formed

her very own band, The Adult Net, with Smiths-lads Mike Joyce, Andy Rourke, Craig Gannon. Singles *Edie, Incense And Peppermints, Waking up In The Sun* ... album, THE HONEY TANGLE ... shone like dawn sunbeams streaming through indie-rock's Venetian blinds. Yet, despite a Phonogram deal, the pop-stardom she sought with her Madonna-image never came.

50 seconds. Calculated-bimbo vs naive-feminist, Brix was a mixed-up addition to female pop. "Sometimes women are so catty, bitchy and will do anything to step on you," she told Penny Anderson in *City Life*. "They'll steal everything from you ... your clothes to your make up, your style of playing; rip you off blind. You have to watch out ..." Know the feeling?

40 seconds. After *Mr Pharmacist*, Brix' influence enabled a series of increasingly 'catchy' singles, leading up to their 'poppiest' album THE FRENZ EXPERIMENT: *Hey Luciani, There's A Ghost In My House, Hit The North*. Inevitably, they hit the charts with *Victoria*, a Kinks' cover-version.

35 seconds. Mark E Smith's indie devotion led him to set up Cog Sinister, their very own label. Its first release, THE DISPARATE COGNOSCENTI, a compendium of strange works by Mark E Smith's drinking mates, next-door neighbours and hairdressers. Such long-neglected Northern genii as The Hamsters, Obi-Men, Beatrice, God and Mr A Valler! Who? There were also The Lowthers (named after the family Hilda Ogden cleaned for?) and The Next Step, featuring Martin Walsh (later of Inspirals).

30 seconds. Other 'notorious' Mancs included, Jon The Postman, piss-head 'poet' from The Electric Circus' 'good old days' (yawn); and Andrew Berry, 'hairdresser to the stars', singer with The Weeds, erstwhile house-mate of Johnny Marr, most influential man in town. Tony Wilson eat your heart out!

25 seconds. "Andrew used to sit between me and Morrissey when we were writing songs," Johnny told *Debris*. "No-one else was allowed to do that. He and John Kennedy promoted our first gig and, in fact, people first took us seriously because of our Andrew Berry connection."

20 seconds. Too preoccupied with world tours, recordings etc, Cog Sinister failed to fulfil its possibilities, but it did release PALACE OF SWORDS REVERSED, a compilation of their early material for those who'd missed out.

15 seconds. The surreal Fall narratives were translated into visual nonsense for *I Am Curious Orange*, a Michael Clark punk-ballet that played Amsterdam, the Edinburgh Festival and Sadler's Wells. Based on William of Orange, who introduced the 1688 Bill Of Rights, it featured Brix in a swimsuit, pirouetting atop a giant Big Mac, a human baked bean can, tutus and chiffon and ballet dancers playing football in Celtic Rangers strip. Meanwhile, Mark E was well hip, appearing as a 'white rapper' on a Coldcut album.

10 seconds. Where Mark never ever gave a fuck, Brix cared passionately. Where Mark was a contented cult-star, Brix wanted to be the No 1 attraction. Dressing up Madonna-style, Brix' own The Adult Net were far more commercial. By the end of 89, she had become a British citizen, split with Mark, left The Fall. In 90, she was snatching tabloid attention stepping-out with classical violin celeb, Nigel Kennedy!

7 seconds. "There comes a point when you just say, 'The whole world is open to me!,'" burbled Brix, "'I can do anything I want to, learn anything I want, I can *have*, I can *enjoy*, the sun is beautiful, the sky is gorgeous crystal blue, the sea is silver.' You just stand and look around and say, 'Life is wonderful!'. I have those feelings to this day!"

5 seconds. The Fall themselves were not stopping to reflect either. Their last contribution to the indie charts was *Cab It Up*; in 89 they finally sold-out their indie-dom, home for their previous five albums, and signed to Phonogram for their first post-Brix album, EXTRICATE.

4 seconds. After a decade in the business, The Fall finally made it to their *Smash Hits* interview.

3 seconds. William Shaw probably summed up The Fall better than any of those pretentious rock-hacks.

2 seconds. "... Mark doesn't so much sing words as bark them.

1 second. "Onstage he hunches over a microphone with a scowl on his face pouring out a stream of words that are either very meaningful or complete twaddle, depending on which way you look at it."

ALL FALL DOWN!!!

They say normal people don't live in Hulme. Just skinny freaks with skinny dogs. Just kids with crazy-paving eyes, junk up their nose, needles in their arms. Just aspiring musicians, who seek superstardom yet never get past their local pub. Just little rich kids living it rough, sleeping with cockroaches under their pillow, so they can pretend they're as tough as the rest.

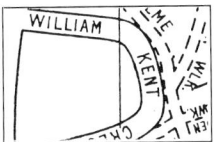

KinGs of the Slums

5 *And God Created Manchester*

Hulme, with its Lego-style low-rise crescents. Hulme, a folly of the 60s, built as a joke by a man with a very bad sense of humour. The punchline ... to name the Crescents after architects like William Kent. Slabs of concrete, cold and grey as a nuclear bunker.

This is Hulme. The end of the earth. One mile wide and eight miles high. You can disappear here. Sucks you in like a black hole, a lair, a maze. Deeper and deeper and deeper until you can't remember the way out. The perfect suicide dive. You can live here for years, oblivious to the outside world. Like the anarchos, with their dreadie hair, unwashed khaki and mongrels-on-strings. They'll probably never leave.

Planet Hulme. Dubious pubs that the authorities would like to close down. Planet Hulme. Salmon taxi cabs to take you out of there. Planet Hulme. The Aaben Cinema, erstwhile down-market haven for anarcho film-fanatics. Planet Hulme, perfect home for people just 'passing through'. Even the Stone Roses and James lived here.

"*So Young* is about when I lived in Hulme," says Ian Brown. "Everyone who lived there seemed to think it was great to stay in bed till tea-time. It's just a waste of life. They could be doing something more worthwhile with their time."

Here come the kings of these slums. Like Mark Hoyle of Dub Sex. He enthuses, "Hulme is full of people who have escaped the poor, over-spill estates like Wythenshawe and Langley. Hulme is poor, but it's far better. There's a cosmopolitan-ness here. It's full of personalities and cultures, it's near the city centre and there's lots going on ..."

OPPOSITE
Dub Sex, 1989.

Here come the kings of these slums. Like Harry Stafford, a gentleman, a ligger-with-attitude, the perfect Royal Garden Party guest. His aristocratic-style led to a rumour that he was heir to Cadbury's chocolate millions!

"It's not true!" protests Harry. "My great, great grandparents are called Cadbury but, unfortunately, they're on the poor side of the family. Honestly!"

When Hulme peaked in musical hipness in the early 80s, Harry's Inca Babies were the definitive sound, transforming their environment into their very own post-apocalyptic film set. Wasted as junkies in a William Burroughs novel; caught up in a mythological Americana of FBI agents and Cadillacs. Harry was joined by Mike Keeble, Peter Bog and Bill Martin. The Inca Babies released a stream of cult records between 84 and 87. All in all, seven singles *The Judge*, *Big Jugular*, *The Interior*, *Surfin' In Locustland*, *Grunt Cadillac Hotel*, *Splatter Ballistic Cop* and *Busters On Fire* on Hulme's own Black Lagoon label; plus four gothy albums *RUMBLE*, *THIS TRAIN*, *OPIUM DEN* and *EVIL HOUR*. Inca Babies' were Manc-Cramps, stumbling blackly between punk, goth and psychobilly. Even some slide guitar! A classic 'cult' recipe for times when everyone in Hulme listened to Link Wray, Captain Beefheart or Duane Eddy.

Hulme pop didn't stop there. A Guy Called Gerald's *Voodoo Ray* echoes through The Crescents like a ghost of former times. Slum Turkeys, Dub Sex, King Of The Slums, rockers Ratfink, Metal Monkey Machine and Harry's new band, Hound God With A Tumour, all turned their horrid environment into horridly noisy records. Best of all Ruthless Rap Assassins and Kiss AMC, making most mileage out of 'The North Hulme Sound', name-dropped on their *KILLER ALBUM* (Syncopate/EMI).

"People let their dogs run all over the place. There's more dogs than people in Hulme. You can't walk in a straight line for very long," sniggers Kermit of Rap Assassins.

Kiss AMC's Anne-Marie is more angry, "We know the real story behind Hulme because we *live* here. Most people are just passing through, living here because it's trendy. The thing about them is, they can go when they want to."

"Hulme's amazing!" says DJ Jon Ronson, proving the point. But would *he* move there? "Fuck no!"

Pity those stranded here. Fact! Accepting the British 'norm', if you live in Hulme you are seven times more likely to commit suicide; 31 times more likely to be the victim of crime; 41 times more likely to be murdered.

"Some people actually choose to live here. People with middle-class parents, slumming it!" said Chris of Dub Sex.

Mark Hoyle is even more to the point, "I'm not embarrassed about being pure filth, why should they be embarrassed about being rich! If I was the son of a millionaire, I wouldn't be here."

Hulme had its own squatters' radio station in 87. Transmitted from a tower block, DIY Radio was unique. Manchester's other pirates served Moss Side, spinning soul and reggae, while DIY were cultural terrorists into hardcore, indie and house. Techno-whizz-kid founder, Pik, also had grand plans for PTV, pirate telly, but disappeared without a trace. Smart idea, especially as everything good about Hulme is illegal!

There was also the now-legendary Kitchen, a cheap eight-track recording studio run by one Jamie Nicholson. In its later days, it doubled as a party-zone open to all free-of-charge once the clubs had shut. Ideal after-hours entertainment when the PSV closed at 2am. The PSV, aka The Caribbean Club, remains the home of hip-hop, reggae, soul and some well-stoned nights out.

Formerly The Russel Club, it was where Tony Wilson, Alan Erasmus and Peter Saville based their Factory Club in the late 70s. Joy Division were virtually the resident band appearing week after week, while UB40, Toyah, Human League, The Undertones and OMD all stopped by.

"There was a very cold winter, 1978 I think," reminisces DJ Dean, waving his walking stick. "Yorkshire bands were very hip at the time but because of the bad weather they never made it over the Pennines, so Joy Division played about eight Saturdays on the run. And they were *crap!*"

Viraj Mendis was one Hulmie who never got to the PSV. A student from Sri Lanka, he stowed-away in the Church of the Ascension just a few yards away. He became handcuffed in a political battle which came to signify more than just one man's fight against

OPPOSITE
Ben, Tools You Can Trust, November 1986.

onkey machin

deportation ... for both right-wing thugs who beat up his supporters and left-wing groups who used him as a figurehead for their cause. The Home Office inevitably had their way and threw him out, leaving behind only his name splashed on every Hulme walkway.

Costa-Del-Hulme, haven for runaways. Quick, somebody call *The Sun*, Elvis is alive! Alive, well and squatting in Hulme Crescents. Imagine it! Just occasionally life is as preposterous as death and the two can become confused. Presley In Mind, aka Jim White, was a legendary star of the Manchester pub circuit, an Elvis impersonator who made a once-weekly appearance at Hulme's Bull's Head. As often as not he was accompanied by Big Ed & His Rockin Rattlesnakes, a looney trio obsessed by Elvis, Tom Jones and football. They scored at home against fellow Manc C&W buskers Skol Bandeleros and the Lonesome And Penniless Cowboys, by managing a deal with anarcho-indies, Ron Jonson, in 86. Just a couple of years earlier they might have trailed Boothill Footapers or Helen And The Horns on the ultra-hip cow-punk scene (honest!).

Eyes down! Eyes down for an album. Yeah, The Rattlesnakes called their LP *BINGO*, their fave hobby at Hulme Hippodrome. Big Ed, Kate and Ernest brought a glimpse of that 'other side' of Manchester. Land of Vera and Jack Duckworth with its working man's pubs, social clubs, bingo halls, chippies, corner shops. The sides of North Manchester and Salford that students, yuppies and trendies rarely tread.

"I'd like to play for a Johnny Cash audience," Glaswegian-born Ed once observed. "We went to see him ... and the bouncer said 'You've got the wrong night, The Clash is tomorrow.' It was all guys with black suits, big stetsons, and an old man with a walking stick."

Elvis is alive! He has put on a tweed suit, a Home Counties accent and a great frizzy beard. He denies being mad despite having turned his flat into a grotto of wood, railway sleepers and teddy bears.

His name is Edward Barton, eternally the most eccentric man in Hulme. Alright, I'm lying, Ed isn't the re-incarnated Presley. He's just the greatest self-publicist, one-man cult and religion since L Ron Hubbard invented The Church Of Scientology.

Let's take an opinion poll. "Edward Barton has more to offer than 99% of the human race," says fat, Irish pop star, Cathal Coughlan. Arty French singer Louis Phillipe has even dafter ideas, "Edward Barton is the best lyricist in Britain." Oh yeah?

In 83, Ed capped No 74 in the pop charts with *It's A Fine Day* sung by Jane (Cherry Red). *NME* called it, "Very English, all alone, no instruments. A wistful little song about fields and the weather. Apparently still sells well in Japan. Played at 33rpm, sounds like Cleo Laine." The follow-up single, *Nine Holes* (White Label), by his band, The Old Men, was less successful!

Who recalls Edward screaming 'I've got no chicken but I've got five wooden chairs,' live on Joolz-baby's *The Tube*? The best song ever written? It was the birth of Wooden Records. Many releases followed. *Belly Box Brother Gob/Barber Barber*, for example, a double A-side concerning Ed's double-good brother, Pin, and Ed's double-weird hairdressers. Soon came a Jane single, *Lovely*; *Slap My Belly*, a song made in the bath and produced by Manc-soulster Chapter; finest of all, *Born In The North*, a house track featuring A Guy Called Gerald!

A *Viz* character come to life, Edward Barton writes poetry about wood-abuse, bestiality and telephone boxes. 'Knob. Gob. Knob. Gob. I can't get my knob into my gob.' Preposterous tales. Now then! Now then! He even obscenely illustrated this song in cartoon form in his lyric booklet!

Mad, crazy, insane, deranged, loopy, looney, mental, demented, deluded, odd, eccentric, strange, weird ... which adjective would you choose to fit Edward Barton? Edward *hates* them all. "Being 'mad' has its uses, but it's best used by the not-'mad'!" he protests, resentfully adding, "People never write about my music, just my teddies." But what does he expect? And, after all, while the sane calculatedly beg insanity, genuine eccentrics always protest normality. Don't they?

Edward (not his real first name, that's Owen!) picks up babies' dummies from the walkways and hangs them on a 'tree' (twig!) in his flat. He also collects teddy bears, his birthday cakes (which rot on his sideboard for years on end) and *anything* made of wood. He even dragged two disused railway sleepers two miles across town to build a throne. He's the king of junk; Patron Saint of The Unusual; Uncle 'Wombles' Bulgaria, making use of the things that he finds.

Like The Man From Delmonte's Mike West (son of a millionaire author), Ed's upbringing has given him a quirky outlook. Born in Lybia, his parents in the British Forces, he was brought up on a diet of army life, English folk songs and Arabian pop. Then, at the age of nine, he was parcelled off to boarding school in Croydon ... where he discovered T-Rex! Only 'eventually' did he end up in Hulme.

Mr Barton not only owns his own label, draws and paints but directs some excellent pop videos like James' *Sit Down*. When he's penniless, Ed takes a train to another city and busks as a pavement painter. His T-shirts, like 'Cool as Fridge', parody Manc bestsellers Inspirals/Roses/James. This man is a legend ... and he knows it!

Cathal Coughlan and Louis Phillipe both contributed to *EDWARD NOT EDWARD*, a compilation of Barton cover versions! Absurd when you think about it, but Ed lured such celebs as Kiss AMC, A Guy Called Gerald, Stump, 808 State and Inspiral Carpets into covering his songs. The kind of crazy scam that could only happen in Manchester, where all styles of music fuse. It actually came out before he'd released his 'proper' debut album, *HERE IS MY SPOON*.

Hulme is perfect for Ed Barton - disposable! He was once arrested for knocking three flats into one to record a video!

Tools You Can Trust were another typical Hulme band. A Manc reply to Einsturzende Neubaten, Test Department and other pretentious industrialists. Post-punk music for armchair revolutionaries who thought painting your radiator black made you an anarchist and banging metal was an act of musical Luddism.

Tools You Can Trust robbed drums, dustbin lids, corrugated iron, fire extinguishers to make music that had a pulsing 'rock 'n' roll' groove. Vocalist, Rob Ward, and bassist, Ben Stedman, were the Bill and Ben of Noise in their matching shabby suits, greased-back cropped hair and Docs. They were soundly backed by metal-bashers Phil Hughes, Adam Piper and Jill Richardson.

Tools were not *art*. What's pretentious in lyrics about paying electric bills and night shifts? Even so, they fooled many arty types, being the only band ever to have played the thirtysomething Cornerhouse ... as part of the musical-sculpture exhibition *Listen To This Space*. They freaked out the producer of their Peel session who slammed their unorthodox methods on *Whistle Test*.

Tools' three mini-LPs *WORKING AND SHOPPING*, *AGAIN AGAIN AGAIN* and *ECHOES OF VIOLENCE IN THE COURTS* (Red Dynamo Records) were as shambolic as a rush-hour ride on the Northern Line, racing to some raw conclusions about everyday living. A misinformed Motown A&R man once asked for a tape. They sent one. He didn't reply! Tools You Can Trust could *only* be from Hulme.

Hulme smells. Stinks of piss and beer and decay and just plain *fear*. Fear like hospital disinfectant. Fear like sweaty police cells. Fear like a knife pulled in a back-alley. Fear that leaves you screaming in your sleep. Fear that has you digging your nails into your palms until they bleed. Fear like Dub Sex. Dogs grow like their masters and bands *sound* like their homeland. Dub Sex sound like Hulme. Hulme is huge, bleak, dark, eerie, most of all *frightening*. So are Dub Sex. Check front-man Mark Hoyle, a skinny kid with John Lennon glasses, slurred philosophies, an unintelligible accent, going so fast he could win the Grand Prix. He hurls himself into noisy oblivion. *Tripwire*, Dub Sex's debut release on a *Debris* flexi, caught his continual motion, all fraught words, coarse melodies, ricocheting round his estate like a gunshot in a creek, blending with the barks of stray dogs.

Sometimes Dub Sex stumbled like a sub-Guana Batz corpse playing *Live At The Klub Foot*. They weren't psychobilly, more clumsy. Flashbacks to when Mark was a member of Manchester Musician's Collective. He played in The Vibrant Thigh (if you think that's bad, there were also Spherical Objects, The Passage ...) who recorded a song called *Wooden Gangsters* for a MMC compilation. A solo Mark Hoyle track, *Yonkers*, appeared on an Inevitable Records album.

'I used to live in this town/I used to love this town/Til things started spiralling down ...' moaned *Then And Now*, The Dubs first 12" on Skysaw, released in 87. Mark's voice looped somewhere between speech and howls, unmistakable as the thrusting dub-o-billy rhythm. Topside down: downside up.

Mark wrote lyrics so awesome that you just wanted to

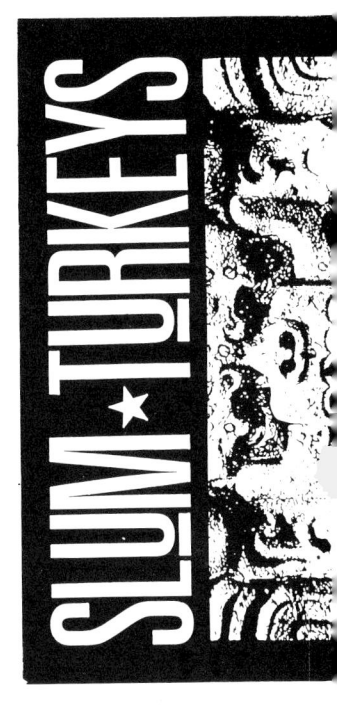

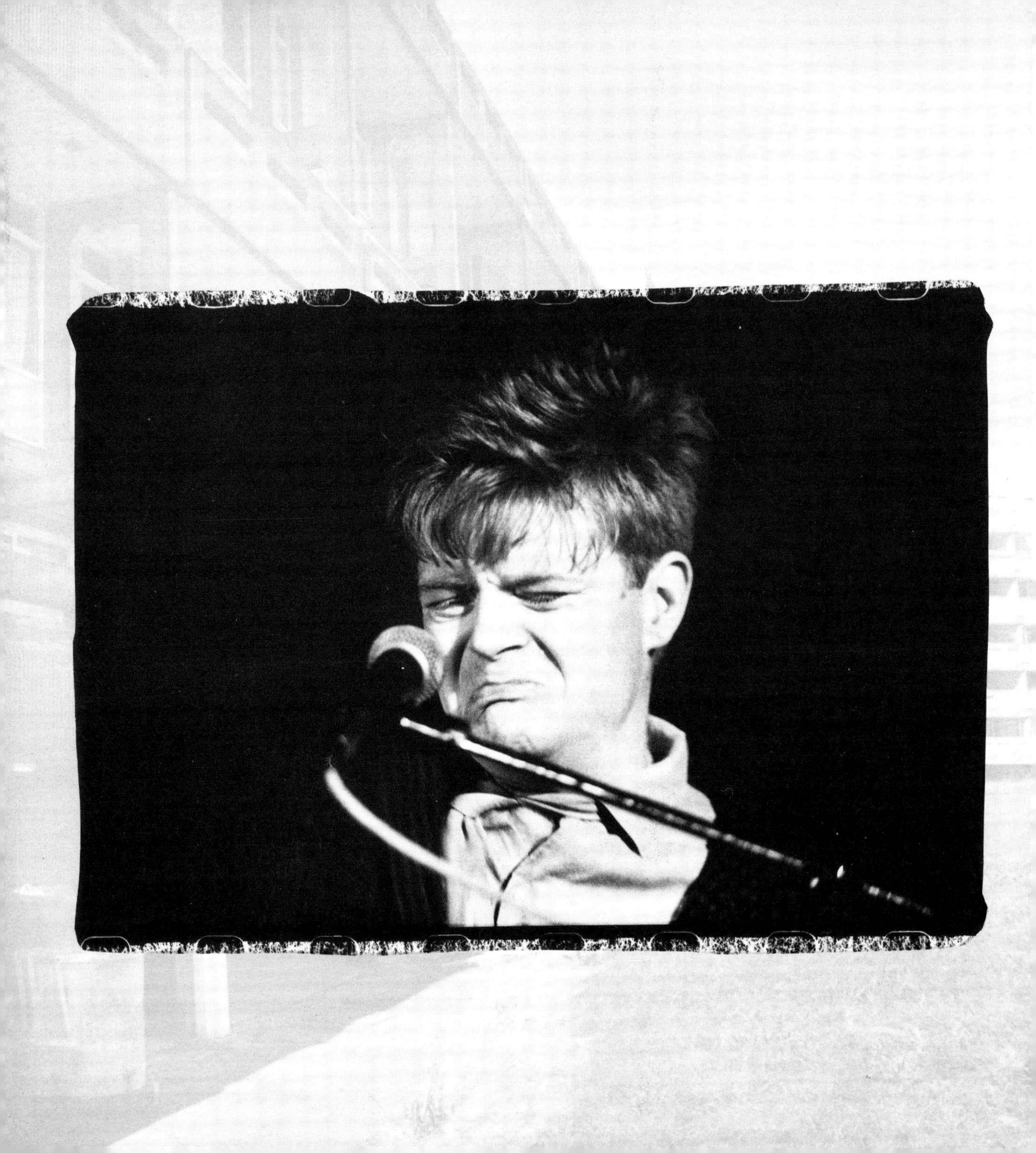

snatch them from the air and hug them tight. 'Conceived in the nineteen-sixties/Ten years in the grip of a snarebeat...' went *The Underneath*, a 12" on Cut Deep Records. 'Someone pushed me/took the skin off my knee/bit my lip so hard I made it bleed/I was loud as an army,' sneered *Playstreet*, from the mini-LP *PUSH!* on Ugly Man.

After a childhood 'in care' in some of the scummiest parts of Manchester, Mark had a lyric-book full of jail-cell recipes, motorway crashes, bullies and criminals. Sounds kinda romantically urban but Dub Sex make sure you feel the real *fear*. Dub Sex became Mark's whole life, his reason for living, the belief that kept him alive and out of jail.

"Lee Pickering, who started Dub Sex with me, got sent to prison," discloses Mark. "When he comes out, he'll be 29 and defeated. That lad's got a lot of worth to get over to people. It's a disgrace that could have happened to him."

Swerve (Cut Deep), Dub Sex's classic indie song of 89, encapsulated Mark's belief in music as the only escape route. "*Swerve*'s about not giving in. It's about having the nerve, believing in yourself, not getting dragged down, keeping out of trouble. Dub Sex saved me personally. I've spent my whole life since I left care trying to set up Dub Sex. I was going totally off-the-rails. Now at least I know where the rails are. The rails are my belief."

As a band, Dub Sex were an odd bunch. Bassist Cathy Brookes couldn't have been more different to Mark. While he was tough Manc scum, she was raised in Maidstone, polite, well-educated, versed in social etiquette, with a BBC accent. She left Dub Sex and in the summer of 90 set off on a world cycle trek in tandem (literally!) with GMR indie-DJ, Phil Korbel, publicising the plight of the rain forests for Friends Of The Earth! "Cathy's dead posh," laughs Mark.

Contradictions, contradictions. *Swerve*, honest and intense, was virtually a 'pop' record, gaining them a memorable *Snub TV* performance filmed live at The Boardwalk. So 89 looked to be Dub Sex's *big* year. Their previous releases *Then And Now*, *The Underneath* and *PUSH!* were combined to form *SPLINTERED FAITH* on Cut Deep. In just one week they supported both the Roses at International 2 and Mondays at The Haçienda.

Yet Cut Deep was in trouble, choking on its own over-enthusiasm so, by November, Dub Sex had switched to Bop to put out *Time Of Life*. It satirised E-culture with all the irony of *Transmission*. 'Are you having the time of your life?' it asked. Are you partying to the end? Dance, dance, dance to the radio. But scallydelia overtook them and, even if they'd stitched all their jeans together, they wouldn't have had a pair of flares between them. They were left behind, the last kids in the queue.

Dub Sex were doomed by their Englishness. Had they been New Yorkers, they'd have been on *The South Bank Show* by now. As DJ Dave Haslam once wrote, "Dub Sex are worth six Butthole Surfers."

Fact! Any old gang of lazy US art-punks are adored, UK 'combos' get stomped on!

Slum Turkeys are more neglected Hulme Noise. They call Manchester, 'the home of insipid indie-pap', and themselves, 'Manchester's definitive Noise pioneers' for their 89 'subversive' single *Ugly As Sin*. "If we were from New York instead of Manchester, people would think we were Gods," says Doc-decked front-man Paul Morley, refuting any connection with Morley, Manc *NME* hack last seen bickering with Wilson on *The Other Side Of Midnight*.

"At the moment people in London think Manchester's a really cool place. They think everyone lives on council estates, takes E, goes to acid house parties and dances on stage with Happy Mondays. We don't fit that image." Hulme's beat was never a part of scally culture which was initially and 'supposedly' about working-class North Manc council estates, not studenty inner-city slums.

Inca Babies, Edward Barton, Tools You Can Trust, The Rattlesnakes. Somehow it all seems worlds away from fashion-conscious Manc indie bands 90s-style. When did things change?

OPPOSITE
Edward Barton, June 1986.

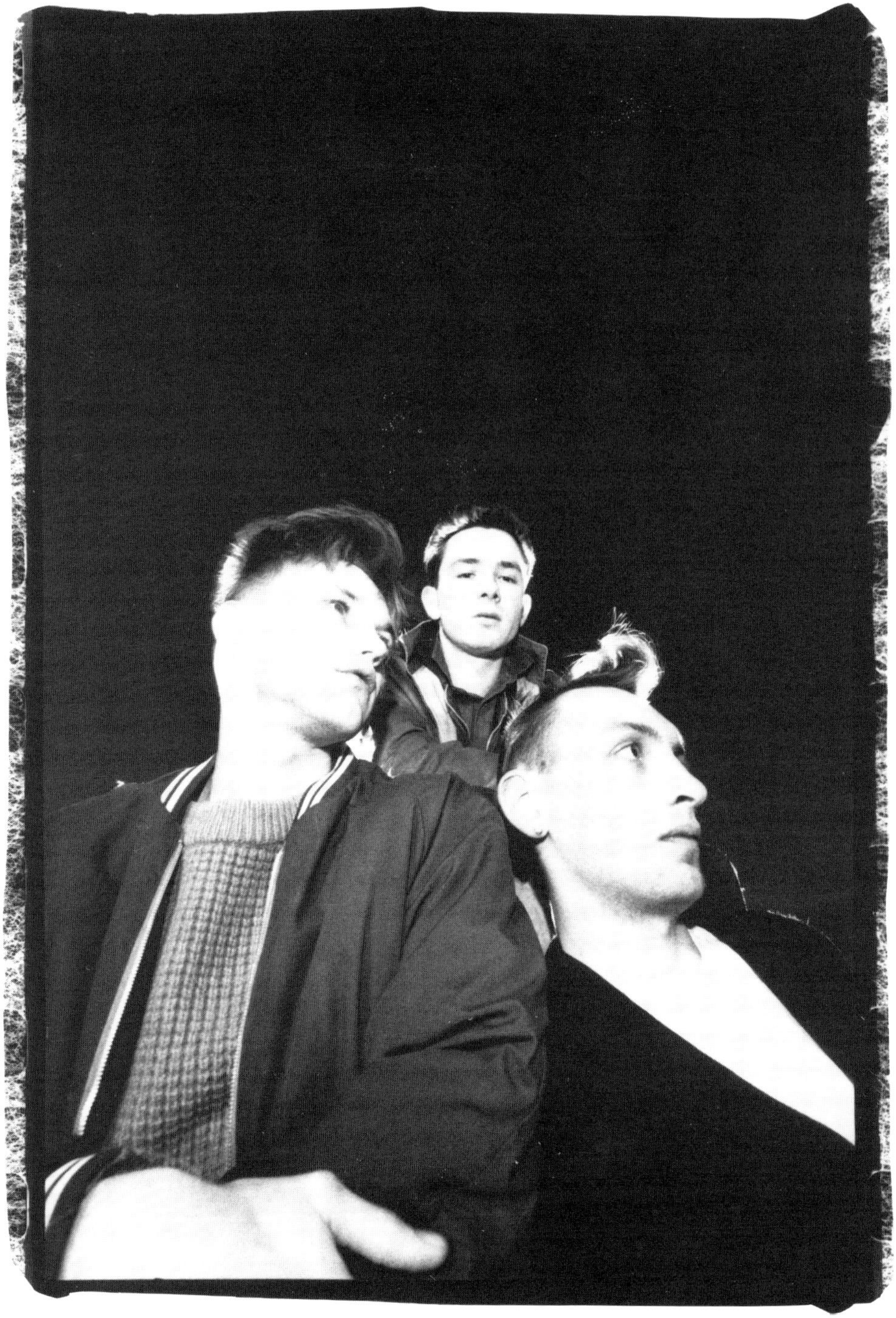

Exit the 70s. Enter the 80s. Death to trad rock. Death to chart pop. Firebomb Radio One. You know when you're 16? When you leave school? When you see your first gig? You *know* then that you can *change* the world. No ifs, buts, hows, whys, just a simple revolution. You know what I'm saying? Well, that's what 'indie' meant in the 80s.

WhistlinG in the Dark

And God Created Manchester

Pop music spent 25 years in the grip of grown-ups and grown-dulls. Then came punk. That's PUNK with capital letters, speeding Sid Vicious to his grave, Buzzcocks to pop-stardom, Paul Morley to a media-life in London. *Fuck* punk! As Sex Pistols' destination plate read, this bus was going 'Nowhere'.

In its Last Will and Testament, punk left only one jewel. Independent Music. DIY records. Suddenly, bands could clamber from the gutter, be as uncivil as they liked, and still sell records in shops.

"We set about to change the world, I think. Or the pop world at any rate," laughed guitarist, Greg O'Keeffe, of Big Flame.

Hulme's Big Flame were mavericks, universally intoxicated by the belief they could alter history. You *need* that faith, swagger, illogical desire, to be *somebody* in pop music. Ask Ian Brown or Morrissey. Talk to any stubborn musician.

"We were naive enough to think that, if we had a good enough product, it would sell. We provided a positive alternative, rather than a whining, negative alternative," reasoned Big Flame

Fired by an equally positive attitude, the scene was best documented by obnoxious fanzines circulated like political propaganda - the 60s had psychedelic comics, punks wrote mags like *Sniffin' Glue*. The term 'fan-zine' was coined. From *C86* pop-zines to 90s rave-rags, from goth bibles to Marxist trash, it came down to kids/fans/inspired youth having *their* say.

Musical and political idealism was the tone of early 80s indie music. Working-class Stretford kids, Andy and Ivor Perry were angry. So, they started a band,

OPPOSITE
Big Flame, 1985.

played their first ever gig supporting The Smiths at Dingwalls in 83, signed to London, released *Coming Up For Air* in 85. Easterhouse were born, named after a hellish Glasgow housing estate.

"If pop music isn't dangerous, then it's drivel," Andy told *City Life*. "The Sex Pistols were exciting at the time, but now it needs a lot more substance."

It was the Red Wedge era when Billy Bragg and The Redskins, revelling in the Miners' Strike, took on the Tories; yet the revolutionary stance of Easterhouse was different. "The working-classes don't want to be the proletariat. They want to dress up and escape. The Redskins are public schoolboys dressing down to be the proletariat," ranted Andy in *Muze* magazine, October 85. While The Redskins held hostage shopping malls with the Socialist Workers' Party, Easterhouse carried the flag of the Revolutionary Communist Party.

The Miners' Strike brought out the best and worst in people. Every hip band in town rallied, doing benefits, ranting in the music press.

"People phoned up and went, 'We're on the barricades together'. And you'd go 'What?'" remembers John Robb of The Membranes. "Then they'd ask you to play in Hull for £40. You'd tell 'em you needed £100 and they'd go 'Are you capitalists or something?' The Miners' Strike was used to get loads of bands to play cheap gigs. A shambles."

While Easterhouse praised the IRA, they condemned the fairy-tale soft-left image of the working-classes. Their second single *Whistling In The Dark* (Rough Trade) slammed Arthur Scargill. "Two weeks after the Miners' Strike began, we saw these posters going up saying, 'They Shall Not Starve'. Who was starving? I thought they were going out to win a strike. They perpetuated this vision of miners where you'd get this big fat bloke knee-deep in water, squashed between two seams, hacking away with his chisel, his butties in his pocket and no shirt on his back. It's not like that any more!"

Easterhouse's album, *CONTENDERS*, was hyped as Manchester's most important debut since Joy Division's *UNKNOWN PLEASURES*. Yet, only weeks after its release, the band had split. Easterhouse became a solo Andy Perry project, allowing him to develop some quirky views.

"I'm not 18 any more, I'm older. Now I say that music serves a function. It's not spiritual or creative," he told *Sounds* in 89. He aimed to make Easterhouse as MOR as necessary to get his message across. Thus his album, *WAITING FOR THE REDBIRD*, and single, *Come Out Fighting*, were politico-rock as clichéd as Bruce Springsteen's *Born In The USA*. Andy Perry posed in leather jacket, arms up-lifted like a godly Bono. Everything that Easterhouse had originally fought against.

Death to trad rock. Big Flame had nicked a big fuck-off music-biz Merc and were doing 90 down the indie motorway. In the back seat A Witness, Vee VV, Bogshed and The Mackenzies, jostling for a glimpse out the window. Overtaking in the fast lane, The Three Johns, Yeah Yeah Noh, The Nightingales, The Membranes. A speedway of fast bands who believed discordant 'pop' would shake multi-nationals to the ground.

Call the cops! Call the fire brigade! Call me a cab and follow that car! Big Flame were really motoring. *Sink*, *Rigour*, *Tough*, *Cubist Pop Manifesto* and *Why Pop Stars Can't Dance*. Big Flame created five 7" EPs for Ron Jonson Records. That's one for every finger, wrapped up as colourful as Christmas presents. Remember 7"? A symbol of artistic purity, clean as mountain water, spiritual as incense, collectable as First Day Covers. Pre-house, 12" was considered an evil cash-in.

"I hope to God we never do an LP," Greg prayed back in 85, recoiling at the very thought. "In fact, we never will. The fact is, singles are fucking ace! All the best records are singles."

Big Flame cut a precise groove, stole electro/jazz/rock and speeded it up into jagged funk noisescapes. Stop-start, cut-up, fold-out, wah-wah pop. Shouting, not singing.

"Put your guitar through a mincer and try to play what's left," wrote Leeds 'zine *Attack On Bzag*. "Get the bits of the strings that are too tight to strum, the bits before the pick-ups, and scrape them with a nail. High-pitched, more jerks than an American comedy show. Spinning the wheel of a bike, then touching the spokes with a stick."

"We're interested in being a lone shining spark that says, 'Fucking hell, *this* is it and *nothing* else counts!'

enthused drummer, Dil Green, exuberant as ever, "We're trying to produce exactly, concisely and precisely as possible what we want to get across style-wise, musically and lyrically in Big Flame. No outside influences are going to tell us what Big Flame is or could be."

Big Flame's demise was as choreographed as their rise, chopped short, with no second thoughts, at The Boardwalk in October 86. By this point they'd snapped out of their naive daze. Wised up. Got serious. Got cynical. Got off the motorway. Dil became an architect; vocalist, Alan Brown, formed The Great Leap Forward and Communications Unique Records, with a studio at 23 New Mount Street; Greg blagged a one-off Factory deal.

Greg's cavaliers, Meatmouth, were Manchester's Beastie Boys. *Meatmouth Is Murder*, their one release, died like a fly in a washing-up bowl. 'We are young and we are tough/The underground North is rising up/We're going downtown, going on a bend-oh/chatting up girls outside The Haç-i-end-oh …' a rhyme to grate your teeth to! As a matter of historical trivia, it was Greg who first coined the word 'scallydelic' in a drunken brawl at The Boardwalk, September 89.

Stockport's A Witness were another Ron Johnson band. Metaphorically-speaking, they shared Big Flame's dirty needles, drank the same blood, breathed the same petrol fumes . Albums *LOUDHAILER SONGS* and *I AM JOHN'S PANCREAS*, had a pervy twist-of-words like that line, 'Bag over right shoulder,' from *Sharpened Sticks* on *NME*'s C86. John Peel was reprimanded for the extremity of A Witness' session. So he repeated it immediately!

Unlike Big Flame, A Witness had no three-year plan. Long after Big Flame burnt down, came *Red Snake*, *One Foot In The Groove* (Ron Jonson), *Sacred Cow Heart* (US Import LP) and zappy *I Love You Mr Disposable Razors* (Vinyl Drip).

John Robb has a lot to answer for. His band The Membranes, fanzine *Rox*, and record label Vinyl Drip, were to the noise-pop scene what Roses and Mondays are to scally. Fact: there have been more fanzine pieces on The Membranes than Billy Bragg, The Smiths and New Order put together. *And* they once reached No 6 in John Peel's Festive 50, beaten only by The Smiths, New Order and Cocteau Twins.

"Another great last rock 'n' roll band, pop songs, but so deformed, so loud, so noisy. Pulling faces, going red and looking concerned, that's not passion. The other definition is doing something stupid for a long time with no tangible success, so it must be passionate," ranted John Robb in Rochdale's *Another Empire* in 85.

The Membranes, raunchy rock 'n' roll for punky cheese-heads and hitchhikers in anarcho-khaki. Fans would punch the air, punch each other, roll round on the floor, dance under bedsheets, push-and-shove, sending bags full of shredded newspapers whirling in the air, gobbing at each other, stage-diving. Really more of a kerfuffle than a riot, like a rough-and-tumble of rowdy little boys at prep-school.

"We've got this really odd following. Like punks who wear anoraks with the arms ripped off. The fat spotty kid with the National Health glasses is always there as well," John told *The Yellow Book*.

The Membranes were satirical pooonk-rockers whose catalogue included *Spike Milligan's Tape Recorder*, *CRACK HOUSE*, *SONGS OF LOVE AND FURY*, *KISS ASS GODHEAD*, *DEATH TO TRAD ROCK*.

"The reasons people have for hating us are all the good things. They think they are insulting us when they say we're loud, noisy and dirty, but that's what we think of ourselves as." John Robb was a rock star who'd wear leather trousers and strip to the waist, but he was ageing fast so switched to being a full-time rock-journo for *Sounds*!

Following The Membranes' footsteps to fame, Vee VV moved from Blackpool to Hulme in 85. They rhymed 'pink cadillac' with 'Jack Kerouac', took their name from a 20s Dadaist rag and robbed their album title from the American Constitution.

Kindest Cut/Romance Is Over, on Glasgow's Cathexis had Leslie Crowther as cover star … because in Roman numerals VVV is 555 and Leslie's old show *Crackerjack* was on at five-to-five on the fifth day of the week! Smart, hey?

BOOMSLUMP EP and album, *LIFE LIBERTY AND THE PURSUIT OF HAPPINESS*, followed. Vee VV spat back at money-makers and manipulators, phone-tapping, bribery, corruption, knives in backs. 'Lay off, lie back, here comes your kick in the teeth …' a song about the Miners' Strike, that could equally describe their career. Ricocheting between Bunnymen/Chameleons pop and Big Flame-funkiness, their album was a mish-mash scraped together from a Piccadilly session, Constrictor single and *Debris*-flexi.

This was LIFE LIBERTY AND THE PURSUIT OF HAPPINESS, a promise of the American Constitution, where profit mattered more than people and money equalled power. Without these, Vee VV were doomed. Born into a Blackpool no-mans-land, prisoners of the small-time. The romance was over.

Punk influence was perverted by electro and rap. Northern indie acts had been corrupted by funk from the start of the 80s. *Debris* fanzine discovered Twang and cut a flexi, *What's The Rub*. Wrote Dave Haslam, "Twang's pervy disco rhythms are the product of Twang boys' love of mutant hip-hop dancefloor beats. The influence of dancefloor rhythms on independent music has a history: from A Certain Ratio and The Fire Engines through to The Cabs, Chakk, Big Flame and Twang. One of the richest seams ever cut."

Sharp, tight, abrupt, funky, brutal, Twang songs never lasted more than two-and-a-half minutes. A cool foursome, Dave Hindmarsh, Lenny Penrose, Jon Sergeant and Andy Ladd (later to work for Eastern Bloc). Sneered Preston fanzine, *Noise Annoys*, "If you're a goth, hippie or rocker, you might as well keep your head up your arse than listen to Twang, because you will not like them. Twang are the *new* faces, the *new* style, the *new* sounds and definitely the *new* band ..."

In a just world, bands like Twang and Big Flame would have been pop stars. Maybe. Justice? Pah! No such thing. When the school bully nicks your dinner money, you realise life's no easy ride.

"We've got completely sick of the independent ghetto," said Dil of Big Flame in 86. "Records get played, say, five times on John Peel but, if you miss that, you don't get to hear the record unless it gets in the indie charts. The independent scene is full of worthy people who essentially don't want their records to sell a lot."

The DIY dream turned into a nightmare. People wised up. They had no choice. Everything had to be financially viable. Death to trad rock. Death to chart pop. Firebomb Radio One. Exit 80s. Enter 90s

OPPOSITE
The Membranes, April 1987.

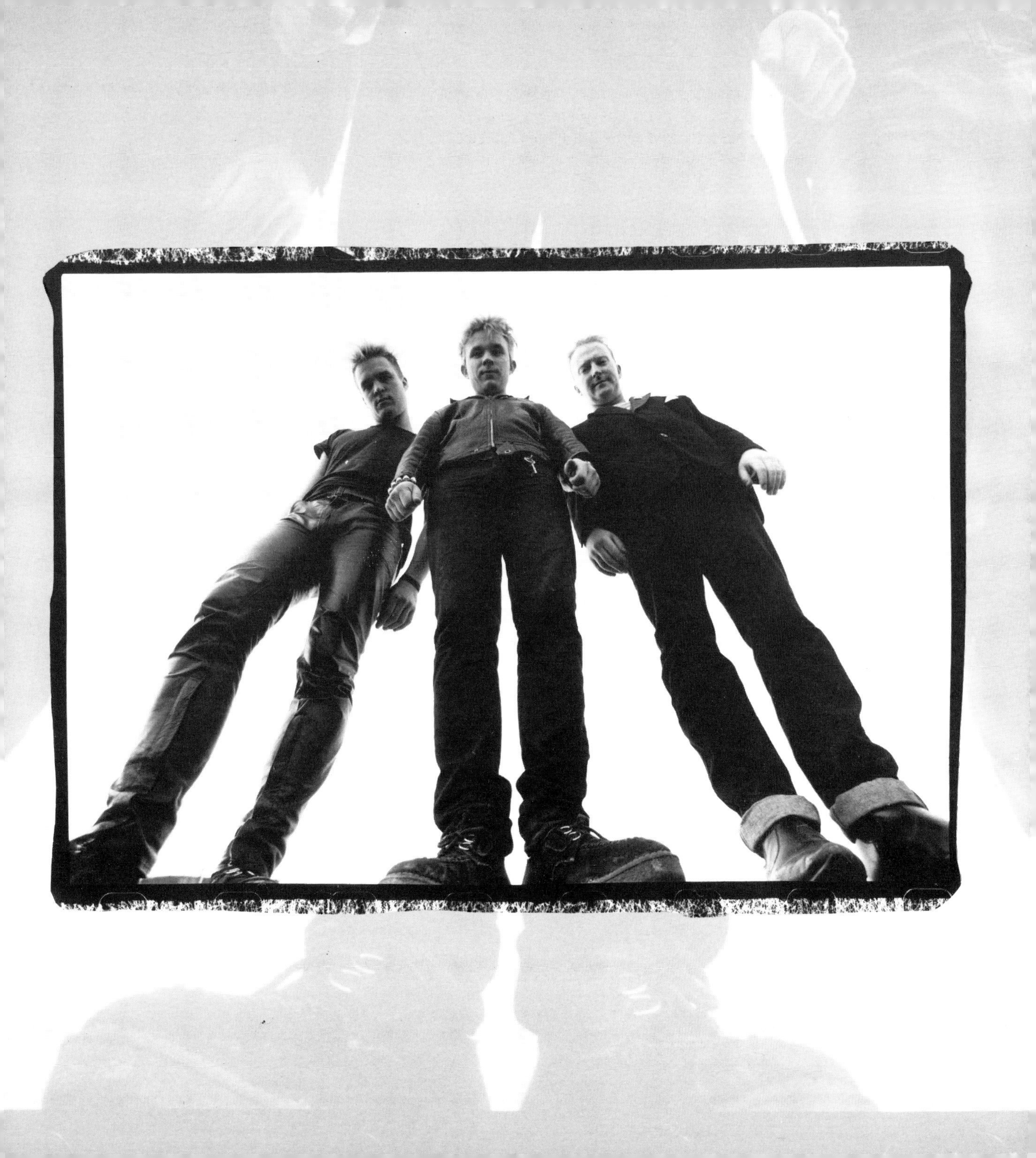

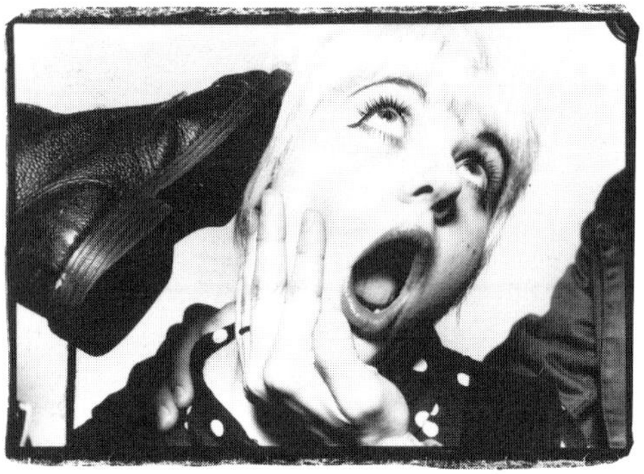

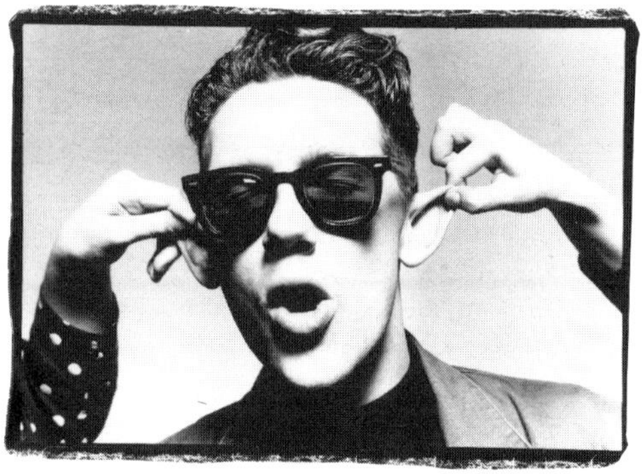

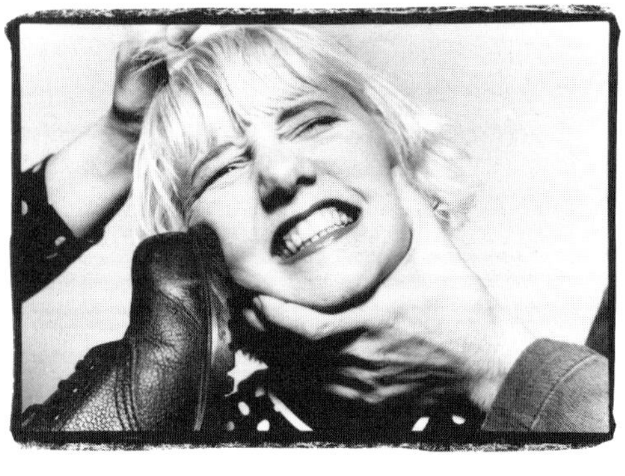

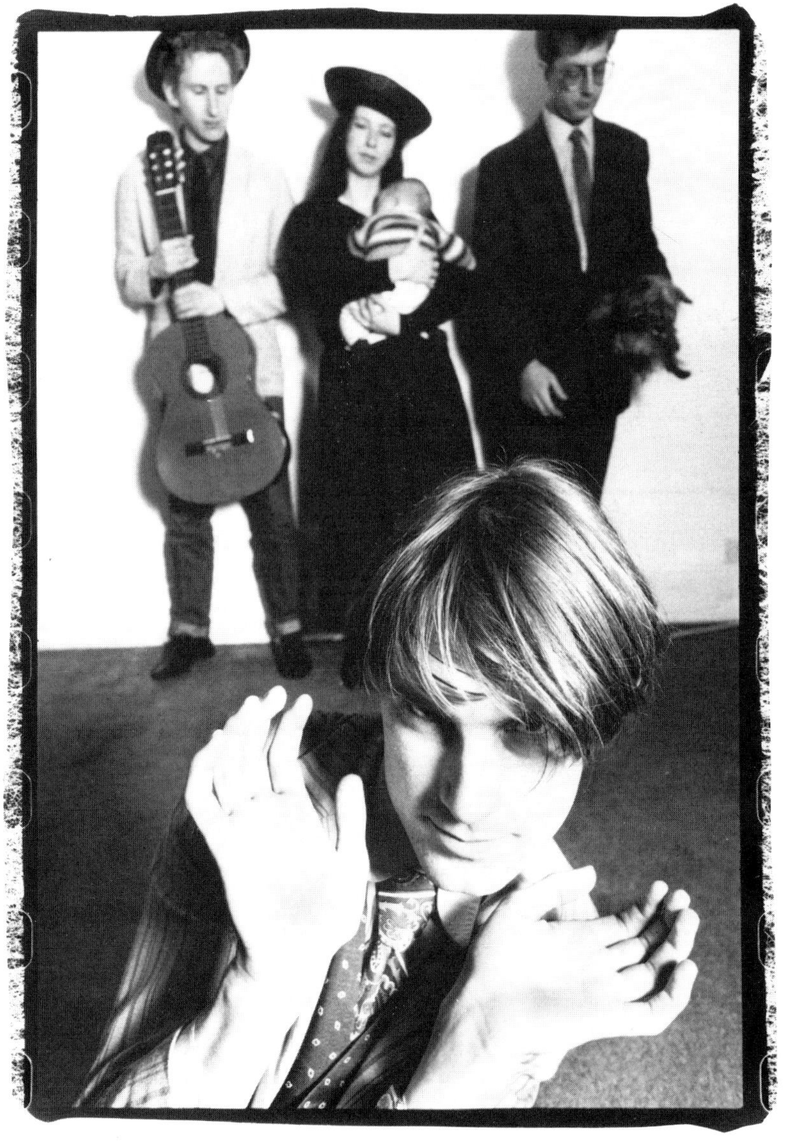

Manchester La La La

7 And God Created Manchester

'Manchester, La, La, La!' A football anthem, idiotic slogan, fanzine, a chant that has travelled worldwide with Manchester bands. Particularly favoured by indie pop-kids. You know the sort ... posh kids, rich kids, spoilt brats, screwed-up grammar-school boys. Scallydelia gave them a chance to dress working-class. Before that, they just had Morrissey and a Mr World of cute, pale-faced pop bands.

Click! Captured on photo, those silly smirks, cutie grins. Yeah! Bands with ordinary day-jobs, simple songs about love. Wooosh! A 'la-la-la' chorus and riff stolen from the Beatles. Swoon! The hearts of boys and girls across the nation leapt. Indie pop became a new religion, discussed in sacred tones. An 80s kind of beatnik. Fringes, polo-necks, anoraks with toggles, Enid Blyton, *Blue Peter*, *Swallows And Amazons*, Winnie The Pooh badges. Manchester tra-la-la-la. Plink. Plink. Fizz!

In 86 serious, earnest, intense young men promoted throwaway music, 'like bubble gum when the flavour's gone'. *Pop* tunes, released on flexi, sold out of carriers at gigs. The ultimate disposable product. Ruled by The Smiths, the Manc scene was well-stewdie.

The hippest new venue was The Boardwalk. Run by Colin Sinclair and his dad, Don, it was a converted school hall hidden in warehousland near The Haçienda. The original site for The Green Room, it doubled as rehearsal rooms. The first gig was a private party, featuring The Railway Children and James, packed to its 250 capacity.

Nathan McGough and Dave Haslam promoted Boardwalk gigs under the guise of Workhard, a series of classic Saturday nights out which featured many embryonic indie-stars. Pop Will Eat Itself, The Soup Dragons, Primal Scream, Sonic Youth, The Primitives, plus all the bands who appeared on *NME* indie sampler *C86*. An early finish enabled you to go on to The Haçienda. A golden era for live music.

Creation Records had a lot to answer for. It was the

OPPOSITE
The Man From Delmonte, March 1987;
Tot, August 1987.

logical next step for boss, Alan McGhee, who had been in London since 80, fronting his own band, Laughing Apple, scripting 'zine *Communication Blur* and promoting indie club, The Living Room. The label owned up to Jesus And Mary Chain, Primal Scream, The Weather Prophets, House Of Love, Felt, Ride, Momus, My Bloody Valentine, The Telescopes ...

Creation's only Manchester signing were The Bodines. "We're complete outsiders when we go to London," said vocalist Michael Ryan in 86. "All the other bands know each other. Especially the Creation bands, they're all good pals."

God Bless, *Therese*, *Heard It All* were The Bodines' classic *pop* singles. And, yeah, they were fringed pretty boys: John, Paul, Tim and Michael, as 'ordinary' as could be. Their debut gig was at The Haçienda, the night Spear Of Destiny pulled out. They were managed by Nathan McGough in his 'pop-kid' days, before he was corrupted by the Mondays. Bought out by Magnet, The Bodines were promised the world. Yet, after their album, *PLAYED*, a summer sound sensation, failed to make them Top 40 stars, they soon found themselves back on indie Playhard.

Like a ballroom dancer trying to body-pop, Miaow were out of step with the other acts on *C86*. Survivors of an early-80s jive, dominated by *City Fun* magazine and the Manchester Musicans' Collective, they were fronted by journalist Cath Carroll. Bright sparks Miaow, with two Factory singles *When It All Comes Down* and *Break The Code*, played indie jazz-fusion. Cath was poised to join other ex-*NME* hacks, Chrissie Hynde and Bob Geldof, on *TOTP* ... yet, by the time Iceland's The Sugarcubes caught the groove Miaow had been striving for, Miaow had vanished!

Other Factory babies were The Railway Children, who'd written perfect indie singles *Brighter* and *Gentle Sound*. "One of the squarest guitar bands in the area, with a reputation for sitting on the fence, not living on the edge," said *City Life*. The Railway Children didn't grasp the *C86* vibe ... they were wet rather than twee; pompous rather than lovable; serious rather than fun. After an earnest album, *REUNION WILDERNESS*, they signed to Virgin; LPs *RECURRENCE* and *NATIVE LAND*, singles *Over And Over*, *In The Meantime*, *Somewhere South* were moulded into stadium pop and aimed at the US. Front-man, Gary Newby, was nicknamed 'The Crystal Kid', handsome guy with an empty head.

If The Railway Children had been nicknamed 'The Rallies' and The Man From Delmonte were affectionately known as 'The Delmontes' ... What did that make The Waltones?!

Chorlton's The Waltones sang in rhyming couplets about girlfriends, spilled gravy down their jumpers, tripped over kerbs and pushed the 'pull' doors. Pop as in 'popcorn', signed to Medium Cool along with The Raw Herbs and The Corn Dollies.

James Knox was the lead singer who never grew up. Singles like *Downhill*, *She Looks Right Through Me*, *Spell It Out* wrote a teen movie script of their own. Two Tokyo college girls flew round the globe to see a Waltones' Manchester University gig. After Bros, The Waltones were their fave pop band, managed by Anthony Boggiano, who would later leave them to snatch his fame looking after Inspiral Carpets.

"I don't think there is anyone is the world who writes a better melody than us," beamed guitarist Mark Collins. He meant it. He believed it. He really did. Their album, *DEEPEST,* crisscrossed through country and stadium pop, stealing melodies from Elvis Costello. It was so, so, so ... so 'normal'. So 'ordinary', that it was to be taken as a part of everyday living (morning, evening and after meals).

From *nice* boy pop bands to *sexy* girl bands.

First there were The Flatmates, Shop Assistants and Tallulah Gosh, going 'sha-la-la-la-bomba'; pouting, grinning, giggling; inane, innocuous. Soon the Biz saw a mainstream selling point. Peroxide Pop was born. First The Primitives then The Darling Buds, Motorcycle Boy and Transvision Vamp. Selling Marilyn Monroe bimbo sex appeal, the money-*men* cashed in.

Manchester had only one peroxide pop trio. Tot were Debbie, Rachel and Tony Martin, fusing la-la-la pop with hip-hop rhythms. Age Of Chance meets Tallulah Gosh. *NME*'s John Munro called the girls, "a right little pair of Margi Clarks." Disco-gals straight out of *Letter To Brezhnev*? "Dressed entirely in white and carrying matching vanity cases!"

"Once a week, we'd get all girlie and do one anothers hair and ... try each others clothes on," said Debbie. "We're not dumb blondes though," added Rachel. "No, we've got brains as well."

OPPOSITE
The Bodines, February 1987.

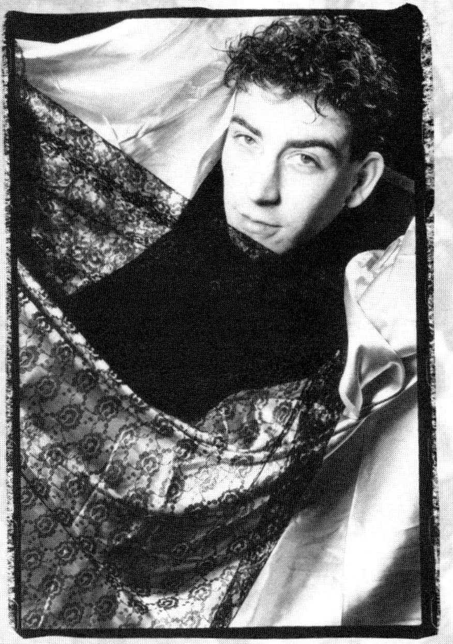
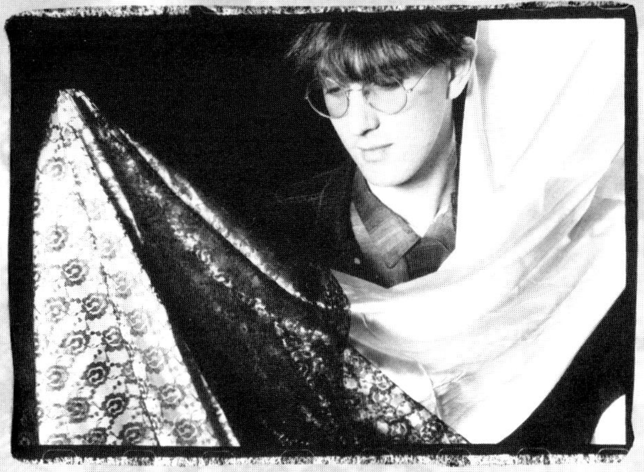
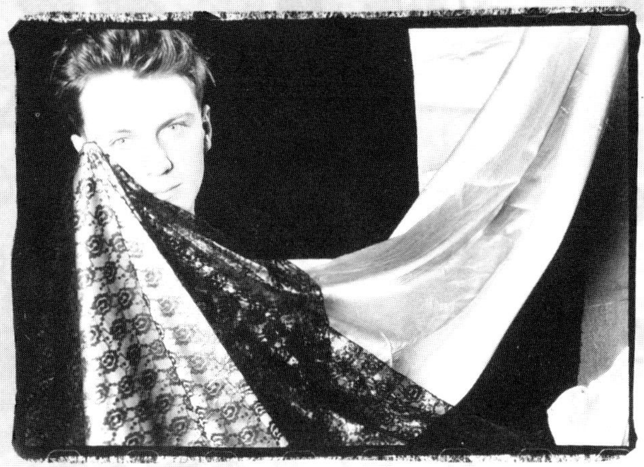
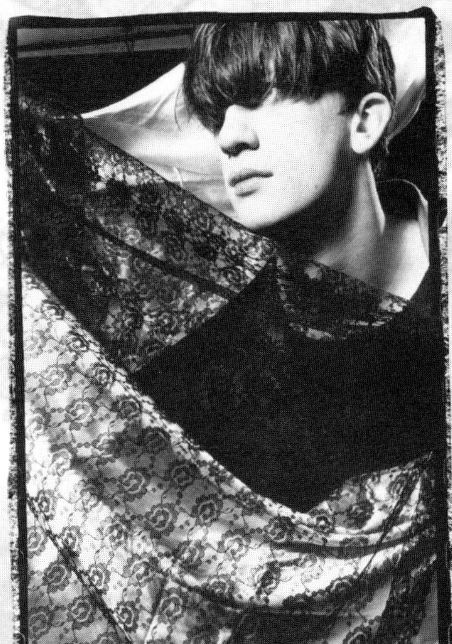

"It's just that nobody wants to see the brains."
"And everybody wants to see the blonde."
Tot! An indie Pepsi and Shirlie, a Mel and Kim, Bananarama even? Gigs at The Haç, supporting ACR at The Ritz and Kathy Acker at the Free Trade Hall, a single *Kill All The Boys* (Rough Trade Germany) and a track on Playhard compilation *HEAD OVER EARS* and Tot were gone. They re-appeared in 89 on house-track *What UR* (DFM), a production job with Debbie's vocals.

After Tot, Twang, Dub Sex and The Bodines, another Dave Haslam/*Debris* discovery was Laugh. "Laugh conjure up a million images of normal England. Arndale girls in short skirts, cheap barber shops, popular cafés, double-decker buses and grey-faced pensioners. This is 60s Merseybeat stretched into the grittier less-optimistic 80s. It may not be what everyone wants to hear, but it's a *goddam* important pulse." *Irresponsible Spirit* fanzine enthused,

Take Your Time Yeah! Take a bus to town. Take a window table in a café. Take time out. Time to talk, smile, think, giggle. Time to *laugh*. Their first release, a *Debris* flexi, *Take Your Time Yeah!*, was a Morrissey fave. A happy-go-lucky tale of eating spaghetti at the Alasia, a greasy café just off Piccadilly.

Take Your Time Yeah! reached vinyl via Remorse Records, followed in 87 by *Paul McCartney* and *Time To Loose It* in 88. Laugh should never have been part of the jangly la-la-la hyperbole. Sixth-form 'zine, *Gloomy Place,* wrote, "I can see heaven in Laugh, but I can still peer in deeper and not see the bottom. Laugh? I think I'm in love again ..."

Laugh got funkier, a mod-band displaced in time. More like The Redskins or The Jam, than The Bodines and Railway Children. Vibrant Northern Soul, Laugh's debut album, *SENSATION NUMBER ONE* (Sub Aqua), appeared in 89. Yet, despite psychedelic soul bass-lines, they were left behind like unlucky prospectors after the Gold Rush.

Ugly Man Records didn't see the 90s Manc boom either. Baby of Guy Lovelady, Longsight-based ad-exec, UGM picked up a bargain ... Colin Vearncombe's Black, described by *NME* as "*The* band of 83", but dropped by WEA after two failed singles.

Play-listed by Radio One, Black's *Wonderful Life*, Ugly Man's debut, shot to No 3 in the indie charts and 70 in real world. Suddenly A&M stepped in and stole Black away. *Wonderful Life* sold a million, Ugly Man barely broke even and Colin's street-cred now shares the same grave as Mick Hucknall's hipness.

"I remember writing to A&M and saying, 'Give us £3000,'" sighs Guy. "... We said 'We've just done all your A&R, broke Black on Radio One and TV and you're gonna make lots of money.' We were naive enough to write it and believe they'd give us it.

"I phoned the head of A&R, this plummy, toffee-nosed git, who probably goes round in jogging suits and sneakers, 48 but pretending to be 28. He said 'No way!' I couldn't believe it! The rejection was so upsetting. What was £3000 to them, when they'd just had a hit with every track off Janet Jackson's album?!"

The Desert Wolves were more Ugly Man hopefuls who had been heavily hyped on Piccadilly's *Last Radio Show*. Puffy guitar boys in a fairy-tale world of Parisian street cafés. Singles, *Speak To Me Rochelle* and *Love Scattered Lives*, had them cruelly condemned as, "a cross between The Barron Knights and Haircut 100."

Guy Lovelady, who came last on a Kenny Everett game show, chose bands he was friendly with. He released The Country Fathers, a swamp-pop steel-guitar trio, Phil Walmsley, John Clayton and Piccadilly Radio's Mark Radcliffe. So too The Danny Boys' *Days Of The Week*, featuring *Record Mirror*'s Craig Ferguson who, with graphic artist, Mick Peek, later formed Raintree County, Aztec Camera-style popsters responsible for *Nice Time At The Disco* on *MANCHESTER NORTH OF ENGLAND*.

The last three Ugly Man Records were paid for by the bands as Guy had run out of cash; Fallover 24, Ambitious Beggars and *Hurry On Down* by Too Much Texas which featured skinhead Tom Hingley soon poached by Inspirals and made to grow his hair back! However, it was The Man From Delmonte who were Ugly Man's biggest discovery, heroes of every camp public schoolboy in the North. Effeminate popsters who were the middle-class antidote to scally. Teetotal art college graduates! Glasgow-born bassist Sheila Seal, graduated from the Royal Northern College of Music, set up and ran the Castlefield Gallery; guitarist, Martin Vincent, was a painter and *City Life* art critic; Drummer, Howard Goody, attended Winchester School Of Art ... "We have all the trappings of the

---

Debris
* 2nd Birthday Party *
with
The Bodines

At a secret location in Manchester

middle-class, but none of the earning potential. People look at as and say, 'You're white, you've got a nice accent, have a loan!'"

Vocalist, Mike West, the son of millionaire Australian author, Morris West, was once asked, "Has a book ever changed your life?" "Yes!" he replied, "*The Devil's Advocate* ... by a quarter of a million pounds!"

The Man From Delmonte started life like the Stone Roses, managed by Howard Jones. A trashy first demo, *Bachelor Flat Affairs* and *One Day My Prince Will Come*, was produced by Martin Hannett. "I thought I could cope with him," said Howard, "but that was before he was sick out the window of my car!"

With Morrissey ambiguity, hand-me-down melodies, silly-string image, The Man From Delmonte released three Ugly Man singles in 87/88, *Drive Drive Drive*, *Water In My Eyes* and *Will Nobody Save Louise*.

Mike West wrote about old friends in London, David Hughes and Sarah Louise, cruelly naming them in songs about Italian boyfriends, bachelor-flat affairs, alcoholic professionals. He'd later be in trouble for a chorus about Deborah Ann Turner, plus a track which gave a Hulme address and the infamous, *Expecting Ian Brown*, about waiting for the Roses at an hotel! "The songs are rude, blatant, vindictive," Mike told *NME*. "And I use their names and last names as well. You want it to be clear, not vague." But then Mike never had tact, his career as a *NME* stringer cut short by the volume of libel threats!

The Man From also took on The Del Monte Fruit Corporation and were very nearly sued for damaging the company's 'noble' reputation and 'commercial interests'. Another Man From Delmonte 'scandal' involved them being banned in Queensland.

"One song I heard openly commends tranvesticism. Another romanticises a bi-sexual love-triangle," a Gold Coast alderman told *The Brisbane Courier*. "It's not just the kids I want to protect ... I don't want to hear this smut myself!" The truth of this story is doubtful. No member of The Man From Delmonte was gay, but Mike West toyed with sexual ambiguity. 'If you take me dancing, I'll wear my mother's white court shoes and dress like a millionaire ... I could be your Miss Monroe and you could be my Joe Di Maggio ...'

The band were seen as wacky, quirky, fey, insipid and trite ... and those were just the compliments. Hip supports for James, The Darling Buds and The Fall did no good. The press *hated* them! *Sounds* summed them up, "Stadium rock for the under-fives."

Throwaway pop at its daftest. Fans wore dangling braces and tried to recreate Mike's ridiculous fringe. Their 'notorious' manager, Jon Ronson, signed as many autographs as the band, while their mascot, Roger the terrier, demanded a can of Mr Dog before every gig (by contract!). Faves on kids shows *No 73* and *Hold Tight*, they played at the opening of Blackpool Illuminations in 89. *Look In* comic stated that their video, *Water In My Eyes*, was the cheapest *ever* shown on *The Chart Show*, costing just £25!

They signed to Bop for an advance of 25p and played The Boardwalk in January, 89, a frantic affair recorded for *BIG NOISE*, their Bop live LP. Singles *Waiting For Ann*, *My Love Is Like A Gift*, and Greatest Hits tape, *CATHOLIC BOYS ON MOBILETTES*, followed.

Without hype, The Delmontes' following rose from 100 to 900 in just one year, their audience doubling every gig. They'd headed the Albert Square CND Festival in July 88, above Inspiral Carpets. The same year they played an historic International gig organised by Radio Manchester's *Meltdown*, supported by lesser-acts Inspiral Carpets and 808 State!

The Man From Delmonte live was an orgy of screaming girls and tearful boys flinging themselves at Mike West's feet, spawning an array of sychofantic fanzines including *Manchester La La La* and *Sounds Like Singing*. At International 2 in November 89, a huge stage-invasion was saved on video by Jettisoundz. The ultimate sixth-form teeny-bop band.

"I've seen the future of rock 'n' roll ..." wrote a sarcastic Tony Parsons. Get serious!

"Twee pop is for middle-class Surrey kids," said Mike West, a middle-class Surrey boy. "It's an internal, private world of touching pop rather than a mass movement like Manchester scally vibe ..."

Swoon! The Bodines, The Delmontes, The Waltones? Pale-faced pop bands for pale-faced pop-kids. Songs about love for people with nothing else to worry about.

Manchester, La, La, La! A football anthem, idiotic slogan, chant of a generation ...favoured by indie kids ashamed of the fact they're actually from Cheshire!

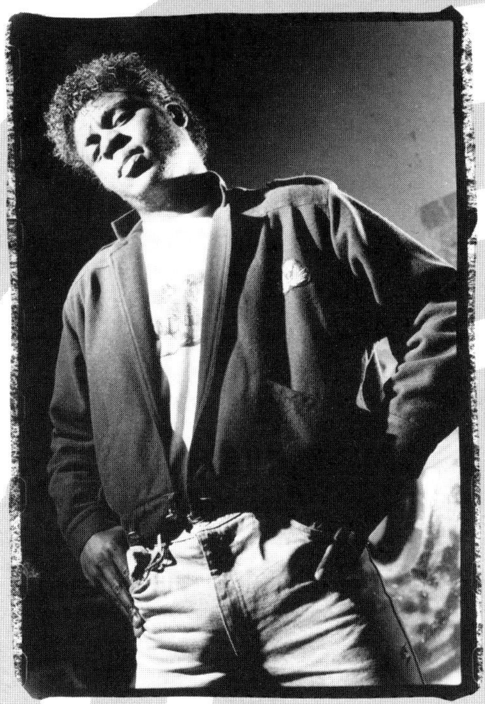

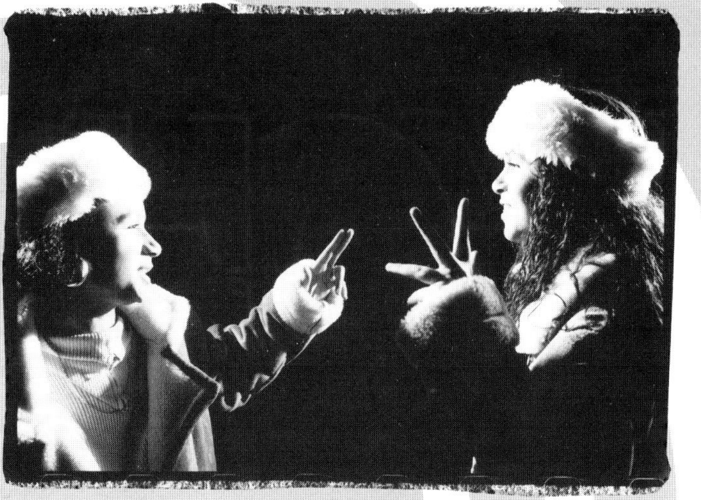

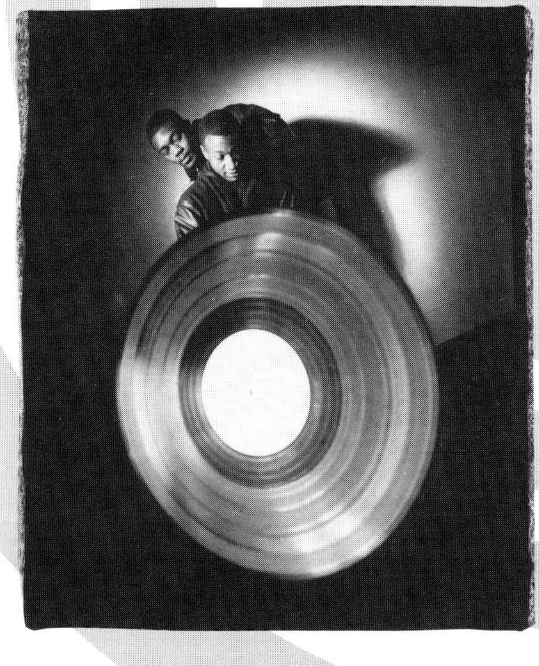

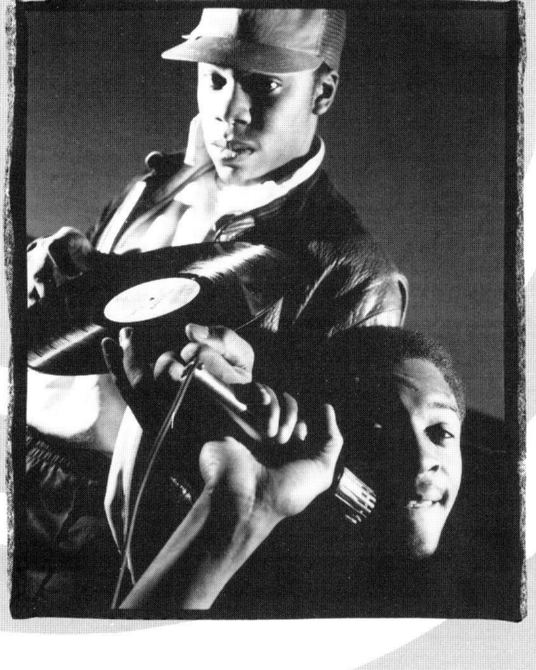

Adventures of the wheels of steel. Street corners, shopping malls, school playgrounds. A youth uprising! Electro charted in a techno-colour ticker tape parade. Breakdancers on the catwalks; body-popping on *TOTP*; graffiti on the buses. Moon-walking, robotics, double-Dutch. Rappers in flash tracksuits. Zany records held together with wacky samples, scratching, mixing and Sellotape.

Wheels of Steel

IN THE NORTH IN '8
starring the Country's TOP
GREG WILSON * MIKE S
COLIN CURTIS

8   *And God Created Manchester*

Maverick Mancs were sharp as a needle, hooked on electro's pulse-beat grades before it chart-busted. This black American ghetto-beat gripped the North West's urban sprawl. Raw like sushi; tough as Rambo. "The whole black side of Manchester has been completely ignored," says Greg Wilson, Manchester's first electro DJ, on the wheels of steel at Wigan Pier and Legends in 82. A disco-chemist, he experimented with mixing and NY's new styles. Secret ingredients included The Peech Boys, electronic black kids turned-on by Kraftwerk's European robotics.

Manchester's old-school DJs *hated* it, clutching even tighter their 'oooh baby baby' collections. Just as the rock biz disliked punk, the black establishment despised electro. Legends stepped out a whole 18 months before *The Face*'s cover feature caught up. Wilson's wild-style competed with Placemate 7's The Main Event, yet still sold out, drawing ravers from Yorkshire, Birmingham and London.

"It orbited!" enthuses Greg. "Legends was jam-packed every night, queues right up Princess Street. It was a state-of-the-art disco. Up till this point, black kids on the Manchester club scene had been stuck in little hovels. It was 80% black."

By the start of 83, white hipsters were changing channels, switching from doom-rock to dance beats. ACR, New Order, Swamp Children and the like tuned in to Legends. Inspired, New Order's *Confusion*, an Arthur Baker-produced electro tune, entered Greg's mixes, while hi-energy-style *Blue Monday* churned up dancefloors like a road drill on concrete.

OPPOSITE
Clockwise from top left
Prince Cool, December 1987;
Peps & Poochie, December 1987;
Johnny J and B Sharp, October 1987;
Master Jam and Owen, January 1988.

53

"In all the things that have been written about Manchester, the thing that has led the way hasn't even been mentioned! The black-white mix! Even when the students arrived, the black side kept its identity and everyone began bouncing ideas around," argues Greg Wilson.

By mid 83 pop's radar was homing in on electro. Haç promo-boss, Mike Pickering, employed Greg. Until then The Haçienda had been an 'alternative' club, with John Tracey spinning Aztec Camera, Animal Nightlife, Siouxsie ... square as a Lada. In 84 Greg passed on his Legends spot (and others) to St Helens teen-DJ, Chad Jackson who pumped mixing to its limits. Even though Piccadilly DJ Mike Shaft loathed electro, he gave both Greg and Chad on-air mix-time. Like bread and butter, chips and gravy, Morrissey and Marr, electro and breakdancing were an inseparable double-act. Manchester's first crew, Reflex, danced out of Moss Side in 79. Invigorated by Grandmaster Flash, Africa Bambatta and docu-movie, *Wildstyle*, Manc jazz-fusion crew, The Scorpions, formed. Led by extrovert Kermit, Broken Glass was moulded in Piccadilly Gardens in 83. *The Tube* filmed them live with Greg - the first mixing on UK telly!

Soon Street Machine and The Supreme Team took over Northern youth club gymnastics. "Breakdancing was so radical," smiles Chad. "How can you take dance to a further extreme?"

Like a restless kid on *Multi-Coloured Swap-Shop*, Greg Wilson exchanged DJ-ing for production. An English re-mixer? Unthinkable! He'd once won an Imagination re-mix competition ... they never released it. So he produced his own material with Martin Jackson of Magazine and Andy Connell (later Swing Out Sister). Together, in 84, they concocted UK Electro for Streetsounds, the label marketing electro compilations to schoolkids. It reached No 60.

Meanwhile, Manchester electro had hijacked youth club culture; DJs, like Owen D, Leaky Fresh and Johnny J, working the under-age party scene. Real club nights at Rafters and Cloud Nine had melted into trouble. "The kids were a bit wild. It was packed out, but they kept wrecking the place, so we got thrown out," said Johnny J who, in the summer of 85, set up a hip-hop jam at Cheetham Hill's Satellite Club.

"That went brilliantly. It was completely full every week. Again it closed down 'cos the kids were getting out of control. At that time, breakdancing was really big in Manchester. It wasn't underground any more. You'd walk out into the street and there'd be kids trying moves."

On every spare square in town, kids rolled out mats and spun on their heads. Unruly lads moon-walked backwards down school corridors. Anyone sporting trainers or tracksuits under £50 was a 'tramp'. You could buy breakdance instruction booklets on doing The Windmill; glossies examined graffiti as a 'cultural' phenomenon; *Breakdance, The Movie* came out. You could even get a copy of Herbie Hancock's *Rock It* by collecting tokens from Kellogg's Cornflakes!

"Electro was one of the great musical revolutions," says Chad. "You could draw a family tree that traces house and rap back to electro and electro back to Kraftwerk. Electro was a lifestyle, an attitude, a frame of mind. It made you tough."

One day, electro became hip-hop. Where DM shoes/501s were symbols of student chic, Def Jam patches/sporty anoraks became synonymous with youth club hip-hoppers. Electro was reincarnated bigger, badder, Deffer than ever. Breakdancing's death was the birth of British rap.

Chad Jackson won the World Mixing Championships in 87, organised by Technics and Disco Mix Club. He battled DJ Cheese on a Champion compilation, travelled the globe, spreading Manchester's reputation, Sefton The Beatbox in tow. Fellow Manc mixers in the running, Owen D, Leaky, Chris Harris and Bury's bedroom-boy, Grand Groove, responsible for *Let's Dance* on Rham Records.

Everyone was on the move. Mike Shaft had long since left Piccadilly and moved to GMR, replaced by the more streetwise Stu Allen. Spin Inn had evacuated its cramped Cross Street basement, home since it opened in 72 as a Northern Soul import store. Spin Inn 2 reflected dance music's changing audience, a bright ground-floor suite close to The Arndale.

"We tried to get away from our identity of being a black music shop," explains ex-manager, Kenny. "Soul music had changed from being just black music to anyone with ideas. All the kids used to be in on Saturday mornings. Tunes, Gerald, Spinmasters ..." Def Jam was now *the* label, umbrella for a lifestyle.

OPPOSITE
Ruthless Rap Assassins, 1989.

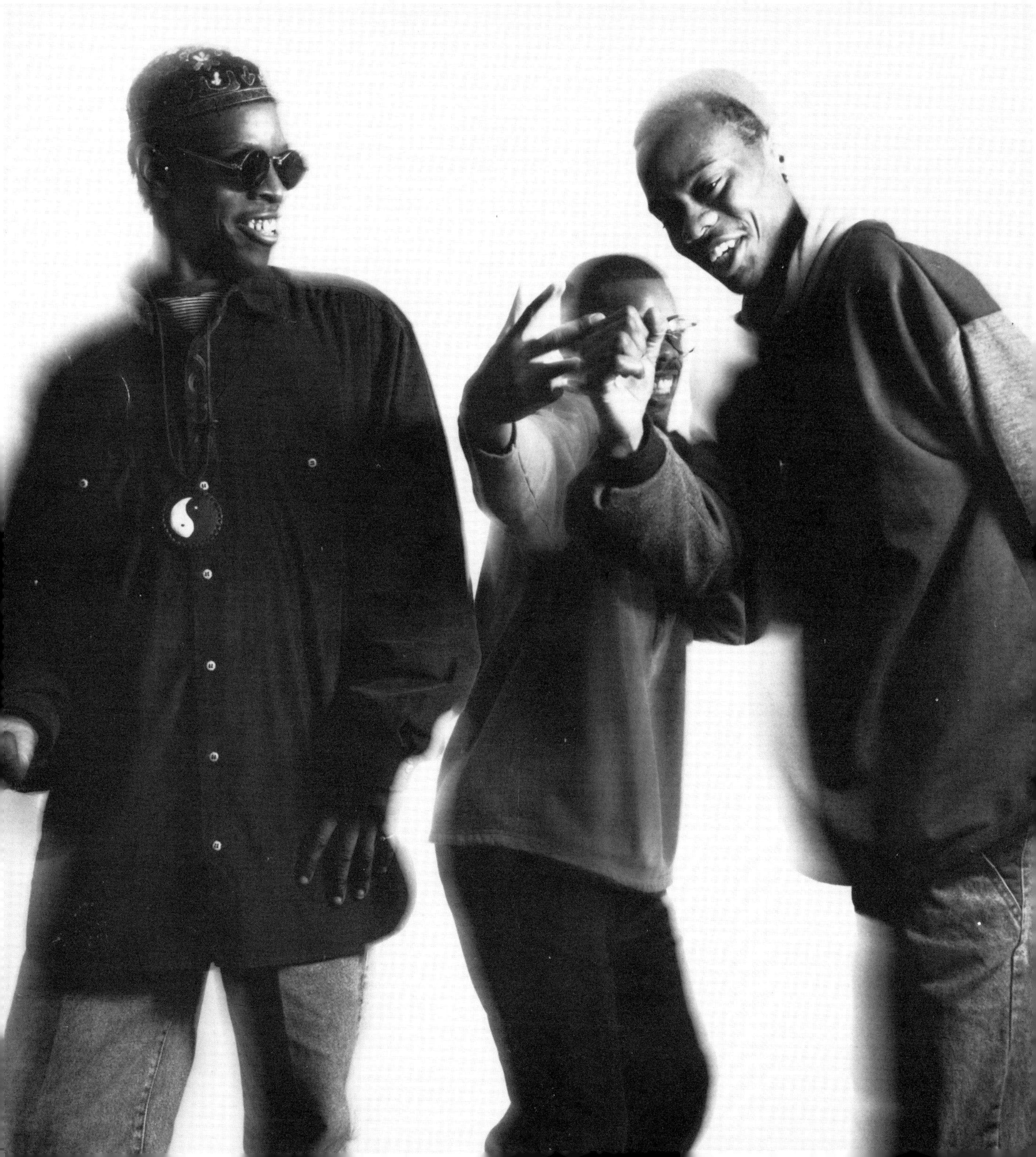

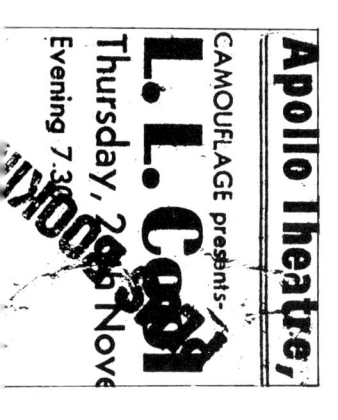

The 'kids' chilled-out at The Gallery, greeting each other with a 'Yo!', hung around Spin Inn, tuned in to *Bus Dis*, sneered at punks and zig-zagged through town scrawling their names on walls. Breakdance gear was jumbled in favour of gold chains, Kangols, sneakers, machine guns, the inevitable baseball hat. In November 87, Beastie Boys hit town. The most contrived group in the history of pop. Ex-punks who swore at cripples, drank Budweiser, had an inflatable penis on stage, locked go-go dancers in cages ... pages of tabloid sensation!

"In Manchester, they welcomed them with stolen Volkswagen badges and arms out-stretched," wrote *NME*'s John McCready. "Outside the Apollo Theatre, the police were three deep. You'd have found more trouble at a Subbuteo match." Not so at Liverpool's Royal Court where the crowd rioted, ripped out seats and threw tear gas.

The Beasties ran home to Mom and Pop in tears! Spoilt wimps.

Def Jam grooved North again with LL Cool J and Eric B, followed by Public Enemy at International 2 in May 88. Hip-hop jams nationwide had been banned due to terror stories of shootings, stabbings and muggings and at International 2 Derek B pre-empted anti-London violence by wearing a 'Manchester North Of England' T-shirt!

Public Enemy were less tactful. Wailing sirens, criss-crossing spotlights and their Security Of The First World Militia holding Uzis symbolically aloft ... Chuck D, Flavor-Flav and Terminator X, an un-Holy New York trinity ... dislocating, uncompromising, deranged ... bringing terror to red-neck America.

"Because I'm pro-black some of the tabloid press in London say I'm anti-white," lectured Chuck D. "They got us banned 'cos we reach too many people and they don't want us to be together like this."

Mancs were getting the message. Forming posses, rapping, buying turntables, samplers, writing tracks, choreographing routines. UK Electro may have been a scam, but this wasn't.

"It's a street thing," Stu Allen told *City Life*. "Sounds clichéd I know, but they can identify more closely with what rappers are describing, than they can with Rick Astley. Punk meant you could grab a guitar and thrash the same chords as the Sex Pistols. Now you just need a record deck to scratch like Cut Creator. If you know someone who can rap, then you've got a crew. It's as easy as that."

A month after Public Enemy, Moss Side's MC Buzz B played Spin Inn Records to promote his debut single *Slaphead/Hard To The Core*. The shop was stacked with 14-year-olds, straight off the bus from school, ties skewwhiff, bags crammed with football kits, blowing whistles. *Slaphead* was anti-school and dedicated to South Manchester's Wilbraham High: 'He was bald from the nose to the crown/You could see your own reflection everytime he bowed down ...'

Spin Inn was *the* meeting place. Yet, by 90, they'd been overtaken.

Eastern Bloc pioneered the house/new beat scene; Decoy on Deansgate was ahead for blues/world; the re-opened Piccadilly Records cleaned up on indie-tunes; while Expansions, on Corporation Street, filled the 'purist' soul market which Spin Inn had been so keen to leave behind.

"Expansions is Manchester's least trendy black music shop," laughs ever-energetic manager, Dean. "We sell very obscure American house, black gospel, rare soul. It's like black music shops used to be." As an import label, Expansions had quietly, and without hype, released some 20 singles in Britain! Spurred on by such enterprise, Spin Inn's Kenny and staff were planning a runner to open a new shop/record label. "We're not being given backing by the owner. We want to advance."

The Manc hip-hop scene was like a High School play. Badly publicised, disorganised, under-funded, riddled with childish in-fights. Few clubs, no cash. Having won the DMC UK Rap Championships 87, Prince Kool only once made it to vinyl, *Here Comes The Judge* on a *Debris* compilation, *HEAD OVER EARS*. Despite kickin' demos, Baby Di, Peps 'n' Poochie, Cold Chillin' MCs, Mouth In Motion and Separate Identity never even got that far.

Adopted by Dave Haslam's Playhard Records, Buzz B became The Bodines' step-brother, thus accepted by the indie scene. He was backed by Rock The House, a posse organised by DJs Johnny J and Karl. Much rap/DJ talent existed in pockets of inspiration, strewn over Northwest council estates like wreckage from a crashed plane. Stu's *Bus Dis* show was a vital contact point for like-minded hip-hoppers, a bit like the BBC World Service linking ex-pats. Other outlets were Radio Lancashire's *On The Wire* and GMR's *Meltdown*. Stu even set up his own label, 061 Records, but only released *Loud Ladies* by Lady Tame.

Hip-house 12"s came from girl-rapper, Zusan, produced by Mike Pickering (Deconstruction) and from Hit Squad MCR, an embryonic 808 State featuring MC Tunes.

Withington's world label, Bop, manufactured a token rap cassette *What's My Name* by MCD. Like many early British rappers, he mimiced his US heroes with fantasy tales of girls, guns and big cars!

One day hip-hop became rap. England's rappers adopted second-hand Bronx streetspeak. Kids who couldn't afford a mountain bike rapped about BMWs. Yet Manchester had a crew, too gifted to play that game ... Ruthless Rap Assassins.

The Assassins, Anderson, Kermit and Carson, and sister act, Kiss AMC, Christine and Anne-Marie, were competing with Derek B, CJ Mackintosh, Cookie Crew, Coldcut. *NME* tagged them one of Britain's foremost hip-hop hopes.

"Rap to us is about where we come from and what we can identify with," said Anderson. "British rap shouldn't be just a diluted Yankee sound."

Electro exiles (see Broken Glass), they hooked up with Greg Wilson, a business friendship that would last. A white label, *We Don't Care/Kiss AMC*, in June 87 and a *Meltdown* session began a buzz. Their Haçienda Zumbar gig, February 88, blagged an EMI deal, retaining Murdertone Records' identity.

Where The Darling Buds ruled disposable pop, Kiss AMC were princesses of throwaway hip-hop. *Let-Off*, their debut, was pure hubba-bubba nonsense, a frivolous, up-tempo nursery-rhyme pop song.

Christine Leveridge and Anne-Marie Copeland, seemingly with pea-green eyes, posed erotically with their tongues down each others' ears! Greg mailed out inflatable Kiss AMC 'pink lips' for bath time. 'Ban These Wicked Sleaze Girls' was the slogan! "I'm not a feminist," admitted Christine, "Just a girl who wants to have fun ..."

Haçienda cloakroom girls gone centre-stage. Two North Hulmies with freaky-deaky tastes. "The best thing about signing to EMI, is that they gave us each a huge cardboard cut-out of Morrissey," smiled Anne-Marie. Most rappers would rather die than confess that. Kiss AMC never wore a tracksuit in their lives. "We both love indie music. The Bodines, The Smiths, Cocteau Twins. In fact we'd really like to make a record with an indie group! Perhaps we could make a record with Morrissey now we share the same label" A wish came true. Or nearly! Instead of The Smiths, their second single was *A Bit Of U2*, stealing *New Years Day*'s riff (with Bono's blessing!), followed by *My Docs*, fashion advice for hip-kids, in June 90.

Yet Kiss AMC never got big enough to swap lipstick tips with Salt 'n' Pepa.

"We're separate entities now," Kermit told *Blues and Soul* in June 90. "They had their chance and blew it, so they're on their own now. Don't get me wrong, I'm very close to my sister, but that's the way it is."

If Kiss AMC were the *Tiswas* of rap, then Rap Assassins were *Panarama*. 'What happens to the brothers when they try and they fail/ You wanna know the answer, take a look at your jails/ I'm living in a system and you tell me it's just/ But there ain't no justice. Just us ...' from their *DRONE SESSIONS* EP, limited edition 12" from 89. Just a taster, showing off their catalogue of samples, Happy Mondays, Maze, Steppenwolf, Hendrix ...

Rap Assassins are no caricature brag-rappers. They are real people. Kermit collects *Marvel* and *Superman* comics; Carson chills-out; his brother, Anderson, has a Humanities degree and part-owns a sports shop in Moss Side. They moved out of Hulme, sick of junkies/ stewdies spoiling their estate. Their *KILLER ALBUM*, summer 90, was no second-hand hip-hop story. It is about *their* experiences.

Soul-styled single, *Just Mellow*, was followed by *And It Wasn't A Dream*, the story of their parents' generation who emigrated to *Great* Britain in the 50s dreaming of that wonderful civilised country that led The Empire! 'Mum packed her cases at the age of 19/She was gonna go to England, she would live like a Queen/She would build her own house, she would raise nuff kids/ Sometimes I know she wishes that she never did/ Residential areas gave a message to Mum/You were OK in the jungle, you'll be fine in the slum ...'

England, land of the free, state of democracy? "I'm proud of being from Manchester, but I'm not proud of

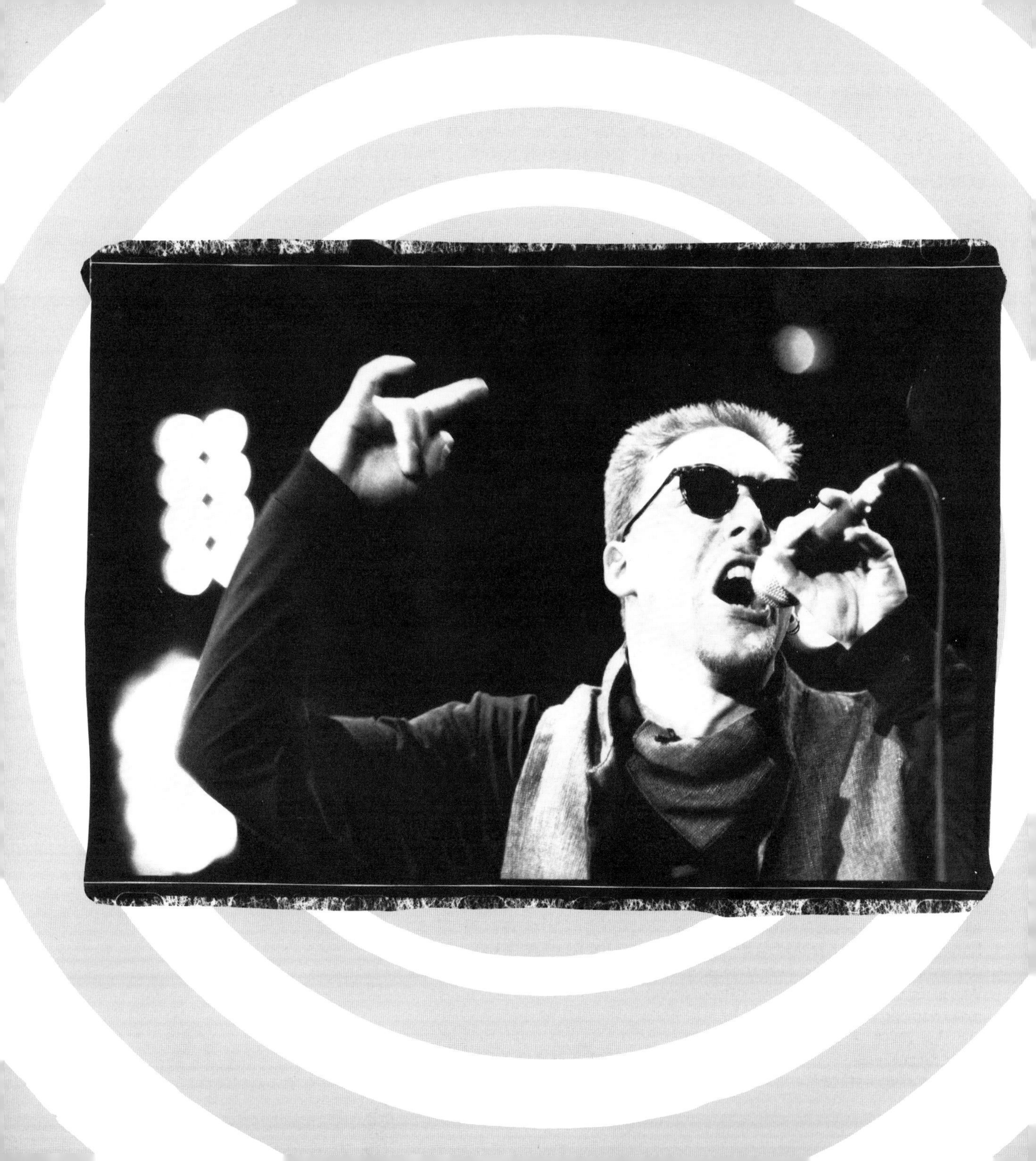

being from Great Britain," says Anderson. "Britain will never be Great."

KILLER ALBUM was a milestone in both Manchester music and rap history. Locally, it ranks with STONE ROSES, Joy Division's UNKNOWN PLEASURES, The Smiths' THE QUEEN IS DEAD, Happy Mondays' BUMMED. Internationally, KILLER ALBUM is a rap landmark as vital as De La Soul's THREE FEET HIGH AND RISING, Run DMC's WALK THIS WAY and Public Enemy's NATION OF MILLIONS.

Simply, the best British rap album ever!

Only MC Buzz B could ever compete. His Playhard singles, How Sleep The Brave, The Sequel and Hard To The Core, refined a new mellow, jazz-influenced form of rap, a genre of his own. He played live across Britain supporting Happy Mondays. "I get on well with the Mondays. They're laddish, but it's to do with what they're about, where they're from, where they've been and where they see themselves going. I used to be the same. I used to be reckless."

Under the management of flash, used-car salesman, Charles of Manchester, Buzz B signed to Polydor. His new material had the cool of Cameo, the class of George Benson, the style of Courtney Pine. He became Mr Cool, Mr Sophisticated and Mr Soul. The 90s single, The Last Tree, was a mellow eco-anthem. 'I bit the air, it tasted plastic/I swallowed man's profound pursuit of things so drastic ...

Rappers against the bomb! Hip-hoppers for peace! Since Africa Bambatta and John Lydon formed Time Zone, since Stetsasonic recorded Africa, since KRS1 said 'Stop The Violence', since the biggest names combined to form Hip-Hop Against Apartheid, rappers have been sloganeering for peace and freedom.

Buzz B preached more personal politics. "Utopia is peace within the mind. You can travel all over the world, but you won't find Utopia. It's to be found here, inside your head."

All aboard the love-mobile. Free tickets all round. Next stop Utopia. MC Buzz B is the driver, philosopher, psychologist, thinker, scientist of hope ...

Without Buzz B, Playhard went on hold. Also on the roster had been Leeds' duo, Breaking The Illusion, and Dee Lawal. A cocky teenager, Dee was the loudest mouth in the classroom, the most vivacious kid in the disco. Her debut single The D Don't Play was a catchy hit, coupled with Stop The Skeezin', a self-explanatory rant at bastard-guys. "It's for a guy who has two children, lives with a girl, but says he wants me. It's me saying 'No way!'"

More stubborn Manc rappers: Elle, a Moss Side girl-duo whose hip-house cut Give It To Me came out on Rham; Krispy Three, kool Chorley trio who appeared on HIT THE NORTH; First Offence, scally-rappers from Little Hulton, mates with Mondays and politically dubious; Bop's Lavinia, teen girl-rapper doing PA's for her single Wasting My Time while eight months pregnant; P Love And Blue, whose Time In The Studio was the finest mix-track since Coldcut ...

All the breakdancers, scratch DJs, MCs kicking round since the days of electro, had their big day out in 1990. Chad Jackson at No 6 in the charts; Rap Assassins on EMI; Buzz B on Polydor ... and most preposterous of all, MC Tunes in Smash Hits!

MC Tunes was a problem child, wider than Broadway, with a scar for every year of his life and an opinion for every bristle of his flat-top. Manchester's most haggard teen idol, with a gipsy-glint in his eye that says he has been there and done it all. Blues brother with an authentic tragic story and a bunch of daft phrases (like 'nish!') forming his very own rhyming slang.

"I was brought up a hippy," he told Smash Hits. "My Mam was a hippy! I was wearing beaded headbands when I was six/seven months old. Me Mam took me to Glastonbury when I was three. Jimi Hendrix was my favourite ... I like trees. I'm gonna buy me son a forest - when I have a son. I did have a son, but he passed away..."

When he appeared on Snub TV, doing a shifty 808 PA, it was underground in every possible way, playing in Eastern Bloc's basement! No-one could have forseen him ending up on TOTP, sampling The Big Country on The Only Rhyme That Bites, doing a scally Thriller routine! Rap beatnik with a goatee beard.

"There is no acid, no indie, no soul music," says MC Tunes. "It all falls into one category now, and that's dance music. If you can dance to it, it's a tune that's worth playing ..."

Adventures on the wheels of steel, where E stands only for Electro.

OPPOSITE
MC Tunes, 1990.

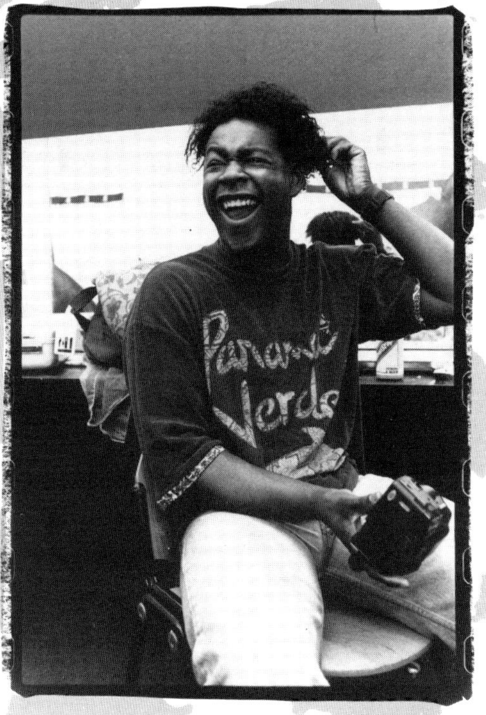

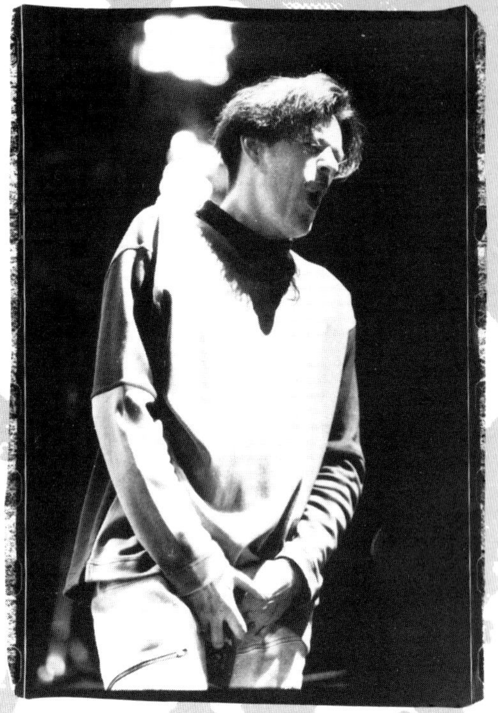

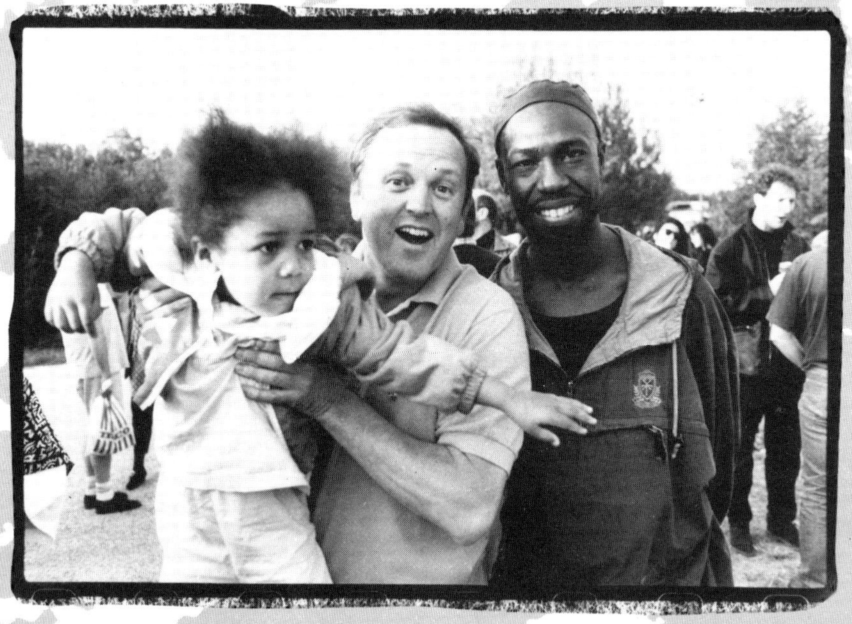

All aboard the groovy train. House from gay Chicago. New York garage. Detroit techno. New-beat built in Belgium. Eurohouse from Italy. Balaeric Beats, Ibiza-style. London rare groove. Industrial Sheffield. Every street, every town, every great conurbation in the globe stamps its own distinctive style on the beats that pump its dancefloors.

On the GroovY Train

And God Created Manchester

The North of England has always been one step ahead in its fave grooves. Like every man is a son of Adam, Manchester's dance culture has a line of descent which goes back to Northern Soul. Soul became disco, disco was overtaken by jazz, jazz faded into electro ... and at this point it diversified into rap, hip-hop, house with all its fusions. Simple, huh? All aboard the groovy train to jazz-city Manchester. Jazz dancing emerged from Blackpool's Mecca in the 70s, where Northern Soul was superseded by disco. Mecca DJs, Colin Curtis and Jon Grant, then pioneered jazz in Manchester in the early 80s, notably Colin's night at Berlin. It first gripped black clubs, then white stewdies infiltrated.

Factory acts, ACR and Swamp Children, caught on quickly, while four enthusiastic Moss Side dancers formed their own crew, The Jazz Defektors.

"People started dancing to jazz so the best of the bunch could parade their new moves ..." said Salts, Defektors' main-man, in 84. "Jazz is here to stay as a sub-culture, but there needs to be some groups in the pop market."

Despite being the hippest foursome in town when *Absolute Beginners* was filmed, The JDs failed to corrupt the charts. "The JDs were mega, pull a crowd anywhere in the country," said Basil of Yargo. "Whether it was dancing, gigs or records, they'd go for it ... whatever pulled the girls! The fact the majors didn't do business with them...well I could cry."

Thirty years after jazz had first bopped England, Sade, Matt Bianco, Everything But The Girl and The Style Council abused the term 'jazz' in the pop arena.

OPPOSITE
From the left
Gerald, May 1990;
Martin, 808 State, G-Mex, March 1990;
Basil, Yargo, with Gareth (Roses' manager), Spike Island, May 1990.

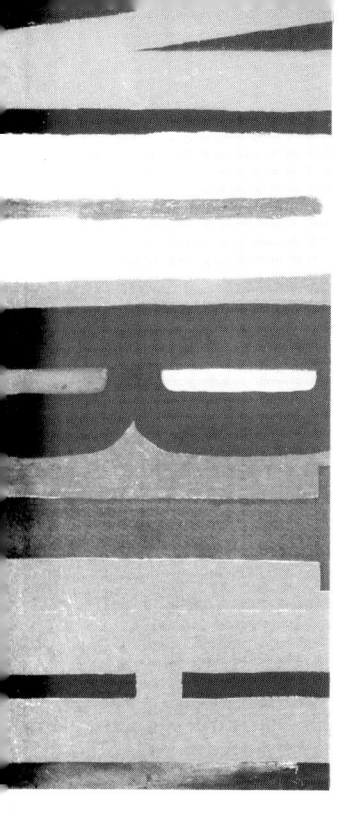

From Manchester, Carmel McCourt, flanked by Jim Paris and Gerry Darby, became UK one-hit wonders with *More More More* from *THE DRUM IS EVERYTHING*. A sparky, excitable, unique debut with unusual covers of standards like *Stormy Weather* and *Tracks Of My Tears*. They left Manchester and became a continental act with grown-up albums like *THE FALLING* and *EVERYONE'S GOT A LITTLE SOUL*, forever forgotten in England, but massive in France (we're told.)

Meanwhile, after one Factory LP, *SO HOT*, Swamp Children changed their name to Kalima and cut a groove with rather more cred. Kalima released Factory long-players *NIGHT TIME SHADOWS*, *KALIMA* and *FEELING FINE*. Where The Defektors did a dancefloor carnival samba, Kalima's vocalist, Ann Quigley, sobbed into her wine, mellow coffee-table jazz somewhere between Brazil and New Orleans. Astoundingly, Kalima pulled-off a hip renaissance on the London jazz-scene in 90.

All aboard the groovy train to electro-city Manchester. Jazz-funk went out: electro came in. The white 'rock' scene picked up electro imports, hanging out at Legends, stealing inspiration for 'weirder' experimental tracks. In return, many Chicago house acts and NY hip-hoppers would later be influenced by these GB mavericks.

Forget T-Coy and A Guy Called Gerald, Manchester's first house record was *Blue Monday*! It became the biggest-selling 12" of all time. Hi-energy artistes stole its beats, notably Divine's *Love Reaction*, a direct rip-off. It was still going strong in 88, when re-released, fitting the new-beat craze.

"When I heard *Blue Monday* I could see New Order understood dance music," said Kurtis Mantronik in *NME*, 87. "That's been one of the biggest club records in New York. You go to any dance club and you'll hear that played tonight. It's like a dance standard. State of the art."

Mike Pickering's Quango Quango were more upfront, white, electro bods ahead of their time. In 85 *Record Mirror* headlined an interview with them, 'More Famous Than Boy George.' Their debut album, *PIGS AND BATTLESHIPS*, sold 8000 on advance, while singles *Tingle*, *Love Tempo*, *Atom Rock* (featuring Johnny Marr), *Genius* and *Bad Blood* drove Quango to an unfashionable, dogmatic disco glory. Mike Pickering, Gonnie, Barry Johnson and Simon Topping were also big in New York where they played to packed houses, famed as New Order's support act.

NME wrote of *Love Tempo*, "Usual fat-yank fancy mix, one foot of plastic aimed at the 'disco' by poker-faced hicks in raincoats, designed to make dumb masses dance ..."

"If Quango Quango were releasing records now, we'd be really popular in Britain, whereas before we were only popular in America. New York DJs would mix hip-hop and Chicago sounds with Fad Gadget and us, while they just used to take the piss out of us in England!" explained Pickering, who played sax in an early incarnation of ABC.

All aboard the groovy train to house-city Manchester. From Quango Quango to T-Coy. Pickering's house trio featured Simon Topping (Harlem-trained percussionist) and Ritchie Close of Apitos, Band On The Wall regulars. Latin, clean-cut, sophisticated, classy, even *real* instruments! T-Coy's debut 12", *Carino*, was Manchester's first official house record. The trio joined Krush and The Beatmasters, hyped as 'The House Sound of Britain'. Singles *I Like To Listen* and *Night Train* followed.

In the wake of compilations of New York Garage, Detroit Techno and London Acid, came *NORTH: THE SOUND OF THE DANCE UNDERGROUND*, an anthology of early Manchester house, eight tracks (six produced by Pickering) over two 12"s. An eclectic collection mixing trumpets, bongos and Roland 303s. Annette's garage; Frequency 9 plagiarising Todd Terry's *A Day In The Life*; DCB, Masters Of Acid and T-Coy's *Carino*.

"North is a statement. You have got to remind 'them' [DJs in the South!] they missed the boat," boasted Pickering, beaming with Manc pride. "The London DJs are loving *NORTH*. Danny Rampling and Colin Faver have been playing it at warehouse parties ... but then they deserve to give us respect as a penance for being two years too late!"

All aboard the groovy train to Liverpool. Across the Mersey in Wallasey is a slice of Manc dance-music history. From a stall in Liscard Market Hall, parallel dance and indie labels, Rham and Skysaw, are run.

They released The Farm, Dub Sex, KMFDM, Marshmallow Overcoat, Manc soul-crews Chapter And The Verse, The Bygraves and mixer Grand Groove but their biggest hit was A Guy Called Gerald's *Voodoo Ray*.

"We met Gerald and said 'Can we hear some of your stuff?'" relates director Barry. "He emptied a carrier full of C90's in front of us! It was really raw, mixed virtually on ghetto blasters, but we heard the first two and said 'Let's go for it!'"

Advance tapes of *Voodoo Ray* first leaked out in August 88. Sparse, hypnotic and trance-like, *Voodoo Ray* rapidly grew into a huge club hit, a lasting classic to be passed down to future dance generations. On *Reportage*, New York's Mark Kamins and Chicago's Frankie Knuckles both paid their respects to Gerald. "I was going to do a record with Spin Inn, two with Rham and three with 808 State," Gerald told *NME*'s Paolo Hewitt. "To try and get money to do something of my own."

The nightmare was just beginning. Warner Bros blew out a licensing deal; Red Rhino went bust, delaying his LP *HOT LEMONADE* till February 89. *HOT LEMONADE* was more of a sleazy, futurist sketchbook than fine art. *Arcade Fantasy. Tranquility On Phobos. Radio Active*. Synthetic, space-age dance tunes built on a budget of only £800! It reflected the fact Gerald loved Kraftwerk, Cabaret Voltaire and Mark Stewart as much as Marshall Jefferson and Derrick May.

"Gerald never sets out to make house music *per se*; he sees what he does as 'un-uniformed dancefloor', universal dance music. That attitude immediately ensures a freshness to the sound, an unpredictability to the music; qualities sorely lacking in much of the British output," wrote demon-DJ Jon Da Silva in *Debris*. The bankruptcy of Red Rhino cost Rham £10,000. They couldn't keep up with Gerald's success and he was stolen away by a London management company and a deal at CBS. Meantime, Gerald's paranoia, naiveté, dole-lifestyle left him with a chip on his shoulder. One helluva bewildered kid. Too much publicity, dealing and money-talk caught him unawares. In five months he rose from unemployed bedroom DJ to cult dance producer. He was forever disappearing, hiding away.

He was officially at war with techno-crew 808 State.

Having programmed their debut mini album *NEW BUILD*, Gerald was angry that he had only received £1000! Not a bad royalty for an obscure record on their own indie, Creed. Gerald also appeared on 808 white labels *Let Yourself Go* and *Massage-A-Rama* and *Pacific State* on 808's *QUADRASTATE* album.

"I think 808 have got a grudge against me," he told *NME*. "When one of them found out Red Rhino had gone bust and I wasn't going to get any money, they were laughing in my face. Fair enough. We'll see who has the last laugh."

Every interview Gerald did, he moaned about money, revelled in the fact he still had to work at MacDonalds despite having a Top 40 hit with *Voodoo Ray*.

Gerald cried poverty one time too many. People lost interest. "We're not envious of Gerald," Martin Price, manager of Eastern Bloc and half of 808 told *Melody Maker*. "We want him to succeed. We always wanted him to succeed, we just never knew where we were up to with him. He never told us what he was gong to do next, and that's what he's done with everybody." 808 State had been sceptical about promoting *QUADRASTATE*. "It's dead old stuff. We've moved on. We just want to forget about it!" Martin said. Promoter Alison Martin persuaded them it was worth plugging, a weird mix-up of ethereal flutes, Miles Davies atmospherics, German new-beat and Detroit techno. At the same moment, 808 employed hefty manager 'Big' Ron Atkinson (no relation). Until then, 808 had been completely underground, promoted only to DJs who walked into Eastern Bloc.

Unexpectably, *QUADRASTATE* orbited in London, dance papers, pirates and club DJs fighting over copies. Everyone homed in on *Pacific State*. Mark Moore name-dropped it in *The Sun*, it went to No 1 in the Blues and Soul charts. Soon every label in town wanted this obscure techno bedroom-band. They signed with WEA/ZTT and *Pacific State* was re-released, striking the charts in November 89, same week as Stone Roses' *Fool's Gold*. It was end record at The Haç for weeks, always a poignant moment following that shiver of silence and football cheers.

Martin's 'other half' was Graham 'dunagrees-with-one-strap-hung-nonchalantly' Massey. He'd been around for a decade, experimenting with sax, trombone, guitars, tapes. His group, Biting Tongues,

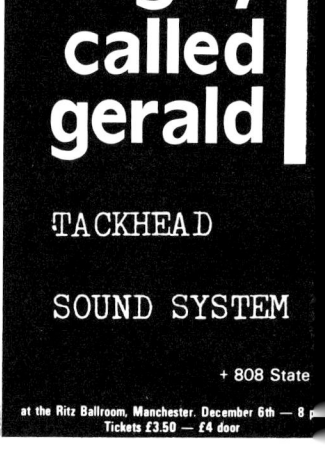

Leghorn Records Presents

a guy called gerald

TACKHEAD

SOUND SYSTEM

+ 808 State

at the Ritz Ballroom, Manchester. December 6th — 8 p
Tickets £3.50 — £4 door

were Factory avant-gardists who juggled muso-terms like 'improvisation', 'jam', 'session'. Formed to perform a live 8mm film soundtrack at The Factory in 79, their releases included *DON'T HEAL*, *LIBREHOUSE* and two video soundtracks, *FEVERHOUSE* and *COMPRESSOR* (Ikon).

"We were into John Cage and Miles Davies," reflects Massey. "In indie circles we were ahead of our time. In 81 when ACR went funk people didn't really know what to make of it. We wanted to be weird, colourful, different, instead of dead morbid like Crispy Ambulance." Graham tuned in to the house groove during his time at Spirit Studios School Of Sound Recording ... as recommended by *The Sun*'s 'From Postie To Pop Star' Massey exclusive!

808 State became a foursome, adding authentic 'kids' Darren and Andy to the line-up, teen-DJs who started DJ-ing the Salvation Army disco then ended up with their own show on Sunset Radio. The 808 State show was an upfront club-style mix of house/new-beat and freaky 60s gear. MC Tunes presented, nattering away in his well-top-sound-nice-one North Manc drawl, huge streams of dedications to scally E-head listeners Baz, Gazza, Wazza, Sharon and Tracey of Wythenshawe. It took over from Stu Allen, with the catchphrase, "A shout going out ..."

"I know what a banging tune is," said Darren. "We hear them when we go out. In Manchester at the moment, if you are not out dancing or listening to forms of house, then yer back home doing dot-to-dot or *Guess The Word*."

In a ridiculously rapid move, on signing to ZTT, 808 State recorded their third album, *NINETY*, in six days. *Magical Dreams*. Detroit techno meets 90s new-age groove, kicking back to the progressive 70s.

Like New Order's No 1, *World In Motion*, the England World Cup song, 808 State supported Manchester's bid for the Olympics with a single, *Olympic State*. "If Manchester got the Olympics it would be the cherry on top of the cake," Martin told *Melody Maker*. "One thing about 808 is that we want things to happen commercially for the city, we want to bring money back here, keep the local economy afloat ..."

808, 'The Bash Street Kids of dance culture', also appeared on *FREAK BEATS*, a sampler of experimental house sounds from Manchester, Liverpool and everywhere in between. Ethnic tunes were stolen, torn apart and synthesised into club grooves. From the aboriginal chanting of Black State Choir to the distinctly eastern Where's The Beach, Suns Of Arqa and Third Wave. "I hate the indie connection with house music," spat Martin, condemning the project.

FREAK BEATS was organised by Scam Records. Scam by name; scam by nature. A short-lived label that released some freaky dance records in the last seconds of the 80s. Black State Choir was obsessed by sampling mantras and monks, while AAAK were post-apocalyptic punks combining Belgian new-beat with thrash metal. And Social Kaos, two Asian scallies, Mo Khan and Shaz Acker, who got together a host of dance talents including Graham Massey, Vanilla Sound Corps and rapper Lavinia for their January 90 compilation, *FREESTYLE*.

All aboard the groovy train to soul-city Manchester. Dance label, DFM, was another extreme, an indie-soul company run by Dave Rofe, more concerned with artistic integrity than commercial success. He turned up gems including debut singles from Manc soulsters Fifth Of Heaven and Inside Out; *Smooth Talking* by No How, one of those embarrassing telephone love-chat records with lots of 'Hey Baby's and Tot's *What UR*.

DFM's hottest discovery was Vanilla Sound Corps. Detroit? New York? London? Nope, The House Sounds Of Trafford! Their thumping, camp, almost hi-energy, single, *Back Where We Belong*, featured the awesome Rowetta. Vanilla were then poached by Simply Red's label, House Of Chaos, for a second single *Passion*, while Rowetta sang on *Stop This Thing*, Pickering/Park's green-house (cringe) project under the name Dynasty Of Two. Her hippest break was harmonising on Happy Mondays' *Step On*.

In the meantime, ACR had left Factory for A&M but their *GOOD TOGETHER* album in 89, was Arndale-bland, neglecting to include their huge club classic *Good Together* itself.

"Manchester's a sophisticated soul city," said Mike Shaft. He thinks Lisa Stansfield is wonderful, "You can slag her off for being pop, but she has still got one of the most soulful voices in the country. You can't fake that in Manchester."

Beyond Lisa, Manchester has bands with varying degrees of 'soul': Distant Cousins, 52nd Street and Simply Red to name just three. Andy Connell of ACR and Martin Jackson of Magazine, who'd produced UK Electro and ED 209, formed Swing Out Sister with Corinne Drewery, the Petula Clark of the 80s, and released their annoying hit, *Breakout*. Yet Manchester's best soul/jazz/blues/reggae band (make your mind up which) remained Yargo.

Promoter Phil Jones reckons, "Without a doubt, Yargo are musically the best band *ever* to come out of Manchester."

In September 88 when Roses, Inspirals and 808 were pure nobodies, Yargo were tipped to be the next great Manchester band. *The Tube* said so. *The Face* said so. *NME* said so. And, not being very original, every A&R department in the country agreed. Yargo couldn't fail. At a sold-out Ritz gig on a wet Tuesday, front-man Basil Clarke, agile as an acrobat, mounted the sky-scraper speaker-stack. He wriggled his hips like an under-age dancing girl in a Montevideo disco. Sockless and shirtless he crouched down, screwed up his face and hit an awesome high note.

Yargo, finest musicians in town. Guitarist Tony Burnside pouting like a Cockney villain's side-kick; Phil Kirby, Hank Marvin lookalike drummer, gob wide open, eyes popping, sweat pouring; Paddy Steer, puppet-on-a-string bassist, tottering like a Flowerpot man, goatee beard and a fez on his head, looney tassel swinging; and Basil himself, rolling back his lips to reveal ridiculous Bugs Bunny teeth. Soul men. "Al Green in the throes of sexual testimony," as Sean O'Hagan put it. Singles, *Get High* (Skysaw) and *Carryng Mine* (Racket), led to Yargo's debut album, *BODYBEAT*, released on their own label in November 88. A mix of so many genres: Memphis soul, Lee Perry dub, Fats Comet funk, George Clinton rhythm, Chicago R&B, acid house. The next single, *Help*, was true blues, a tale of adversity ...

"That's about how desperate things can get," Basil told *NME*. "Look around Manchester and you'll see it. People who have nothing, no emotional support, no financial pull, just the fact that everything is beyond them. Y'know, you're soooo bloody skint you can't even go out the house."

So Yargo signed to London. A mistake that robbed them of the fame everyone had predicted. Their theme tune to *The Other Side Of Midnight* evokes that late-night telly feeling. Broadcast once a week as the credits of the Granada show rolled, it should have been a hit, but the label screwed up. Second album, *COMMUNICATE*, was a slow boat which finally arrived with no hype whatsoever. "We sold more records on our own than we did in London. They just printed a token number like 5,000 ..."

"Soul is forever," says Basil. "The expression of what a person is that will never die. All I want to do is express myself. I want to sing the blues. That's where I begin and end."

All aboard the groovy train. Soul City Manchester lives on.

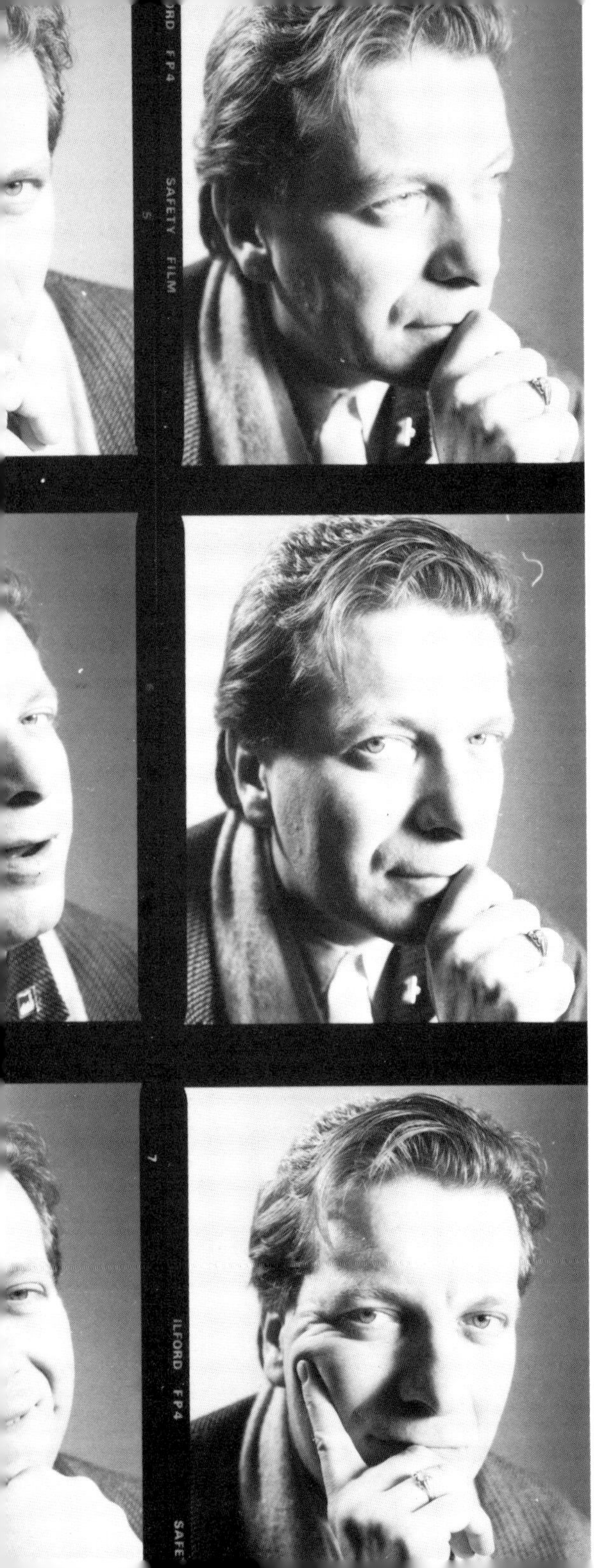

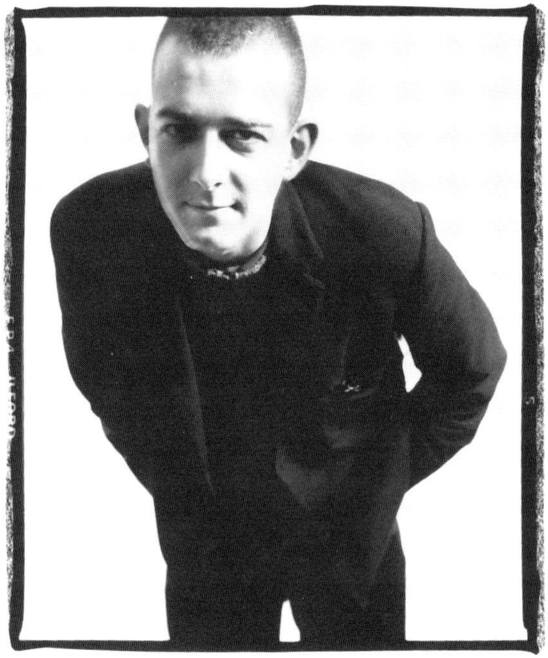

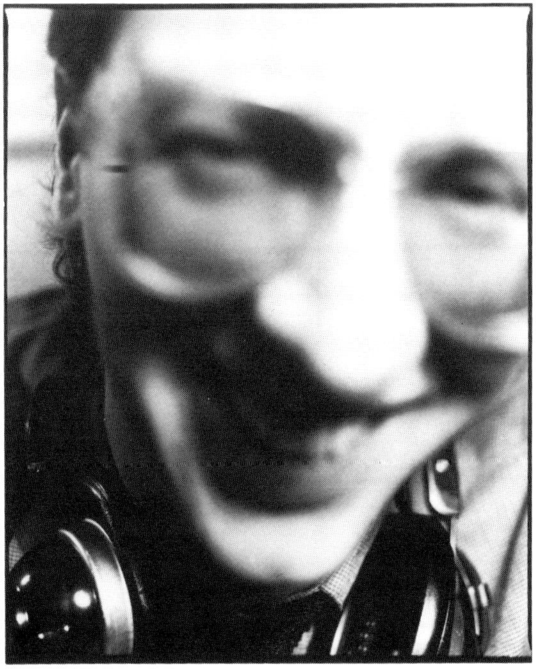

The Manchester Myth. The kids had no record label, so Tony Wilson started Factory; there was nowhere to dance, so he built The Haçienda; there was nowhere to drink, so he opened Dry 201. Manchester's musical myth is the myth of Factory Communications. Simple as that.

Move over TonY ...

And God Created Manchester

"Just because I earn £33,000, a bourgeois salary, doesn't stop me being an armchair anarchist," Tony Wilson told *NME* in 89. Oh yeah? He's a rock diplomat, pop politician, stealing fame and glory from all the other backroom boys. A small-town Melvin Bragg who rules Manchester, but is just another media-casualty in London.

June 88, Granada TV canteen. Tony confessed he felt music was at its lowest low since punk. What about house? He seemed oblivious to The Summer of Love pumping his own nightclub. One year later, Wilson had caught the swing. Obsessed by culture/fashion, he was gifted at snapping-in to the latest style. Punk inspired his *So It Goes* telly show; new-wave had him open the Factory Club; the designer decade built The Haç.

"Factory are getting old," admits Bruce Mitchell, dinosaur himself. "But Tony will argue he's an avant-gardist. He's a media man and he wants to be involved in the next-big-thing all the time."

Few have met Wilson, but all have an opinion about him. Ultimate compliment to any fine self-publicist. If Factory is Masonic, then Wilson is the Master of The Lodge. "Tony is the figurehead ... That's the way it is. There's no point thinking it's gonna be otherwise. There are clashes of ego in private but, when you join, you become loyal to The Company," says Tim Chambers, Haç booking agent.

Joy Division, New Order, Happy Mondays ... pots of gold at the end of a rainbow of failures ... Stockholm Monsters, Section 25, The Wake, Crispy Ambulance? By the late 80s, Factory were weary. They'd lost their quest for raw young bands. In 89, the only new

OPPOSITE
Dave Haslam, 1989;
Tony Wilson, February 1987;
Steve Barker, Radio
Lancashire, March 1986.

artistes were Little Big Band, To Hell With Burgundy and the Factory Classical roster! That's Rob Grey, one-man-band Market Street busker; To Hell With Burgundy, Fairport Convention of the Manc pub circuit; and classical music packaged like pop. Very scally. Very house. Very rap. Very now. I don't think. Just like Durutti Column, the unlikely twosome of Bruce Mitchell and Vini Reilly ... best drummer in the world and skinniest kid in town ... together producing arty music released on Britain's first DAT (played live at Manchester Cathedral). Bruce 'Albertos' Mitchell has done the lights at every Manc gig for the past decade. An anarchist, who couldn't be bothered with ironing, playing music that inspires suicide notes.

"I can't understand why anyone would buy a Durutti Column album," said Vini. "Every single piece is total crap. They're just appalling, pathetic ..."

Bruce revealed more about Factory. "In the beginning, Factory was completely out-of-control. You had Alan Erasmus in his bedroom actually sticking labels on. He was the only one doing the work. Tony was pointing directions, finding the money, chatting up the musicians ..."

"There's a lot of myths," says Railway Children's Gary Newby. "It's just a tiny office on Palatine Road run by three people. We never got an advance and as far as I'm aware, we never earned any royalties."

Without New Order, neither Factory nor The Haç would have brought us Happy Mondays or rave culture. Like most indie labels, they would long-since have been bankrupt. New Order put up £500,000 to keep The Haç alive.

"Somebody had just given us this 'thing' out of *The Face* and nobody knew what to do with it. It took years before people used it as a nightclub," said original Haç-goer Graham '808' Massey.

"If you look at any piece of art, if it wasn't hated in the beginning, you might as well forget it," says Wilson. Manchester *needs* a talking head like this. A respectable, wealthy ambassador to mingle on the international media-scene, arguing the city's case. Yet, often, outsiders look no further. They see Anthony H Wilson (sarcastic media name!) as *the* voice of Manchester. Far from it.

Manchester's success is down to its variety. Factory is just one of 20 indie labels; Haç is one of 40 clubs;

Dry is one café-bar out of 100. Manchester needs Wilson, but it also needs to reject him. Arrogant newcomers should be building their own empires. And so they are!

"Running an indie label is a bit like having your own black hole. It swallows up all of your money, all of your time, your whole life," says Ian Runacres, director of Bop. "Musicians are arrogant, egotistical, self-centred, ruthless, back-stabbing bastards!"

Long, long ago ... when Mick Hucknall was in The Frantic Elevators, Johnny Marr was in V2 and Mike Joyce was in The Hoax, the indie 'scene' formed. In the late 70s, fly-poster king, Tosh Ryan, signed John Cooper Clarke to Rabid Records. Richard Boon, Buzzcocks' manager, sank his royalties into New Hormones boasting thrashy God's Gift, hippie Eric Random, Dislocation Dance and Mozzer faves, Ludus. Finally, TV presenter, Tony Wilson, launched Factory. From this moment onwards, The Manc Empire began to build, brick on brick, layer on layer, wall by wall. Intape 83, Ugly Man 86, Playhard 87. How come every label but Factory has been written out of the history books? Sinster, hey. Like 1984, where The Party re-write their past ...

Take Intape. Geordie Jim Khambatta's love-affair with The Fall inspired him to sign Marc Riley and The Creepers in 83. Rock 'n' roll geezers, T-Rex tunes, songs about motorbikes. Singles: *Favourite Sister*, *Jumper Clown*, *Pollystiffs*, *Shadow Figure*, *Creeping At Maida Vale*, *Baby's on Fire*. LPs: *CULL*, *GROSS OUT*, *WART 'N' ALL*, *MISERABLE SINNERS*, *FANCY MEETING GOD*, *ROCK 'N' ROLL LIQUORICE FLAVOUR*, *SLEEPER* ... Prolific or what?

"The Creepers could have been like The Charlatans. A pop band," says John Robb, "but Marc Riley just got really cynical, bitter and made his pop band into this grungey, noisy stuff to annoy people. If he'd been five years younger and come along in 89, he might have hit the mainstream."

Instead, Riley retired early, realising a far better living drawing Harry The Head cartoon strips for Manc-based *Oink!* comic and starring in their Snatcher Sam photo-strip! He organised *TILL THINGS GET BRIGHTER*, a charity Johnny Cash covers album and ended up employed by Tony Michaelides' radio-pluggers. Fall of a cult figure.

OPPOSITE
King Of The Slums,
September 1987.

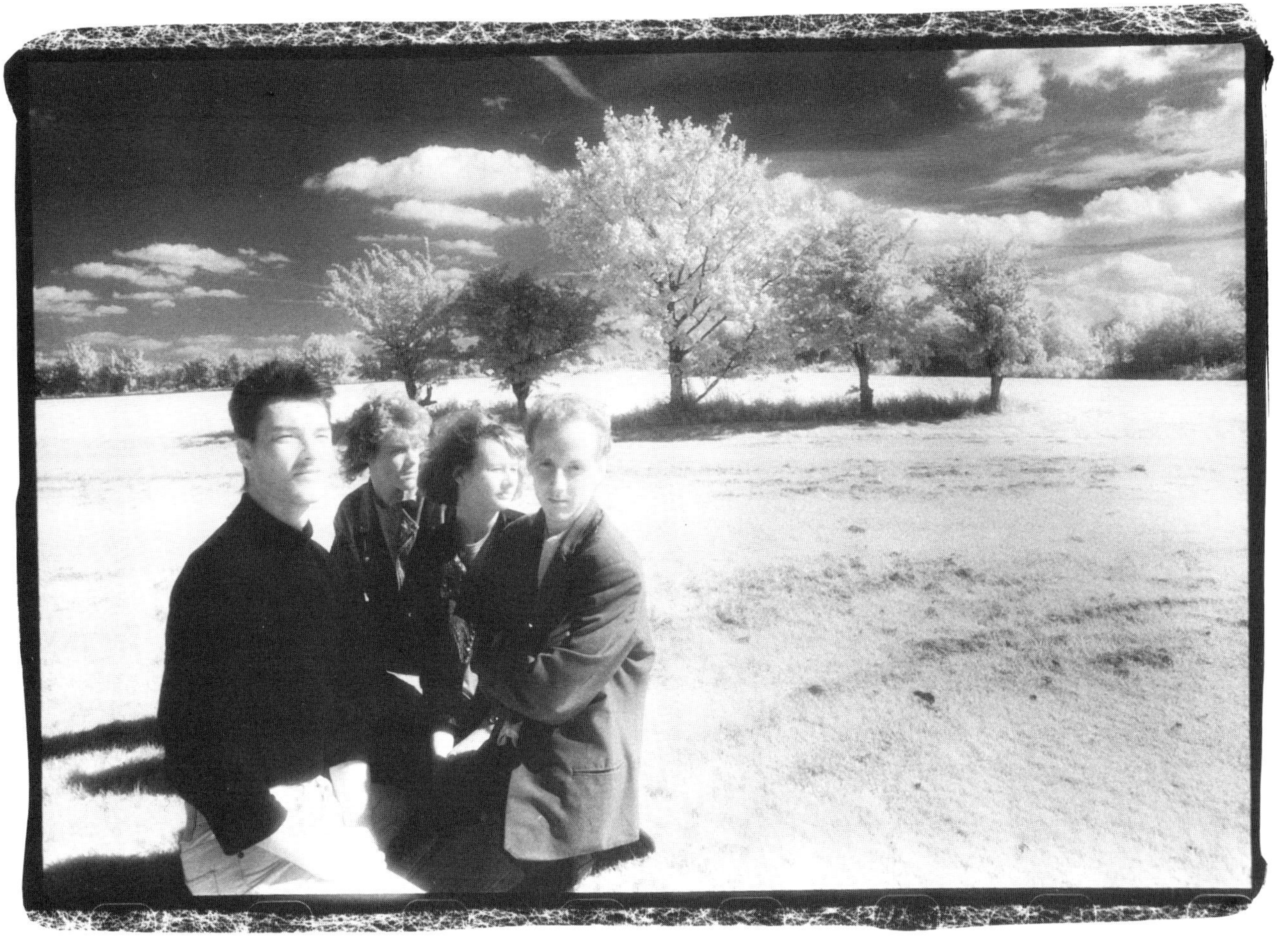

KING of the SL

Intape had Leicester's Yeah Yeah Noh, The June Brides, Implied Consent, The Waterfoot Dandy, Rote Kapelle, The Janitors, Gaye Bikers On Acid, The Heart Throbs and skiffle buskers, Terry And Gerry. "Y'see, I believe in the indie way of doing things," boasted Jim at the time. "I believe it can work. The Smiths proved that."

In 86, he funded Mondays-style lads band, The Weeds, and their doped-up single *China Doll*. The Weeds were fronted by Andrew Berry, mates with Morrissey and Swing's 'hairdresser to the stars.' He was also friends with Mark E Smith, appearing on The Fall's Cog Sinister label with solo, *Unsatisfied*. By 90 he'd sold-up to a major, singing *Kiss Me I'm Cold*. When Red Rhino Distribution (Cartel's York division) went under in 88, they took with them Intape and most indie labels in the North. A new Intape emerged, featuring a less vital roster of Stitched Back Foot Airman, Eva, Robert Lloyd And The New Four Seasons. Plus ... the unsupressible Frank Sidebottom! After years struggling with silly pub-rockers The Freshies, daft records like *I'm In Love With The Girl On The Manchester Virgin Mega Store Check Out Desk* and *If You Really Love Me Buy Me A Shirt*, the diminutive Chris Sievey put on a papier-mâché head, called himself Frank and became an overnight sensation. No-one expected it to last more than a month or so. Frank Sidebottom was a one-line joke that lasted six years, and on into infinity. The original Man Whose Head Expanded. A multi-media industry run by Frank from a bedroom in Timperley (when his Mum wasn't looking).

Frank Sidebottom had his own strip in *Oink!*, fan club, Frank-o-gram service, answer-phone messages to order, slot on Piccadilly Radio and *No 73* kids TV, computer games, pantomime at Timperley Labour Club. He was mascot of Altrincham FC, author of club song *The Robbins Aren't Bobbins*. What next? A Frank doll, cartoon series, or maybe even a 'Frank's World' theme park (in Timperley, of course!).

On Intape Frank penned seminal rock 'n' roll anthems *XMAS IS REALLY FANTASTIC* (featuring *Mull Of Timperley*), *FRANK SIDEBOTTOM SALUTES THE MAGIC OF FREDDIE MERCURY AND QUEEN* and *TIMPERLEY EP* (*Timperley Sunset, Wild Thing In Timperley* ...); plus two albums *5:9:88* and *13:9:88*, involving The Fall's *Hit The North* and Beefheart's *Mirror Man*.

Before that Frank had bought the Regal Zonophone label from EMI on HP through their Christmas Club. This provided *FRANK'S FIRM FAVOURITES* (*Anarchy In The UK, Material Boy* ...); *OH BLIMEY IT'S CHRISTMAS* (*Mull Of Timperley* ...). Other classics? Definitive versions of *Love Will Tear Us Apart, I Should be So Lucky* and *Little Frank Strikes Again!*

Under the football management of Guy Lovelady, Frank released a football annual 90. After the demise of Ugly Man, Guy had launched *Rodney Rodney* footie-zine and label specialising in footie-mad novelty bands like I Ludicrous. Frank appeared on *BANANAS*, *Rodney Rodney*'s anti-ID-cards compilation ... inflatable fever also struck The Waltones, Bradford, Too Much Texas and Half Man Half Biscuit. Unfortunately *BANANAS* was released the week of the Hillsborough Disaster.

'Concept' compilations were real hip. Rochdale's Imaginary Records pioneered cover-version tributes, homages to Syd Barrett, Captain Beefheart, The Kinks, The Byrds and The Rolling Stones. Boss Alan Duffy, a bookie, gave up his day job to pursue this vinyl obsession with the 60s. He persuaded The Shamen, Sonic Youth, XTC, That Petrol Emotion, Dinosaur JR and friends to contribute. Each album also featured Imaginary's unknown local acts, Mirrors Over Kiev, The Reegs and The Mock Turtles.

Building slowly since 87 with 60s-styled singles *Pomona, Wicker Man, And Then She Smiles, Lay Me Down*, The Turtles' album, *TURTLE SOUP*, was lazy, hazy, trippy guitar pop.

Wrote *Melody Maker*'s Dave Simpson, "As much a landmark of contemporary 60s-influenced pop music as was *THE SMITHS* or *STONE ROSES* albums, *TURTLE SOUP* is seriously brilliant."

"Actually, I think it's better than the Roses' album," smirked front-man Martin Coogan. The Mock Turtles were not another indie-crew, but a show-biz band. Backstage it's a real *Who's Who*. Martin is brother of impressionist Steve Coogan; bassist Andrew Stewartson was asked out by Michaela Strachan; guitarist Martin Murray plays Mark Thompson in *Families* and dates Steph Barnes from *The Street* ...

Meanwhile, a six-foot-tall skinhead with trousers two-sizes-too-small and ears two-sizes-too-big still powered the indie scene.

Hulme 83. Dave Haslam had his first baby ... *Debris*, the Manchester fanzine of the 80s. *Debris* watched, listened, carefully analysed. Neat lines of prose, careful, tasteful, mindful. Sombre lay-out, straightforward headlines, artistic white space, classy black and white: a style of its very own, to inspire a zillion copyists ... *Irresponsible Spirit*, *Get Out*, *Scam*, *Recoil*, *M62*.

Debris' flexis broke acts like Inspiral Carpets, Laugh, Too Much Texas, King Of The Slums. Playhard Records was the foolhardy next step. Dave had an open-minded *global* view of music, writing in *M62*, "99% of bands in Manchester are talentless." His first vinyl release was HEAD OVER EARS, an 11-track compendium in November 87. Big Black, Kit and A House, snuggled up next to Manc's Tot, Swivel Hips, Railway Children, The Fall, Prince Kool, Twang and Biting Tongues.

Bitten by the record-biz bug, Dave partnered Nathan McGough and they signed King Of The Slums. This was music-biz *reality*. No big advances. No wages. In fact, King Of The Slums' *paid* Dave Haslam £100! Hilda Ogden vocals, 'quirky' cloth-cap lyrics and a wailing electric violin. King of The Slums were a naive bunch!

Sarah, who spent four years at Royal Northern College of Music, met up with Charley Keigher, and purposely distorted her carefully-studied violin playing. Their obscure first single. *Spider Psychiatry* (SLR Records), was pressed-up complete with hand-drawn, photocopied sleeves. It was never even distributed and remains unheard.

"The early stuff was experimenting with noise. I don't believe in that any more. I hate our first single. It's awful. The singing is out of tune," vocalist Charley admits. Surely all part of the charm? "No, at the time I thought it was in tune!" It ensured gigs supporting Walking Seeds, Pussy Galore, The Membranes, World Domination Enterprises and other noisy troupes.

Before settling for King Of The Slums, they'd been known as Slum Cathedral User and Trash Cathedral User, two names straight out of a Mark E Smith lyric booklet. Charley spent two years in his room writing, believing he was Britain's greatest songwriter, until a CBS A&R rep brought him down fast. It hurt!

Charley listened mainly to classical tunes. "I don't like pop music," he revealed to Deborah Reid of *M62* fanzine. "I've never been to a gig in my life, only the ones we're at ourselves and then as soon as we're off, I want to get out, far too loud."

Playhard releases, *ENGLAND'S FINEST HOPES*, *VICIOUS BRITISH BOYFRIEND* and *BARBAROUS ENGLISH FAYRE* tamed King Of The Slums' sound. Though the searing violin and rockist guitars were kept, there were murky melodies too. Lyrically, Charley followed Mark E Smith into colloquial Northernisms. He wailed about armpit-slums of North Manchester and the Pennines, the only hills on Manchester's sky-line. 'I am a mere Mancunian of no fixed ability ...'

On the downside, Slums' covers depicting Enoch Powell, pastel-coloured Union Jacks and Britannia soon got them in trouble. The 'are they/aren't they' battle raged. Were they 'patriotic' (read 'racist')? "If you mention England within a song, everyone immediately pricks up their ears and eyebrows get raised as if you're some kind of facist. I haven't got any politics," Charley told *Debris*.

King Of The Slums. Politics of everyday Northern life. Bus queues, burglary, plumbers, joiners, whippets, queer-bashing. *Up The Empire*, *Bombs Away On Harpurhey*! They moved to Midnight music for singles *Once A Prefect*, *It's Dead Smart* and the album *DANDELIONS*.

"Frank Sinatra sings about New York. Other people sing about Detroit, Chicago and California ... why can't I sing about Ancoats and Harpurhey?"

Playhard were tokenists. Slums were their rockers; hip-hop came from MC Buzz B, Dee Lawal and Breaking The Illusion; Liverpudlians Kit were their gay-girl pop band; The Train Set were jangly faves, Camel the Fat Controller's band from the tram-sheds of Crewe.

"We've gone out of our way not to create an image for the label. We don't want people to be able to say, 'That's a Playhard band,' because then individual bands can rise and fall with the label and that's not fair," said Dave. "The value of independent music lies in its diversity and we want the label to reflect that."

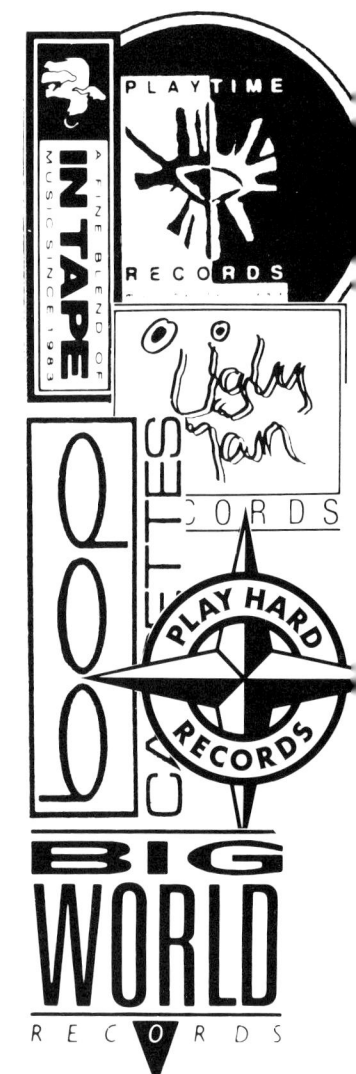

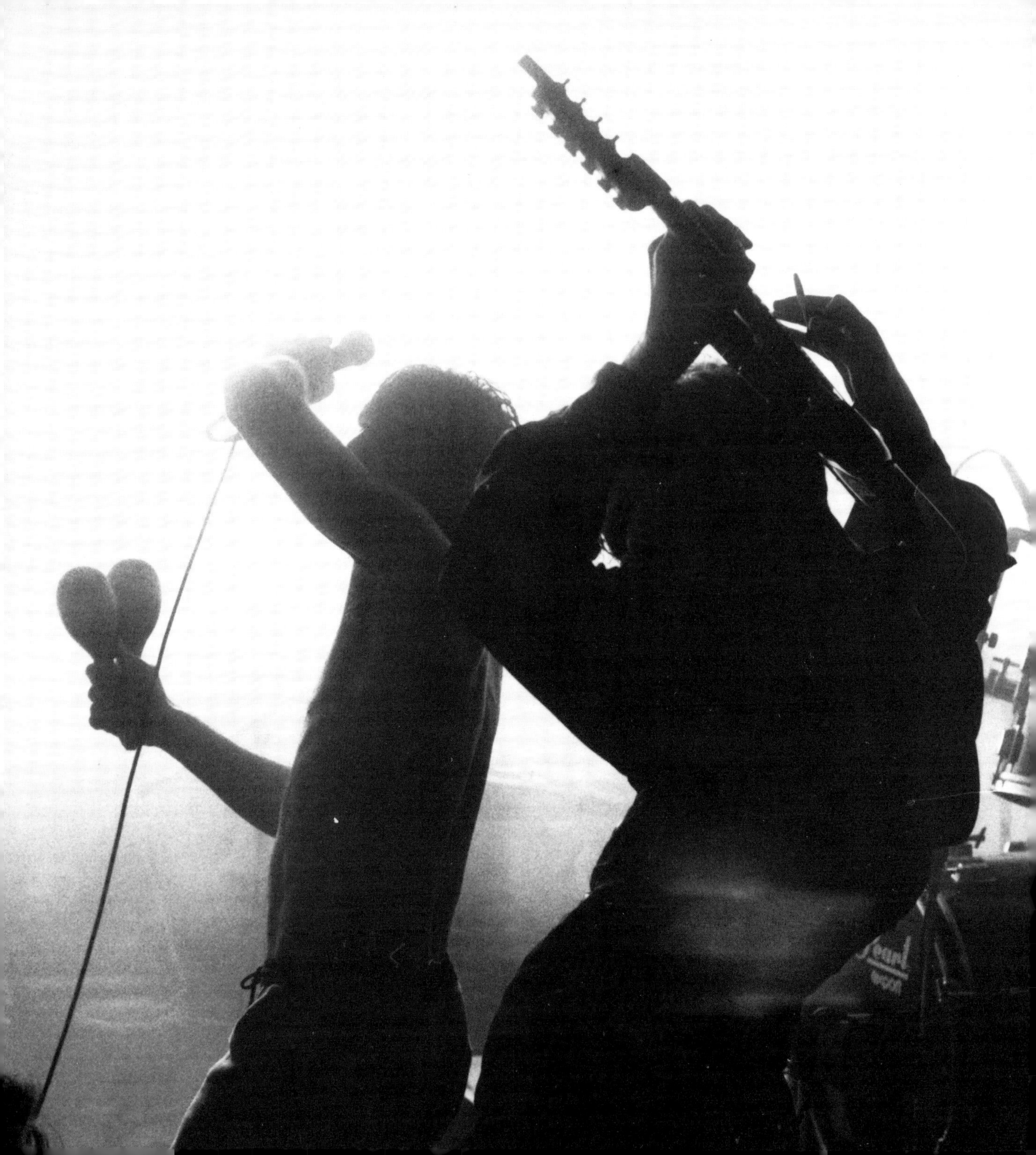

The Exuberants were Playhard's finest Manc jangly discovery. Lads around town. Lads in fights. Lads on the terraces. Salford Lads' Club. Angry young men. Sensitive youths. Uncouth scallies. Smiths, Joy Divison, Mondays, Northside, Charlatans, Inspirals, Buzzcocks ...

What, no girls? Manc pop is male pop. Women remain spectators, girlfriends, groupies pushed aside by a sexist scally scene.

Bands with opinionated females, Kalima, Faye Ray, Beyond The Glass, and Dislocation Dance became marginalised as 'benefit' bands? There's a gap in the market for a 'serious' female idol. And who ever asks Gillian from New Order for a quote?

Business-wise, however, Manc women are very powerful. Strawberry Studios' Caroline Ellery manages World Of Twist; Alison Martin and Sue McDermott direct radio-pluggers, Red Alert; Debbie Reid launched M62 fanzine as a teenager; Dub Sex were managed by Penny Anderson; Saffron Prior runs Cog Sinister; Paula Greenwood manages New Fads and Swirl; Tracey at Factory and Soozi at Playhard organise Happy Mondays; Gina Morris edited Bop City ... while Tony Wilson soaks up the publicity, an army of others do the work.

Jack Kerouac, James Dean, Ian Curtis ... but where are the Angry Young Women?

Enter Muffin Spencer of The Exuberants.

Muffin moved from New England to start a band. "What women write and say is never taken seriously enough. No-one has ever got in the position in popular music that I'd like to be in. I've been interviewed by every journalist in Manchester, but not one has expressed even the slightest interest in my songs."

Fave support to The Man From Delmonte, The Exuberants' intelligent pop of *Bedside Appeal* and *Yeah Yeah Yeah And Yeah* was available on *Debris* flexi and Playhard sampler, HAND TO MOUTH. Exit Muffin.

Enter Paula Greenwood, boss of Playtime Records. "I'd planned it ever since I left college. I'd got experience in almost every field of music. Music journalism, record shops, distribution, venues, a radio station ... Then in 88, I decided 'now is the time.' But it wasn't really. Everything possible went wrong."

Playtime Records' first release was *Different Girl* by folk-popsters Mirrors Over Kiev. Next Inspiral Carpets' debut, *Planecrash*, which began to pick up Peel plays. A second Inspirals EP, *TRAINSURFING*, was recorded but, before it hit the shops, distributors, Red Rhino, went bankrupt. Inspirals left. The rest is history. Paula learnt from her mistakes and launched her own PR company. She signed up Too Much Texas, Tom Hingley's old band and The Rainkings, Steve Holt's new act. Her biggest discovery was New Fads.

New Fast Automatic Daffodils. Gobbledygook advertising-speak that says everything but means nothing. Lead-free petrol, low-alcohol lager, gum-health toothpaste, liquid washing powder in plastic balls ... New Fads beamed from every wall, television and radio. "The words 'new', 'fast' and 'automatic' are always used like they're so meaningful when really they're disposable. If nothing else the name was designed to grab people's attention."

While hip-hoppers were sampling ancient records, New Fast Automatic Daffodils stole advertising slogans and actual lyrics of other songs. Troublefunk and Talking Heads appeared on their debut *Lions*. 'This isn't a song: this is a totally new concept in disposability/Providing only a few minutes listening pleasure, it is then ready for disposal/Burn it, bend it, tear it ...'

New Fast Automatic Daffodils were special. From the silly *Lions* to the insane note-read narration of *Fate Don't Fail Me Now;* from *Your Dreams My Nightmares,* slow, spooky as Sonic Youth's *Starpower*, to the ironic *MUSIC IS SHIT* EP. Third single, *Big*, was an indie hit, a loopy, club dance tune mixed by Jon Da Silva. New Fads gained a James support tour and were filmed live by Granada TV's *Celebration 18-25* ... as ludicrous as The Fall, yet as fresh-faced as The Famous Five.

Meanwhile, Paula's interest in folk music inspired Big World Records featuring Kevin Seisey and Claire Mooney, their albums *STARK RAVING MAD* and *ROCKING THE BOAT*. Both were members of Five Go Off To Play Guitar. This bunch looked like the cast of a disaster movie. An unlikely crowd who'd normally only meet in a sinking ship or a towering inferno. Five desperados. Middle-aged, McCartney lookalike, George Borowski, allegedly *the* 'Guitar George' from Dire Straits' *Sultans Of Swing*. Teenager Penny Priest,

OPPOSITE
Mock Turtles, International 1,
July 1990.

who appeared on *MANCHESTER NORTH OF ENGLAND*; her stand-in, ever right-on Claire Mooney. Plus broad Northerner Kevin Seisey, cheeky kid Johnny Dangerously and Bob Dillinger, step-brother of John Cooper Clarke, son of Bob Dylan.

These faces busked dubious 'cabarets', The Buzz, The Fun Box, Buskers' Night. The dregs of Manchester music. Mark Burgess (ex-Chameleons) covering *Starman* or Mike 'Salford Jets' Sweeney rattling through *Gina In A Cortina* or blond-boy Dave Hulston or politico-folky Jon Poole. And Craig Davies, tagged the Tom Waits of Salford. Geoff Travis of Rough Trade financed albums *LIKE NARCISSUS* and *GROOVIN' ON A SHAFT CYCLE*. Craig sang *Euston Railway Station Blues* about *Big Bad Voodoo Men*, strolled through summer parks into rainy cities and ended up in seedy bedrooms. His ultimate couplet, 'Nothing ever happened in my live worthy of note/until I saw you glide down my thoroughfare like a May parade float ...'

As Bob Dillinger says, "There are three ways to ruin your life: wine, women and song ... trust us to pick the most boring!"

Johnny Dangerously was the real contender, four foot high with an impish grin. The kind of kid who'd let down your tyres if you didn't pay him 10p to mind them. He'd been lead-boy with Hyde's Ignition, great guitar pop band circa 85. After they split, Johnny spent an extended exile in an Abergavenny caravan, while the rest of the band re-grouped as Ambitious Beggars. Johnny's legendary *Black And Blue* ballad appeared on his mini-LP, *YOU ME AND THE ALARM CLOCK* on Village, which also inflicted us with Wigan wackos, The Volunteers, and Moz-faves, Bradford. Johnny was managed by Sandy Gort who also baby-sat *Spitting Image* impressionist, Steve Coogan, and Kevin Kennedy, aka Curly Watts of *The Street*. Curly, sorry Kevin, was the anti-Kylie soap-opera pop star playing the pub circuit with his preposterous new-country act Bunch Of Thieves! "The dirtiest, scruffiest dregs that ever scuttled across a stage," as *Sounds*' Stephen Kingston put it. They didn't have a hit.

All the way from chainstore city, Stockport, and Strawberry Studios, Paul Humphries' Cut Deep Records never made *The Pops* either. Yet in 89 they had a fine roster. Their catalogue included *Swerve* and *Splintered Faith* by Dub Sex; Biting Tongues' house experiment, *Love Out*; What?Noise's *Vein*, single of the week in all the papers. Noise for the sake of noise? Noise for the sake of art? Nope, noise you can *dance* to! Sort of.

What?Noise were a sonic boom for an age when hardcore bands played hip-hop. The trio's unique techno-grunge swerved all over the road ... steering between the unlistenable and the genius, like a drunk-driver on a wet highway.

Chris Nagle, engineer/producer/techno-kid, formulated a sound as 80s as *The Face*; his wife, Julia, was one of a minority of women in the Manc scene. Like a part-time punk, a weekend biker or a day tripper, vocalist Tim Harris juggled an executive career in trade finance with band commitments. "It's a bit like being in a play. I'm acting out a role. My suit and tie is my stage costume," Tim said. "You need quids to do things like finance a band, so it's more fun screwing from the inside than banging on the door." What?Noise philosophy.

Gil Scott Heron said *The Revolution Will Not Be Televised*. Sampling Nick Coleman, What?Noise turned it around and said there would be no revolution while the TV is on. "People would ignore a revolution until the commercial break. TV isolates people from each other." Sounding like a combination of Tackhead, Ministry, New Order and Sonic Youth, What?Noise left Cut Deep for One Little Indian. Their thin debut album, *FAT*, was weird-as-hell. The revolution was coming. Or maybe not.

Rig, more noise-dance from Cut Deep. Lurid gang into Tackhead, Talking Heads and hip-hop, momentarily tagged 'scallies' but actually college kids. Their *DIG* EP had a 'difficult' sound, mixing Dub Sex with Happy Mondays, shouted vocals and a dance beat. Mere youngsters!

Strawberry Studios' talent-inspired brother label, Big Round. Flush with a royalty cheque from EMI Publishing, The Milltown Brothers released their *COMING FROM THE MILL* EP. Flat caps? Newton & Ridley beer mats? Curlers? *Coronation Street* postcards? All mementos on sale in Granada Studio Tours' shop! There's money in t'muck as we say 'oop Norff. The Bros, from Burnley, realised that. They issued a press release in which the first word was 'black'. The second was 'pudding' and so, inevitably, the third had to be 'rain'.

As much a novelty as *Matchstalk Men And Matchstalk Cats And Dogs*, The Milltown Brothers were designer Northerners, videoed in cobbled streets, a Lowry painting on their single sleeve and lyrics praising the red rose of Lancashire. Daintees-style trad folky pop. *Janice Is Gone* appeared on *MANCHESTER NORTH OF ENGLAND* and *HOME* featured *Inkwell*. The Milltown Brothers were too 'Northern' for anyone to take them very seriously.

Other Big Round-ers, Bounce The Mouse, spun *Like Lorraine*, a pale Velvets' tune. Meanwhile, an ambitious Paul Humphries had extended his 90s roster with mafia-house Manchester Vibe In The Area, world-hippies Suns Of Arqa, punk new-beaters Mighty Force and sample-crazy P Love And Blue. Too much! Cut Deep folded in summer 90.

Suns Of Arqa were not lost. Dub-bhangra-acid cut, *Godvinda's House*, appeared on Cut Deep, Antler, Bop *and* Scam Records all within the space of a year. The work of Wadada, an Ashton hippie, maker of eight albums. A mad professor who scoured North Africa, India and the West Indies, searching out musical excellence. He would gather instrumentalists from every outback on earth to record. Quirky contributors like narrator 'Professor' Stanley Unwin, The Manchester Boys Choir, Longsight blues-singer Helen Watson and punk poet John Cooper Clarke, aka the star of the Sugar Puffs adverts!

Inevitably, Suns Of Arqa were on Bop, suburban world music company launched in 87. Veterans, Ian Runacres and Jerry Bullivant, set themselves the 'worthy' task of capturing Manchester's 'minority' spool. Backed by North West Arts, they released cassette albums at the rate of one a fortnight! "Our philosophy is *not* to be a pop label," they said.

So began a stream of obscure Manc releases. Sonja singing Motown soul-funk; jazzers Yes Brazil and The Honkies; Inner Sense Percussion, hippie latin-buskers; soul-jazz of Rhonda's *Black And Strange*; poets Su Andi and Lemn Sissay; Manc-bhangra Betaab Sangeet. Especially successful, their *WOMAD INTRODUCTION TO WORLD MUSIC* series taking in The Pogues, Cocteau Twins, Nusrat Fateh Ali Khan, Remmy Ongala and more.

Once Bop had exhausted all the 'worthy' minority bands in The North, they radically side-stepped into vinyl, indie pop and dance music...*MANCHESTER NORTH OF ENGLAND*, The Man From Delmonte and Scam Records. Notably, Irish guys Toss The Feathers, who regularly filled International 2 with teen-bop Tossettes, mixed a Celtic house single *Skidoo!*

In 90 Bop compiled *HIT THE NORTH*, a cash-in compilation featuring Rap Assassins, Rowetta, Revenge, Paris Angels, Rig, New Fads.

In November 89 they launched *Bop City*, a quarterly Madchester fanzine. It was needed. Manc music has not always been well-documented. All those free-sheets that get round your ankles. The ones used as blankets by sad old guys in Piccadilly Gardens; papers like *Uptown*, flung at early-morning commuters like confetti at a wedding.

People have tried. Most have failed. In the early 80s, there was *New Manchester Review* and *City Fun*, followed in 85 by short-lived pop mag *Buzzin'*, a free-sheet, and *Muze*, a glossy edited by Mick Middles. Sued by Morrissey for suggesting greed had ruined The Smiths, Mick Middles wrote the band's unofficial history (Omnibus Press), slated by both group and media. Slag him as you may, Middles documented Manchester more comprehensively than any other journalist, from punk through to 86 when he became *Manchester Evening News*' pop columnist.

Listings mag,*City Life*, also survived. Launched as a co-op in 83 with £700 by ex-stewdies Andy Spinoza, Ed Glinert and Chris Paul, it was left-wing and multi-cultural with sussed pop-hacks Rob Graham, Dean, Cath Carroll and Bob Dickinson. "It gave a boost to the Manchester music scene," says Spinoza. "It was on a far greater scale than any fanzine and covered all the new bands."

Times change. In January 89, the bankrupt title was bought up by *Manchester Evening News*. Under the editorship of Mike Hill, *City Life* ended the 80s out of step. When *NME* had Northside on the cover, *City Life* had Tor*vile* and Dean. "More people will see Torvil and Dean than will ever see the Stone Roses," said Hill, preferring cricket and Chinese food himself.

"It's a joke. I can't believe it. I'm gobsmacked," said one contributor. "They totally ignored the Manchester hype, when they could have made a mint documenting the scene. No one respects them at all."

After *Debris*' demise in 89, decent 'alternative' reading was scarce. Just a few throwaway pamphlets like Roses-zine, *Made Of Paper*. How come in a country of free speech, no-one has anything to say? *Freaky Dancing* was the ultimate document. A comic written by, for and about kids in the queue for The Haçienda! Such editorial scope. Getting to, in and home from The Haç. It also heavily advocated drug use. An escapist's dream. Why bother writing about pop music, when you can simply *live* it?

If you wanted to *hear* Manchester music, that was another matter. Beyond John Peel, godfather of the whole scene, Steve Barker's *On The Wire* on Radio Lancashire was the best radio show in the country. BBC Sundays no longer meant Alf Garnett and Thora Hird. Broadcast between two and five, *On The Wire* was so extreme that many first-time listeners assumed it must be illegal!

Steve Barker is a fan whose career began by interviewing Jimi Hendrix and Yoko Ono for college mags in the 60s. He became a civil servant, grabbing his first radio-show in 79 as a hobby. "It's a joy to play great music on the radio and say what the fuck I want. Music is the same in 86, 76, 66, 56 ... if you're looking for excitement, a buzz, some intelligence, something articulate, something committed, something to make you dance ... it's always there!"

Steve spun 'acid house' before dance shows would touch it; he was also a reggae expert and Adrian Sherwood's number one fan. He broadcast debut radio interviews with The Smiths, New Order and set up a free Fall gig at Clitheroe Castle Bandstand in 85. Artistes at his 88 Crimbo party included 808 State, Neneh Cherry, Tackhead. Among his cavalry of helpers were soul experts Andy Madhatter, Pete Haig; critic Fenny, Blackburn's Clive James; bluesman Jukebox Johnson ... even Alan Woods playing non-stop hardcore/thrash for half-an-hour at a time! Cult programme for anarchos, homeboys, hippie civil servants alike, *On The Wire*'s signal snakes across Manchester, Lancashire, Merseyside and even North Wales. Inspiration to many, especially GMR's *Meltdown*, launched in 85 and presented by Phil Korbel and Alison Martin.

Meanwhile, Tony Michaelides' *Last Radio Show* on Piccadilly Key 103 is respected by all. Tony mixes local sounds with reggae-blues-country, oldies Neil Young, Bob Dylan and a catalogue of sessions from Pete Shelley to the Stone Roses.

On the box? *The Other Side Of Midnight* and *The New*. Ruling the waves? KFM and Sunset, two of the first 'community' stations on air.

KFM 104.9 was a Stockport pirate run, in the early 80s, by Steve Toon and Charles Turner. They began broadcasting legally in early 90 with a charter to play 30% local sounds. Broadcasts were haphazard, chaotic but vibrant, wall-to-wall Happy-Inspiral-Roses, coolest playlist in the country. Billboard posters shamelessly claimed, the one thing KFM didn't stand for, was 'Kylie Fucking Minogue'! Too good to be true. After just three months of low ad-sales, Charles and Toon were sacked. Uncool Signal Radio took over. One of the new presenters remarked, "They Might Be Giants? Yeah, great new Manchester band ..."

Sunset Radio's first steps were equally fraught. First community station on air and a 'black music' station too, people wanted to see it fall. "We're really gonna kick ass in Manchester. Our aim is to provide the wickedest tunes during the day and a voice to those who've never had it before in the evenings, with various ethnic shows," said director/presenter Mike Shaft. He employed some cool club DJs like Leaky, Hewan and The Spinmasters to spin soul, house, hip-hop and reggae all day round.

Yet ad-sales also faltered. Pioneer Shaft, who'd spent five years dreaming it up, was sacked, then reinstated and eventually resigned to be replaced by Greg Edwards. So it goes. Yet the dream remained alive. Good times gonna come.

"The power is in London and will always remain there," Paul Morley said in 85, determined never to return to his home town. "It's geographical. No-one will ever be able to change that or effectively work against it." Oh Yeah?

The 90s' Manc boom finally brought genuine decentralisation for the music biz. Radio, press, labels, pluggers, distribution ... the Manchester Myth was no longer a one-man-show. Move over Tony ...

OPPOSITE
Frank Sidebottom, November 1987;
Mark Riley And The Creepers, February 1986.

ALTRINCHAM FC

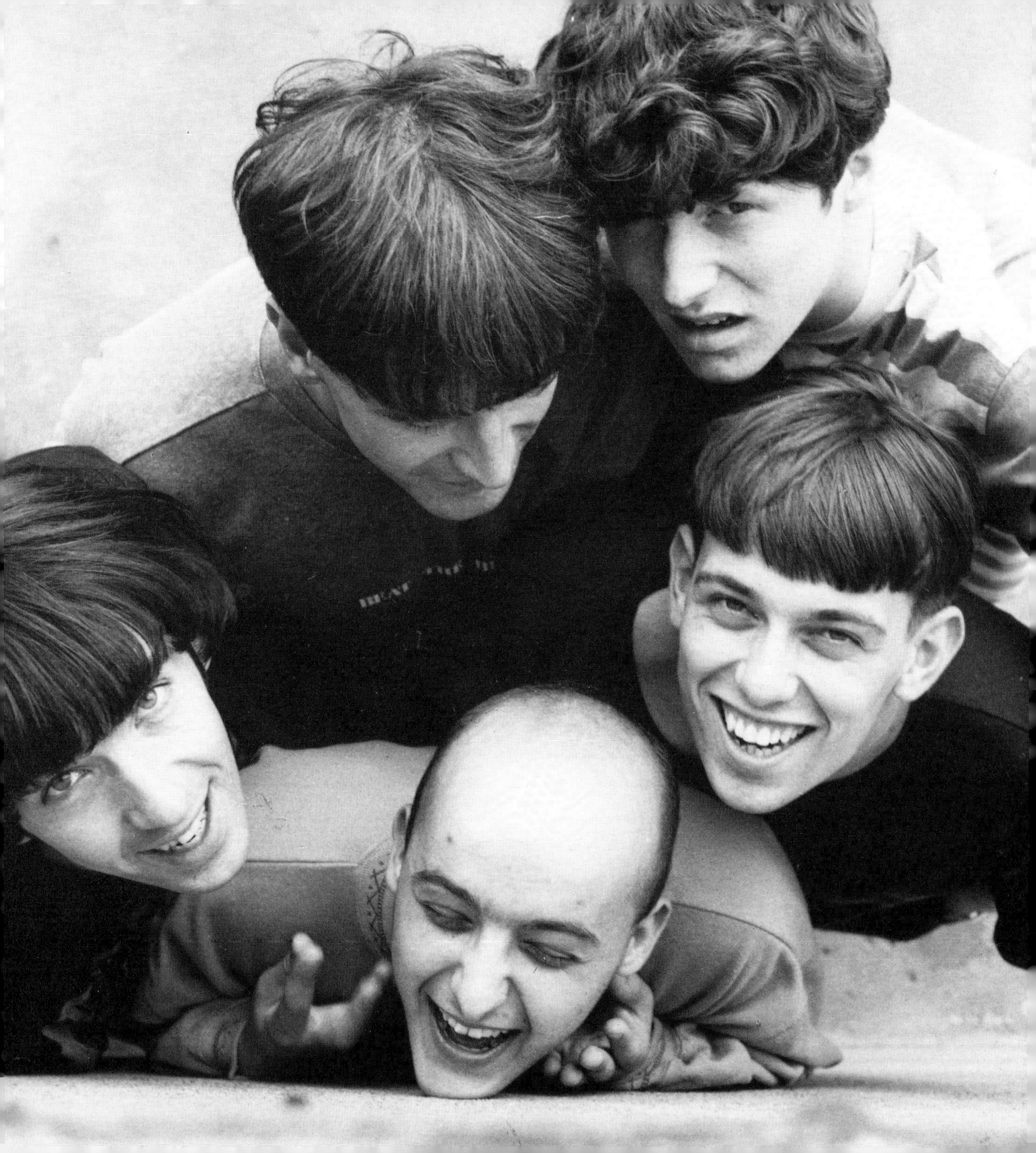

Here they come. Walking down the street. Get the funniest looks from everyone they meet. Anytime, anywhere, just look over your shoulder, guess who'll be standing there. They're just trying to be friendly, go and watch them sing and play. They're the young generation and they've got something to say. Hey! Hey! It's the Inspirals

SPiral Bound

11 *And God Created Manchester*

The Inspiral Carpets are not the fabbiest rock band on earth, roughest pop stars in the Western world, prettiest scally group or most avant-garde dance-combo since Kraftwerk. They leave such exaggerated claims to Roses, Mondays, Charlatans and 808 State. No pretensions here. Simply local lads made good. Barrow-boys who hit the jackpot on a fruit machine. "If you meet a Capri-boy with a pear-shaped nose and a fruit-bowl haircut, follow him," wrote Mike West in *NME*, June 88, "He will lead you to a bed factory in East Manchester, where the fumes are toxic and the employees have mutated into beer monsters. There you will find a cow as big as a Buddha, with spotlight eyes and polyester hide. It is a stage prop built with loving care, verging on bestiality, by Inspiral Carpets." Inspirals, the biggest band from hilly mill-town Oldham since Barclay James Harvest! Hideous haircuts, complexions bubbling like cheese-on-toast, dress-sense as square as a chess board. A Johnny Ramone clone playing a Farsifa organ straight off *Sale Of The Century*. Musically a mix of The Doors, The Freshies and Showaddywaddy. Hardly surprising that, during 86 and early 87, this uncouth band's first demos were largely ignored by the ultra-cool Manc muso-scene! The Carpets were Transit-vanners, bumping round North Manc pubs: The Mare And Foal, The Grey Horse. Their demo, *COW*, whipped at Ashton's The Mill in 87, had four bases like a rounders pitch. *Whisky*, *Head For The Sun*, *Love Can Never Lose Its Own* and *Now You're Gone*, were all popular with their already cow-crazy Oldham faithfuls. Though grossly dismissed by trendy veggie Manc media, Dave Haslam

OPPOSITE
Inspiral Carpets,
September 1989.

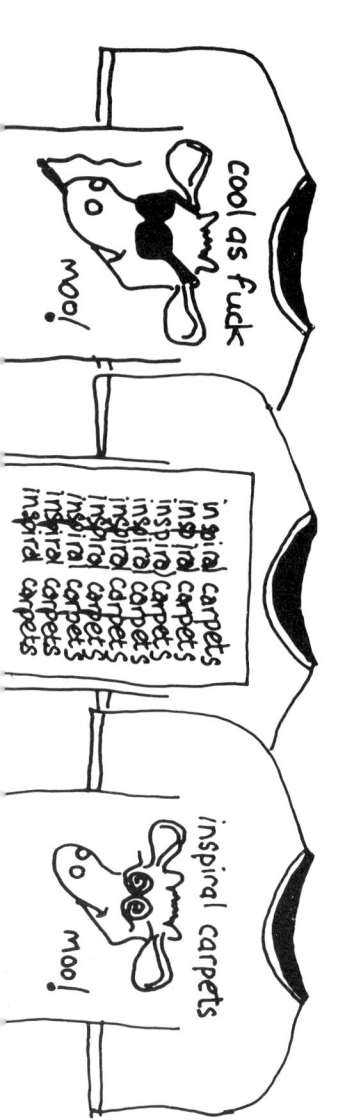

loved them (someone had to!). They recorded *Garage Full Of Flowers*, inspired by the baby-faced Roses' *Tell Me*, for a *Debris* flexi, coupled with Metro Trinity's *Stupid Friends*.

The in-the-know few were hooked. Paula Greenwood, who'd been gaining contacts answering phones for Piccadilly's *Last Radio Show*, put out their first EP, *PLANECRASH*, on her new label, Playtime.

Materialising in June 88, the Summer Of Love, the EP had a pressing of only 1000. Five songs which grappled with a unique mish-mash of swirling, 60s-influenced, sing-a-long pop music. *Keep The Circle Round*, *Garage Full Of Flowers*, *Theme From Cow*, *Seeds Of Doubt* and a cover of *96 Tears*.

The gawkiest band ever, with a complex history. Organist Clint Boon founded the band. He also managed T'Challa Grid, which featured Mani (yes, *the* Mani) and Inspirals' drummer, Chris Goodwin, whose CV also includes The Jerks, Asia Fields, Buzzcocks Foc, The High and more.

In 85 Clint discovered teenage-mutant gingerbread-boy Craig Gill at U2 in Milton Keynes. Craig soon replaced Chris, making his debut when Inspirals supported Zodiac Mindwarp at The Boardwalk. Then Craig chanced upon Graham Lambert in a pub car park. Graham Lambert, a guitarist with a footballer's haircut, had recorded a demo, *Songs Of Shallow Intensity*, with his school band, The Furs.

Somewhere down the line they found bassist Dave Swift and vocalist Steve Holt, 'friendly face like a twin-handled Toby-mug ...'

In local radio's tiny stratosphere, Inspiral Carpets were already notorious, their name uttered with a whisper of dismay. Graham and Clint had been obsessive listeners to Radio Manchester's *Meltdown* show since 87. The programme had an over-generous giveaway scheme, dumping 60 prizes every Monday. Week after week, Graham and Clint called in to harass the phone-girls with childish remarks and claim tickets to all the weekend's gigs. They were seen at The Boardwalk every Saturday night in 88! It reached such an extreme that they were blacklisted for being too greedy!

Fans began calling in, seven or eight times a show, to request Carpets' tunes. Initially, they were dismissed as a snivelling, crap local band. When *PLANECRASH* came out, they came in for a chat. Presenter Alison Martin agreed to send John Peel, a personal friend, a copy. Meanwhile, *Joe* appeared on *MANCHESTER NORTH OF ENGLAND*, a cheap, raw production on a cheap, raw compilation. 'The frostbite took your toes and now it's set to take your soul.'

"He's a tramp who really existed," said Clint. "He used to hang around our studios in Ashton. He died a week after we wrote the song. I wrote it one Friday and the Friday after he died. It's ironic. I wanted to go round and play him the tape, but it was too late."

PLANECRASH, was equally perverted. "It predicted Lockerbie," said Graham. "We're thinking of calling our next EP 'Massive Coach Disaster On M6', there's sure to be one this year. The one after could be called 'World War Three' ... sorry, do we come across as being sick?"

In fact the follow-up was *TRAINSURFING* EP ... more of the same ... *You Can't Take The Myth*, *Causeway* and *Greek Wedding Song*. Partyleader was *Butterfly*, about 'male ego', a kind of indie *Summer Nights*: 'Does she wanna go with me?/I'm crawling round on my knees.' Uh-huh. Uh-huh. 'It's really, really bothering me/She's a butterfly on our breeze.' Uh-huh. Uh-huh. 'You want to see her.' Uh-huh. Uh-huh. 'I'm coming round right now.'

TRAINSURFING, a dangerous sport best left to Bond movies! White labels were pressed in October 88 but, before they could reach the shops, Red Rhino went under. Yet, Inspiral Carpets found themselves at No 5 in *NME*'s Newcomer of 88 readers' poll and No 11 in John Peel's Festive Fifty. *Keep The Circle Round*, was Peelie's fave single of the year.

He told *NME*, "When we go on holiday with the kids, we make tapes for the car which consist of some records for me, some for them and some for the wife. Invariably records like Inspiral Carpets become favourites since they are essentially good, strong, accessible pop music. I come away liking the kids faves like *Rent* which I wouldn't normally. And I would very definitely play The Pet Shop Boys on my show, if I thought Steve Wright would play Inspiral Carpets." Little did Peel know what surprises were round the corner! Just like years earlier when he had promised to retire the day The Fall appeared on *TOTP*. What a shock when *Victoria* reached the Fearsome 40.

Fortunately, they never made telly!

"The fact that John Peel said ours was his favourite record of last year is better than a million ads in the music press," said Clint in early 89. "We could be as big as The Wedding Present by the end of the year. As Brian Clough said, 'The man who doesn't want to be top of his profession, doesn't deserve to be in it.'"

Graham: "He never did get the England job, did he?" Third in line to the throne, the Inspirals played International 1 in November 88, bottom of a bill that included The Man From Delmonte and 808 State. It was buzzing with people who turned out to see Inspirals for the first time. It was broadcast live on Radio Manchester's *Meltdown*.

Hey! Hey! Anytime, anywhere, look over your shoulder, guess who'll be standing there. Grime, dust, muck, dirt whirling around the Carpets' feet as they stood on City Road, opposite The Haçienda.

"It works perfectly well without ears," they chanted in unison, giggling at The Deaf Society's hoarding picturing a brain. "You can say that again!" laughed Graham. The 'in' joke being that Stephen 'Flapper' Holt had exited at Christmas, the International had been the last chance to see him front the band.

"Basically, it started off as a hobby and when it came to the point where it had to be a career, he didn't want it to be his," explained Clint. "He didn't want to be a pop star, didn't want to stay out late at night doing gigs and didn't want to go on the road!"

It might have worked without ears, but having no record company or distributor either was more of a hitch! "It was quite dispiriting at the end of 88. We'd had a brilliant six months going from playing gigs in Manchester for £20 a night to prestige gigs in London. Then it felt like everyone was walking out on us. Our bassist left, then our singer left and because of Red Rhino none of our records was in the shops."

To top things off, Inspiral Carpets abandoned their label, Playtime, in search of a better deal. Something which left a distraught Paula Greenwood in debt. Didn't the band feel guilty?

Clint: "I feel bad about what happened, but our career definitely comes first. We've sacrificed a lot ... like ten years of my life. We're not doing this for a laugh or a hobby any more. We want to escape working in factories and make the band our career instead. Staying with Playtime, that wasn't possible."

Replies Paula, "I sacrificed a lot as well and it's certainly not a hobby. I take it very seriously, sometimes too seriously. I can understand why bands leave small labels, I never expected Inspirals to stay for ever, but I was upset at the *way* they left, leaving me in debt."

Inspiral Carpets were a gang of working-class skivvies. Bungle sold vinyl at Our Price; Graham worked for a printers in Uppermill; Clint was a van driver. Old-fashioned elbow-grease/nose-to-the-grindstone working-class reality.

"Happy Mondays are more streetwise than us, simply because they spend all day scumming round, while we spend all our days working to earn a living. Sometimes we have to go straight from work to a gig without changing or eating ... but rather that than going on the dole, nicking a guitar and farting about in a flat."

Inspiral Carpets were baling out the sandbags, slashing the ropes. Their indie balloon was going up, up, up. They were sharing manager Anthony Boggiano with The Waltones. He'd formerly been Bodge, a runner in Lewis' hi-fi department. Bassist Dave Swift, had left and been replaced with cheeky skinhead Martin Walsh, aka Bungle, member of The Next Step, Mark E faves. "Playing somebody else's stuff is like stepping into a dead man's shoes ..."

"We were happy with Steve, so we always knew we'd have problems replacing him. We need someone who can represent us on the cover of *NME* in a year's time. Someone charismatic, someone with a good vocal range. We're insisting on someone who doesn't smoke and has a sick sense of humour."

They chose Tom Hingley, well-spoken Oxford-born English graduate and office clerk of Too Much Texas, a Manc act who'd released a *Debris* flexi, *Fixed Link*, and Ugly Man single, *Hurry On Down*, an endearing dedication to falling in love at the seaside, with echoes of Bunnymen's *The Cutter*. 'Riding up and down the pier/Different speeds and different gears.' July 88. Too Much Texas hired an open-top bus, and took journalists (well, the one who turned up!) on a magical mystery tour of the city centre, by Piccadilly and out past the Apollo where Bros were playing, past Cornerhouse where real media-people were

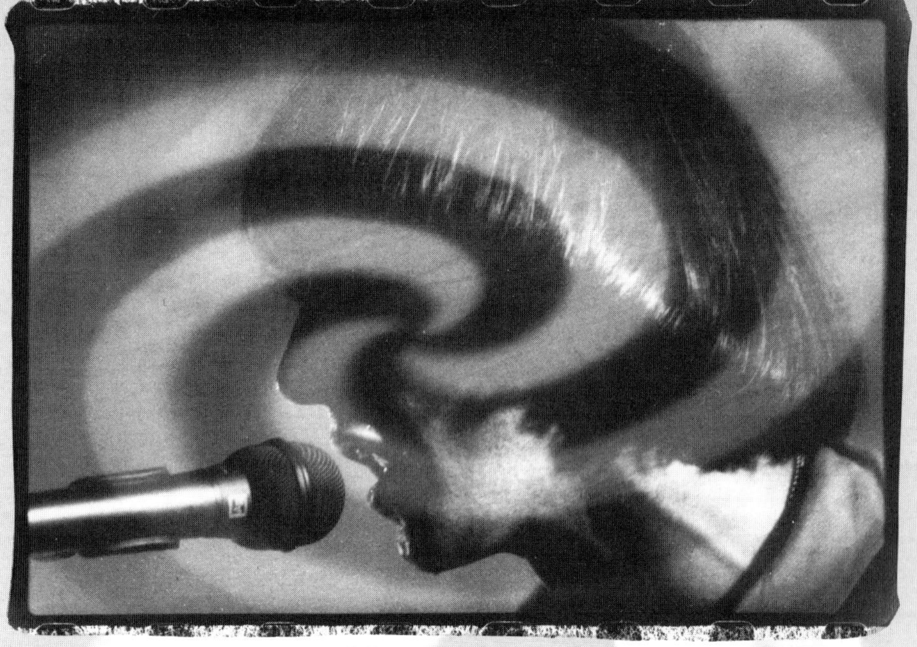

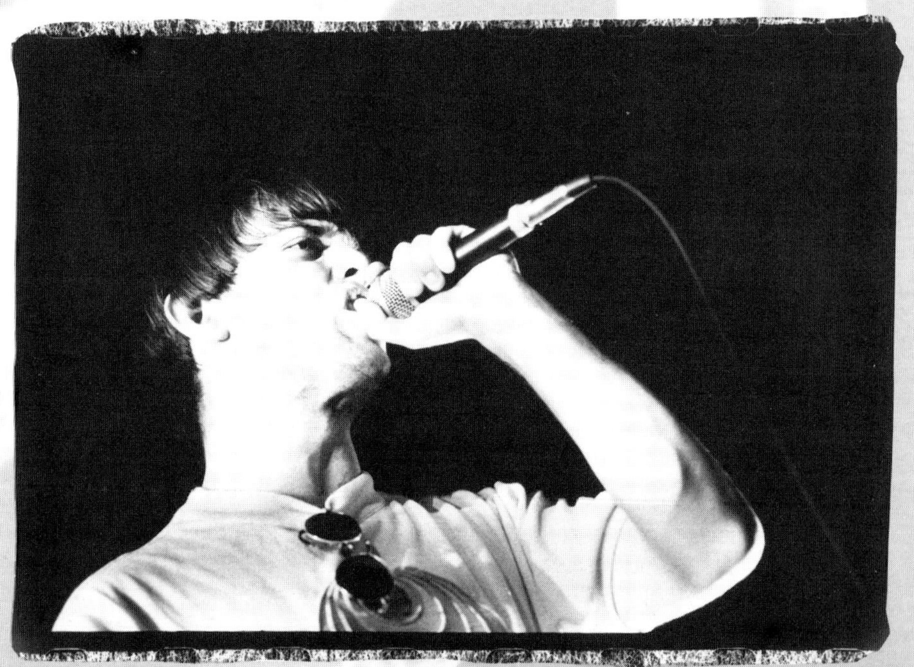

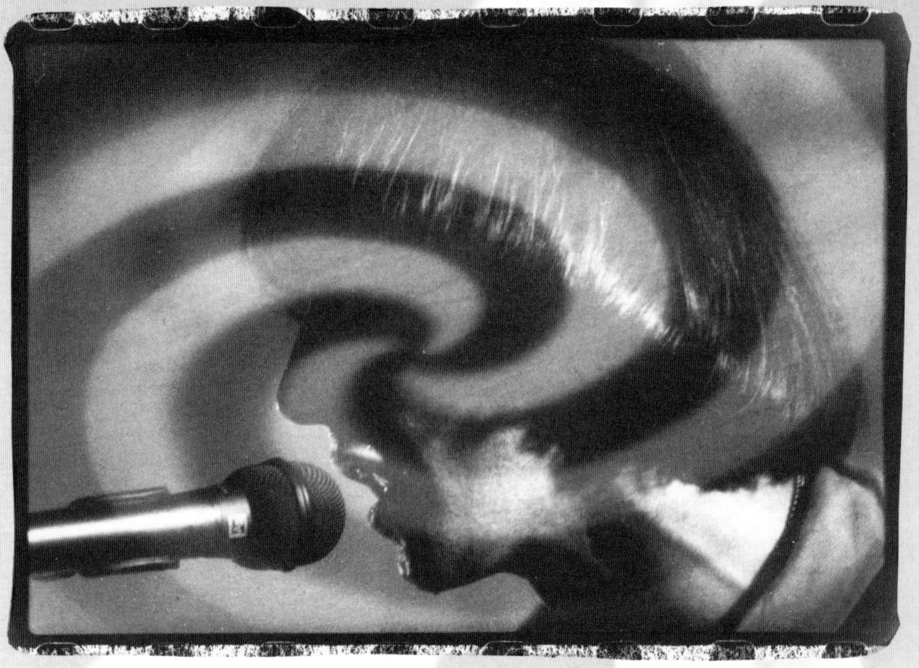

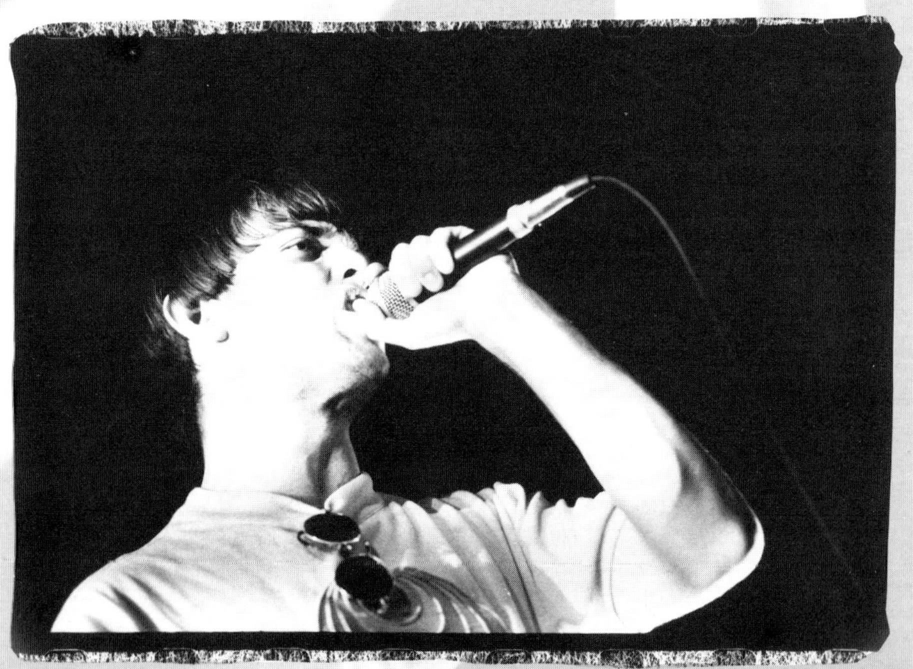

sampling free hair-care products at a Brylcream lig with slicked-back Kalima.

On the bus, Too Much Texas performed their single. Four hippies with uniformly shaved heads, Fac 51 badges, bovver-boots, braces and acoustic guitars. Looking like members of some strange religous cult, they shared one thing ... they all worked as glass-collectors at The Haç!

"Tom Hingley is a star," says Ugly boss, Guy Lovelady. "Even before he was famous he hung off the mike like a big show-off with a voice touching on Julian Cope, Holly Johnson. He was so beautiful. Watching him sing on top of the bus was like kopping off."

Without Tom, Too Much Texas were down and rocking-out for their second EP, *SMART*, on Playtime. Meanwhile, Stephen Holt became Madchester's Pete Best, the 'fifth Beatle', a Julian Lennon, struggling to live down past associations. Steve and Dave's new band, The Rainkings, released poppy-go-lucky *Sunlight Fades*, soon followed by *Get Ready*. Rather than tapping into scally-fervour, they seemed happier playing a trad *C86* lightweight groove.

"I'm not sorry I left," Stephen told *Bop City*. "I'm only disappointed because I think we deserve what they're getting, but I'm not jealous. I don't really like what they're doing. I never did really. I wanted to go one way and they wanted to go another."

Backed by Eastern Bloc and based in the shop's cellar, Inspirals wasted no time. On 4 March 89, the new line-up debuted at The Boardwalk, which was also celebrating. It had just refurbished and extended its capacity from 250 to 500. Re-releases of *PLANECRASH* and *TRAINSURFING* were thwarted. No matter. They'd re-recorded *Joe* with Tom's vocals, started their own label, Cow, and released it at the end of April 89 to coincide with a sell-out gig at Manchester University. The roles had now been reversed and 808 were guesting.

Clint: "Manchester's a community and people aren't snobbish. They're not afraid to be seen mixing."

Inspiral Carpets were a contradiction. A psychedelic band without the drugs. They flirted with late-60s imagery, but it was more mod than hippie; fuelled by beer not acid. Calling Inspirals 'psychedelic' is like calling a Macclesfield folk band 'authentic country and western'! *Joe*'s flip-side, *Commercial Rain*, was their hippest, hallucinogenic track; a Lowrider meets Peter Gunn dub, with a touch of feedback.

"In the old days people said that we were corny for having strobe lights and being psychedelic," Clint told John Robb.

"We've been called Northern, working-class capitalists. We don't deny that. We are capitalising, but we'd be stupid not to." says Clint, who smirks as he says it. If he was the face of 80s capitalism, then it must surely be acceptable!

"Clint's lovely. He stands up on the passenger seat of his car, out of his sunroof and waves going down the motorway! He's wonderful, a star, an old man just starting to enjoy himself. I look at him and think: what am I worried about?! This man only started having fun when he was 30!" lisped Mike West of Delmontes.

Inspiral Carpets 'capitalised' magnificently. Their September 89 single, *Find Out Why*, zoomed straight into the Top 100 with sales of 8000 in just one week. Enough for *another* indie No 1, the week they played a prestigious Haçienda gig, 'The Binsey Meets Monobrow Tour'. Monobrow referred to their roadie's eyebrows, Binsey was Anthony's nickname.

They also played a 'secret' gig in August at Liverpool's Hardman Hotel, entitled 'The Manweb Music Machine' ... designed to boost the Electricity Board's street-cred! Roger Morton, covering the event for *NME*, fell for their riotous sense of humour, writing a feature that portrayed them as obnoxious, sexist beer-boys.

Welcome to The Ministry Of Dung. Introducing, Clint Boon, MP for Cowsville North, named after an obscure member of the Jesse James gang. There's money in muck! The Inspirals Compost Corporation had taken over a new office in tumbling-down Sackville Street. They were going up in the world ... by three storeys, and at least this one had windows. In the same sHaçk-up, Johnson/Panas (Factory's graphic designers) Central Station Design and *NME* photographer, Peter 'trendy' Walsh.

Here Clint's girlfriend, Debs, co-ordinated their growing T-shirt empire. In the previous nine months they'd sold 6000 button badges and 10,000 T-shirts. Enough profit to buy them, say, a small house in North Manchester! Being sensible they re-invested all the profits back in the 'business'. "We want to build something for the future," says Clint.

OPPOSITE
Clint, International 2, November 1989.
Tom, G-Mex, July 1990;

Their most popular shirt, a cool-cow sporting shades, topped off with the slogan 'Cool As Fuck', reputedly stolen from the Milk Marketing Board's 'Cool As Milk' campaign. Even The Harlem Globetrotters were spotted buying them! Fans throughout Britain have been arrested under the obscenity laws!

"Without the merchandising, which was paying for our food, we would have had to have signed to a major to continue," Clint said in *ID*.

Just when we thought we knew exactly what Inspirals were about, a juddering indie steam-train, huffing and puffing along, came *Move* ... as streamlined as a Japanese bullet train, with a bonfire-night sleeve. This was for real. An all-out bid for *TOTP*, with a radio-friendly ballad. While Roses, 808 and Mondays all made it, Inspirals hovered at No 49.

A greater achievement, as it was on their own label. Now they'd done all the hard work, everyone in the country wanted them, offering fractions of a million! They stayed indie, signed to Mute Records. Their next single *This Is How It Feels*, took them to a sell-out at The Ritz and *The Pops*. The cameras hugged Tom, ignoring the rest of this "ugly" bunch. Clint Boon now had a gold chain that Brooklyn rappers would pull guns for. Fun for all the family! From toddlers to grannies, Inspiral Carpets were the biggest '*pop*' band from Manchester *ever*.

Children's *Newsround* father-figure, John Craven, would soon be turning up backstage with his daughter. BBC Manchester invited them to star in their own cartoon show. They declined, but recorded the theme tune to Saturday morning's *8-15 From Manchester*. How soon before they'd be invited to meet a Royal? Sneered Steven Wells of *This Is How It Feels*, "The lyrics read like a cross between The Mekons spoof agit-punk rant and one of those awful Morrissey celebrations of misery, 'Baby's fallen off the table/rats are eating Auntie Mabel/I'd like to help but I'm not able.'"

Next single, *She Comes In The Fall*, was a rat-a-tat-tat marching song, for scallydelic carpet-baggies marching to peace. Flip-side was *Sackville*, 'a different world.' This was Sackville ... where red lights spelt danger. This was Sackville ... where rows of used condoms appeared during the night, adorning bushes like Christmas decorations. This was Sackville ... where a dank canal ran by the Inspirals' old office.

This is Sackville ... biggest gay-town outside London, just ten minutes walk from the Arndale, to the embarrassment of homophobic bigots who write to the *Manchester Evening News*' 'Famous' Postbag, calling for the return of capital punishment. This is Sackville ... gay nightlife mecca: Central Park, New York New York, Napoleons, La Cage, Rembrandt, Clone Zone ... just round the corner from Chorlton Street Bus Station!

This is Sackville ... which Inspiral Carpets translated into an innocent pop song!

"I wrote the lyrics about Sackville Street," explains Graham. "It was early in the morning and it looked really cool. I suppose if I'd walked down the street and some pimp'd beat me, I'd change my mind about the place ..."

The days of Transit-vanning were over for good. They now had a £100,000 tour bus, 'as used by Gloria Estefan.' Their debut album *LIFE*, sold 200,000 copies, in just one week. In just 14 months their audience at hometown gigs rocketed by 2500%!

Oldham had never had it so good! Their Second Division footie sons walked out at Wembley for an FA Cup Final against Manchester United. Meanwhile, their third-in-line pop star progeny, Inspiral Carpets, walked onstage to a sold-out G-Mex on July 21, 90. "We know we can be as big as U2 if we want to be."

"The best thing about the 60s," said Clint, "Is that it was 20 years ago and we weren't there." Hey! Hey! It's the Inspirals. They're the *young* generation, and they've got something to say. Come and hear them sing and play.

FOLLOWING PAGES
Inspiral Carpets, spring 1990;
MC Buzz B, summer 1990;
Twang, winter 1987;
G-Mex, Happy Mondays gig, winter 1988;
Happy Mondays, spring 1990;
808 State, summer 1990;
Kiss AMC, summer 1988;
Stone Roses, spring 1989;
Spike Island, spring 1990;
Northside, Free Trade Hall, autumn 1988;
The Charlatans, summer 1990;
James, summer 1990.

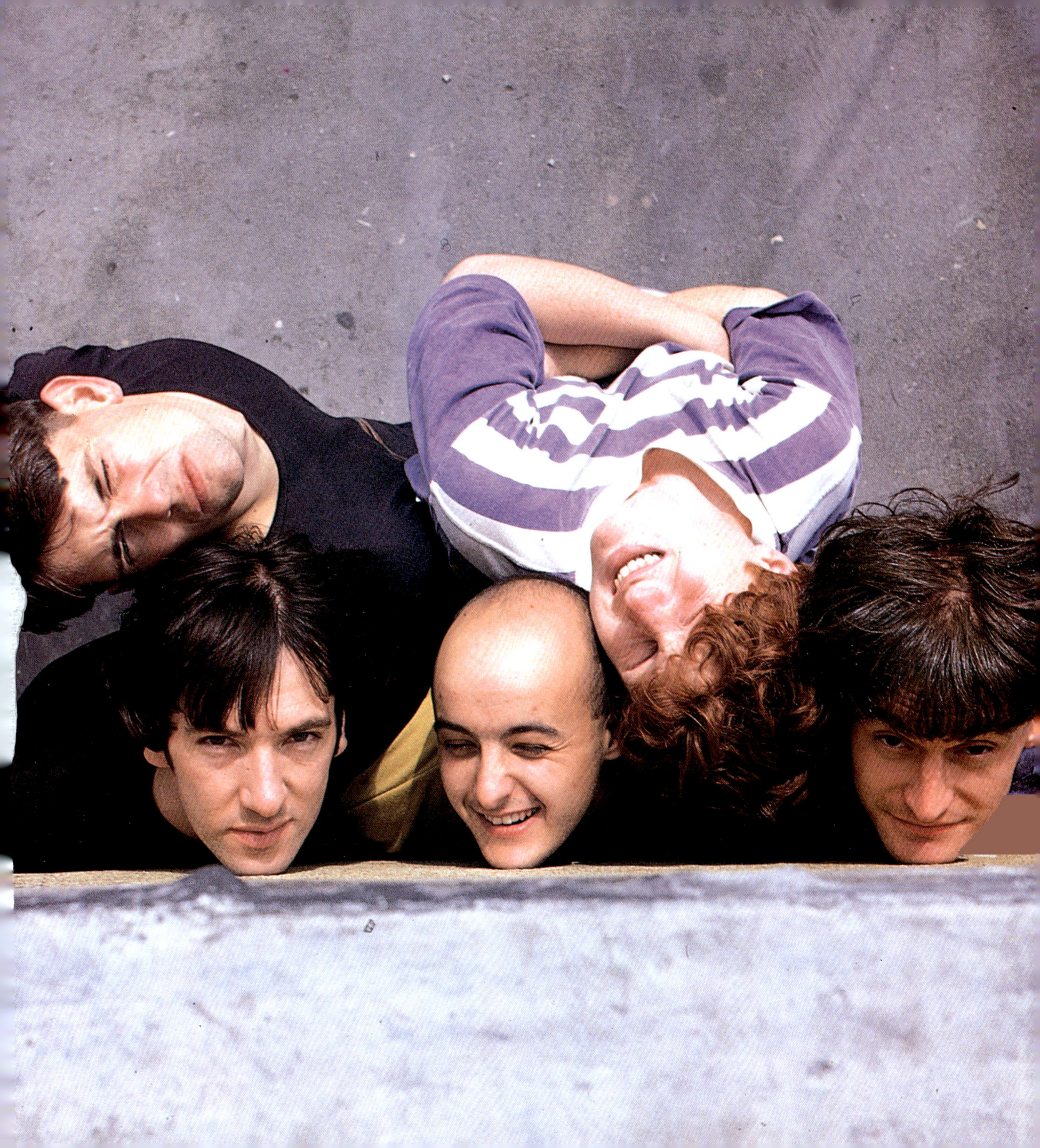

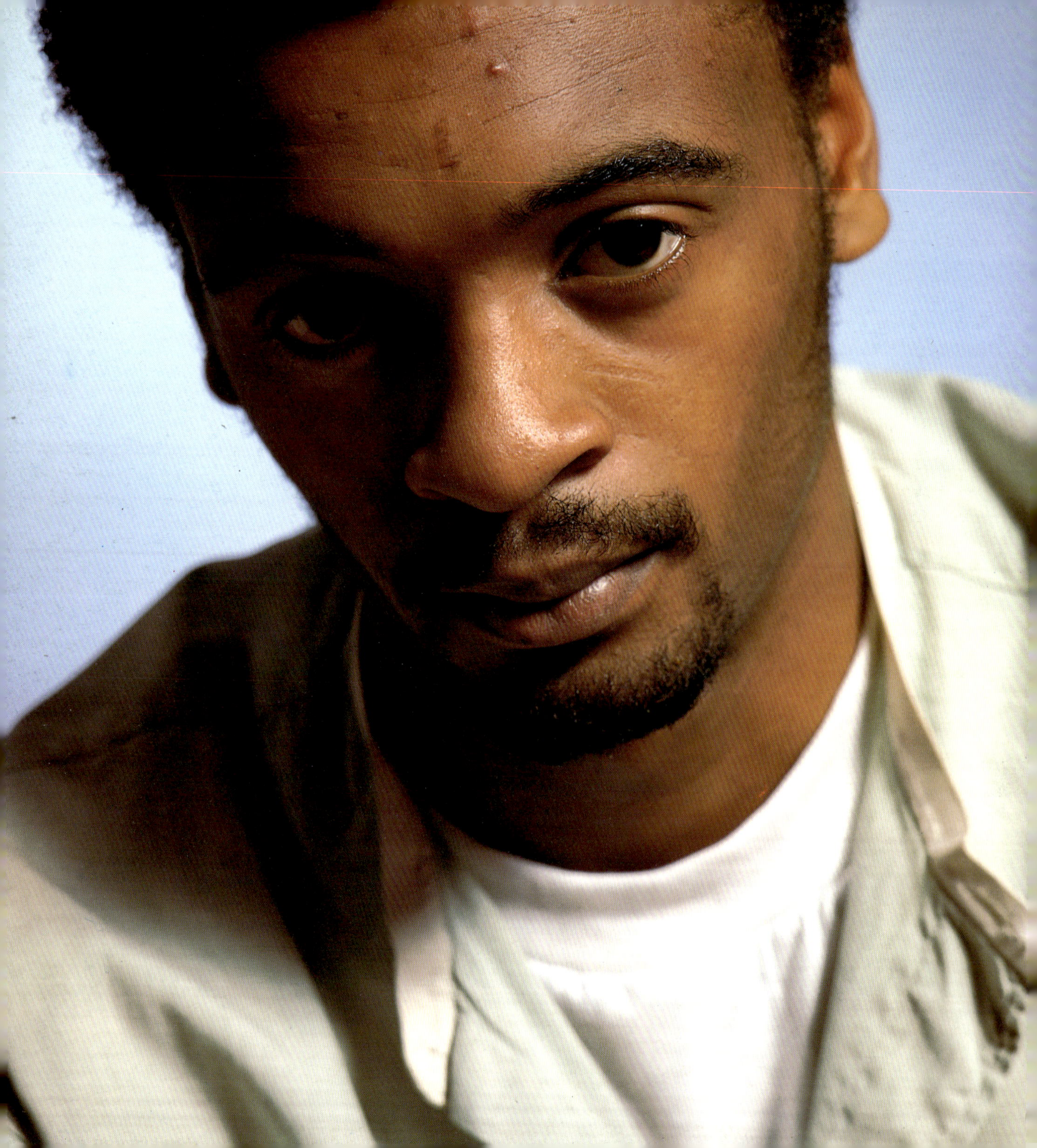

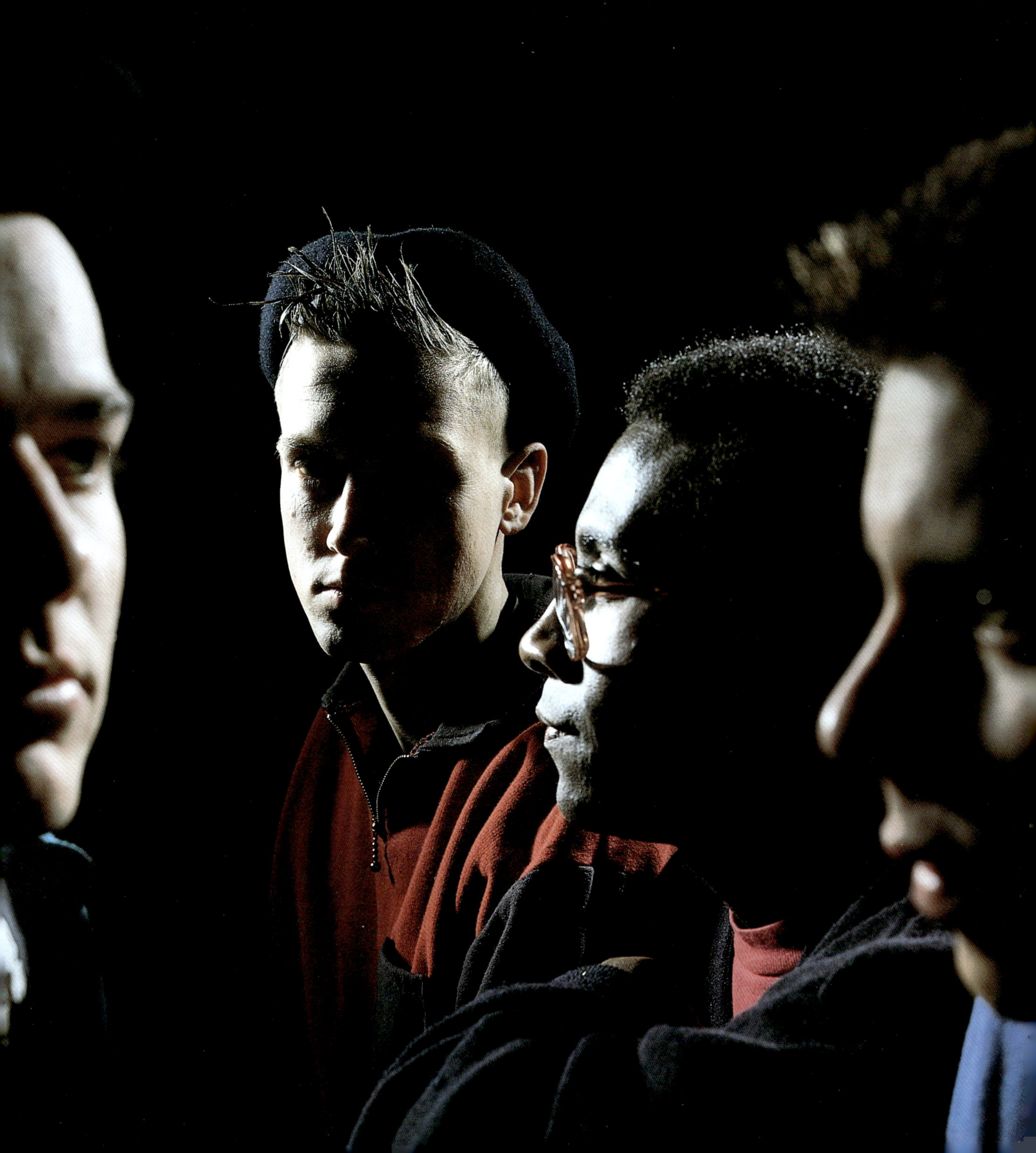

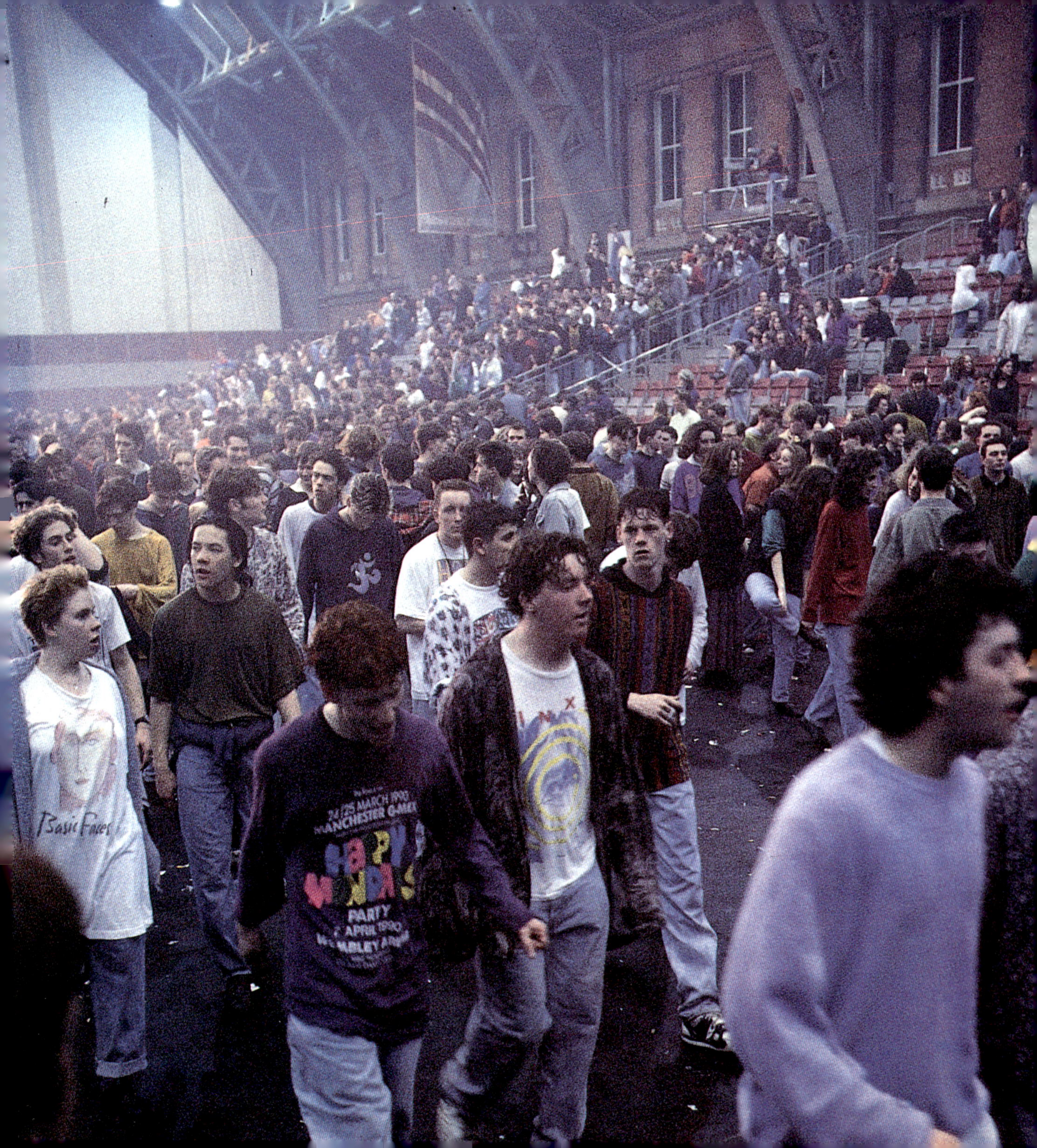
24/25 MARCH 1990
PARTY
Basic Faces

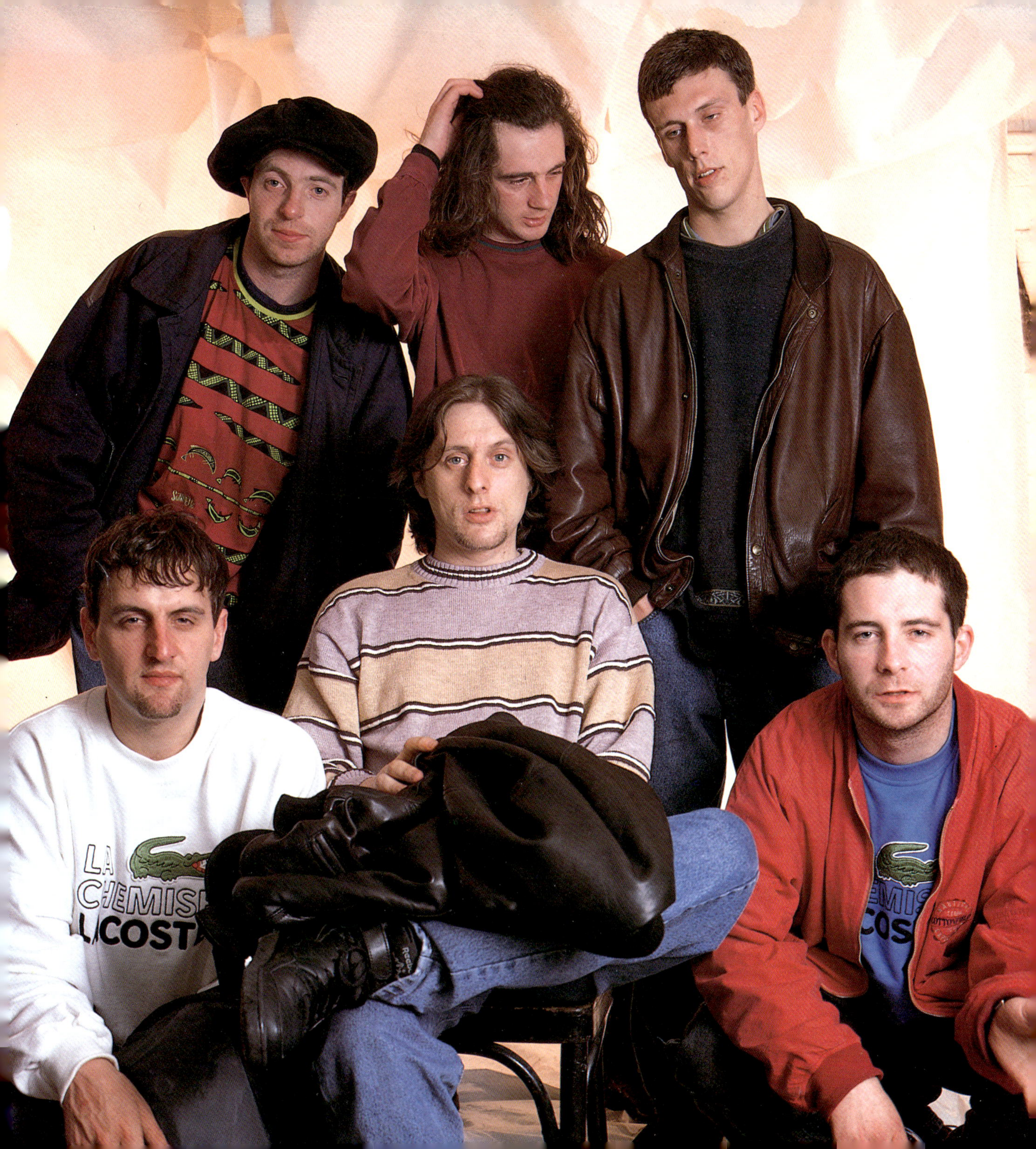

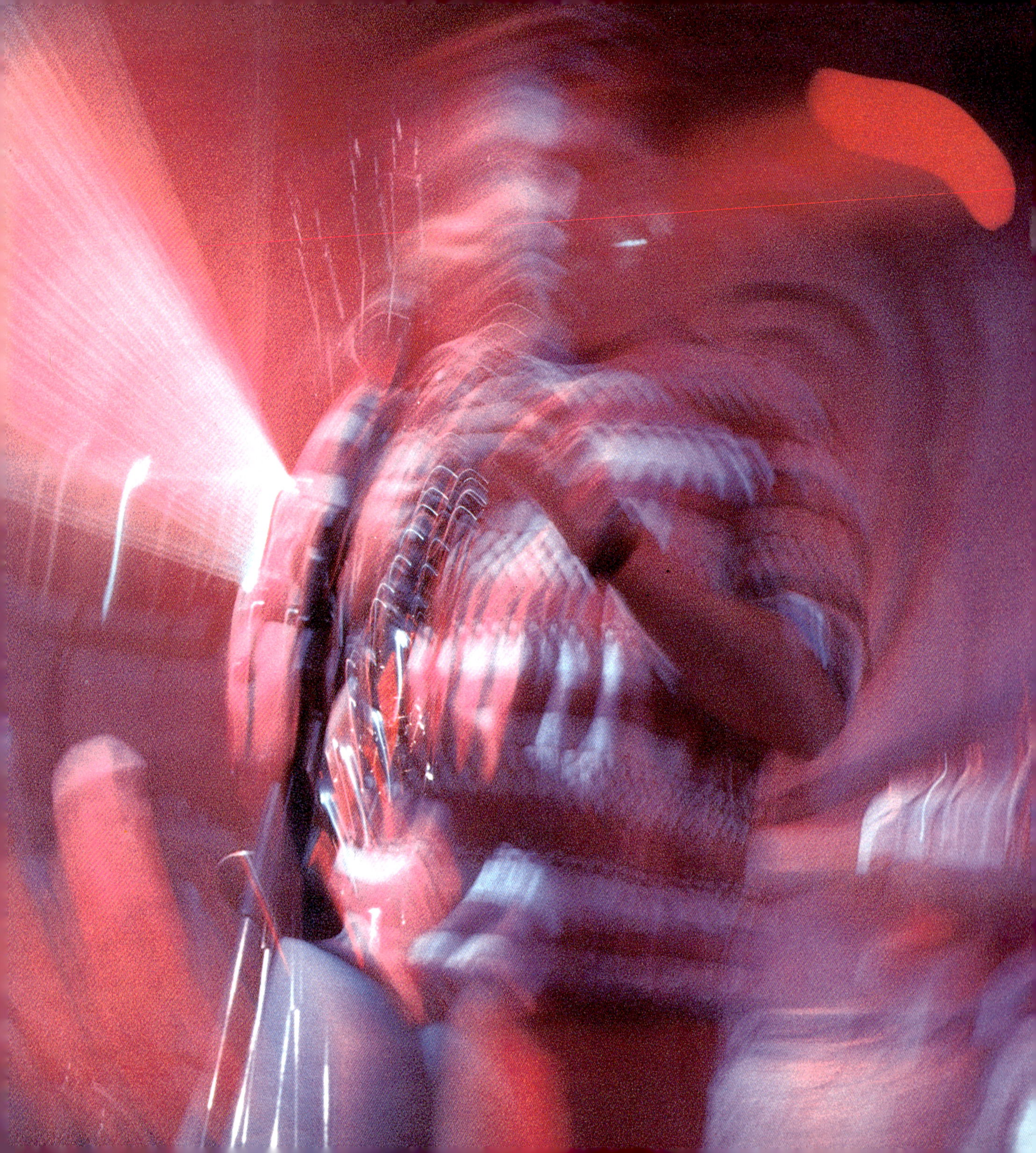

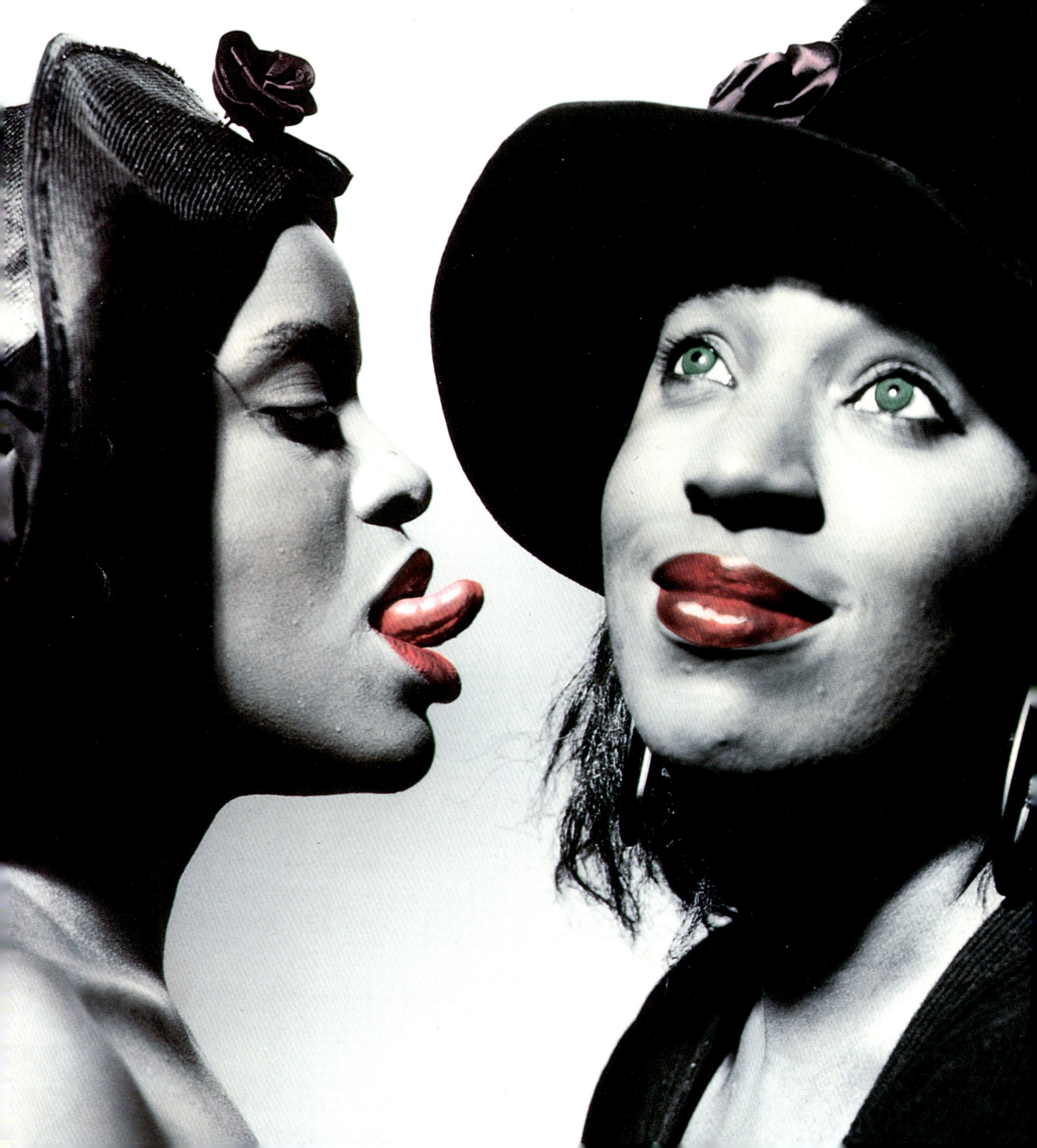

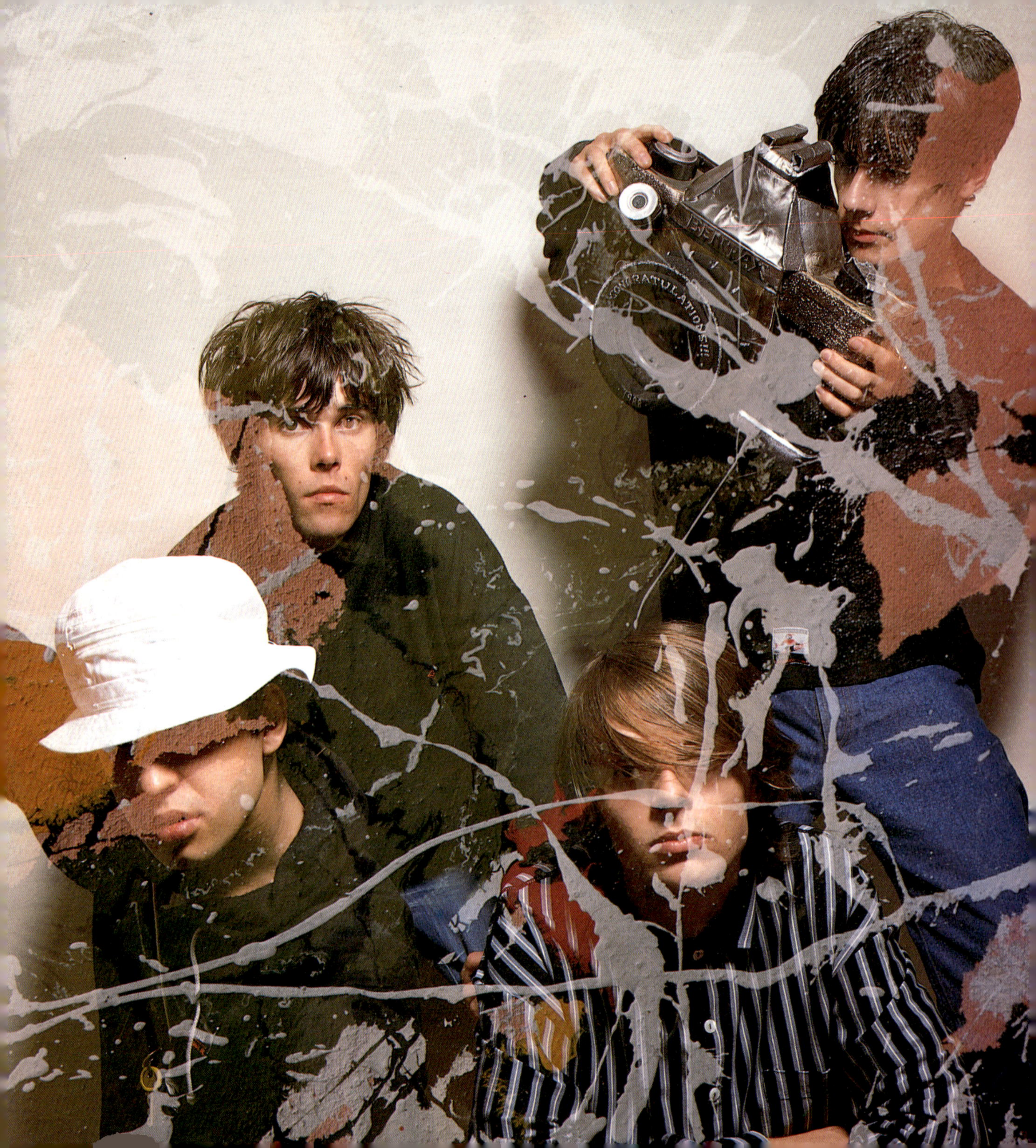

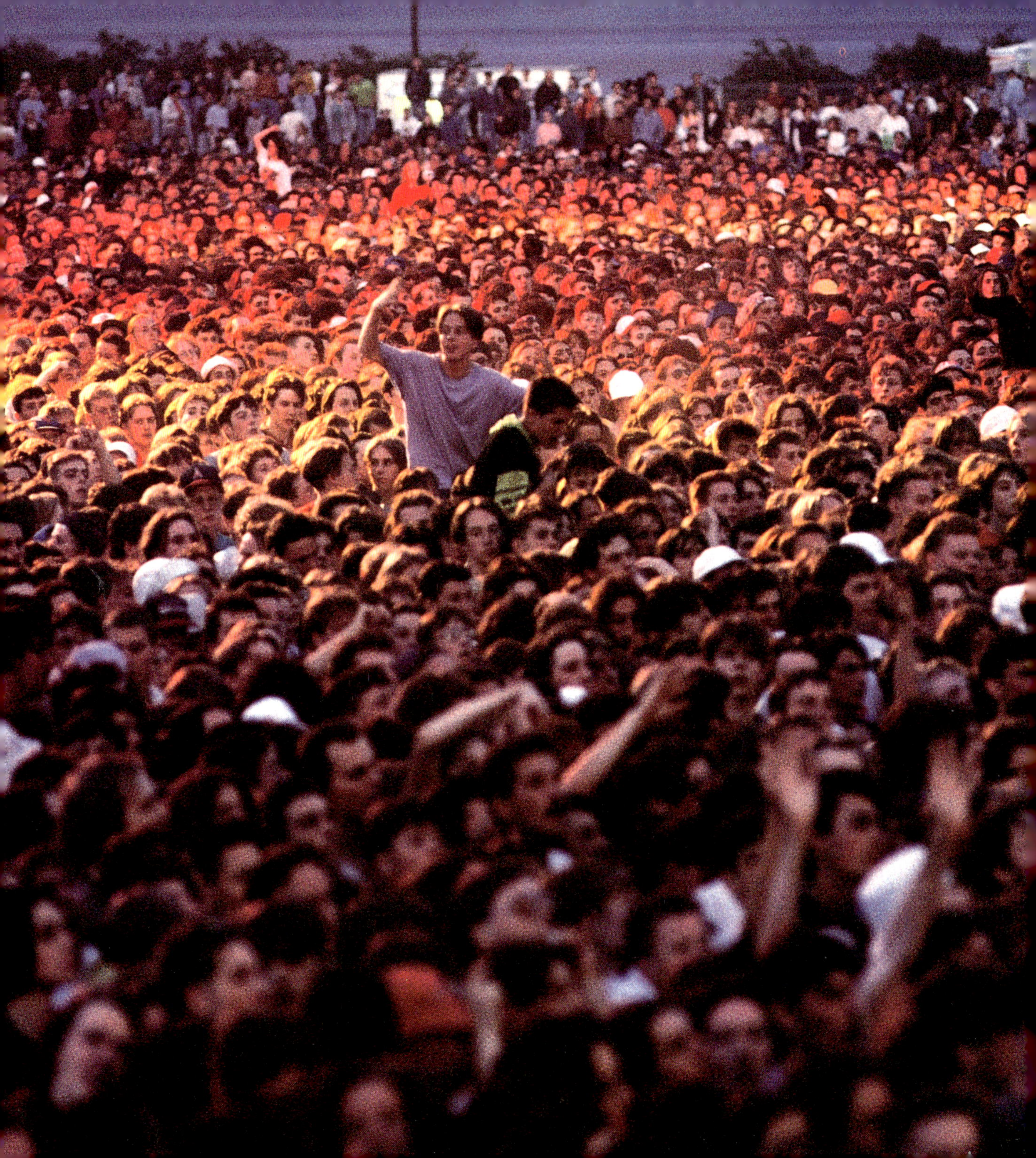

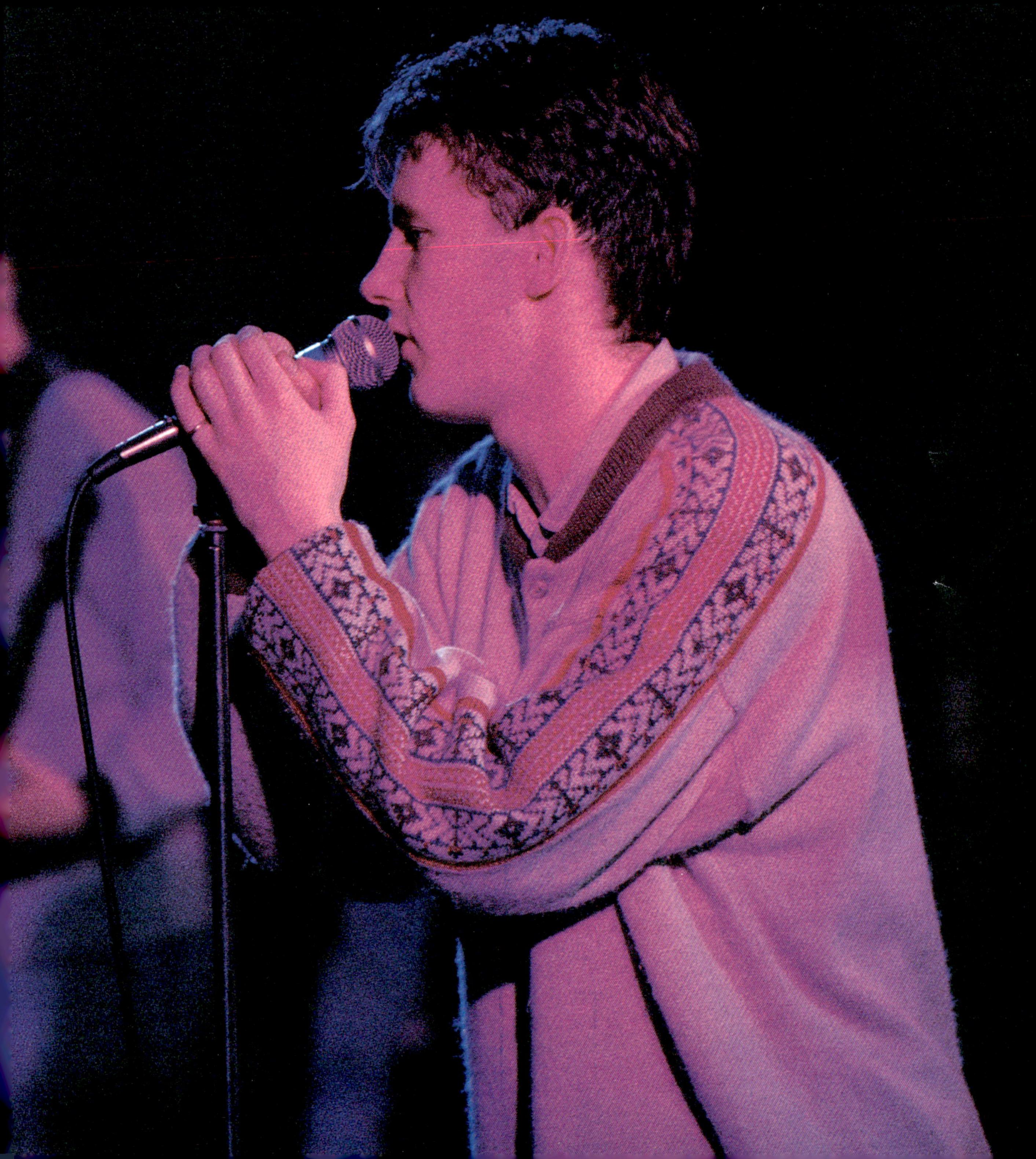

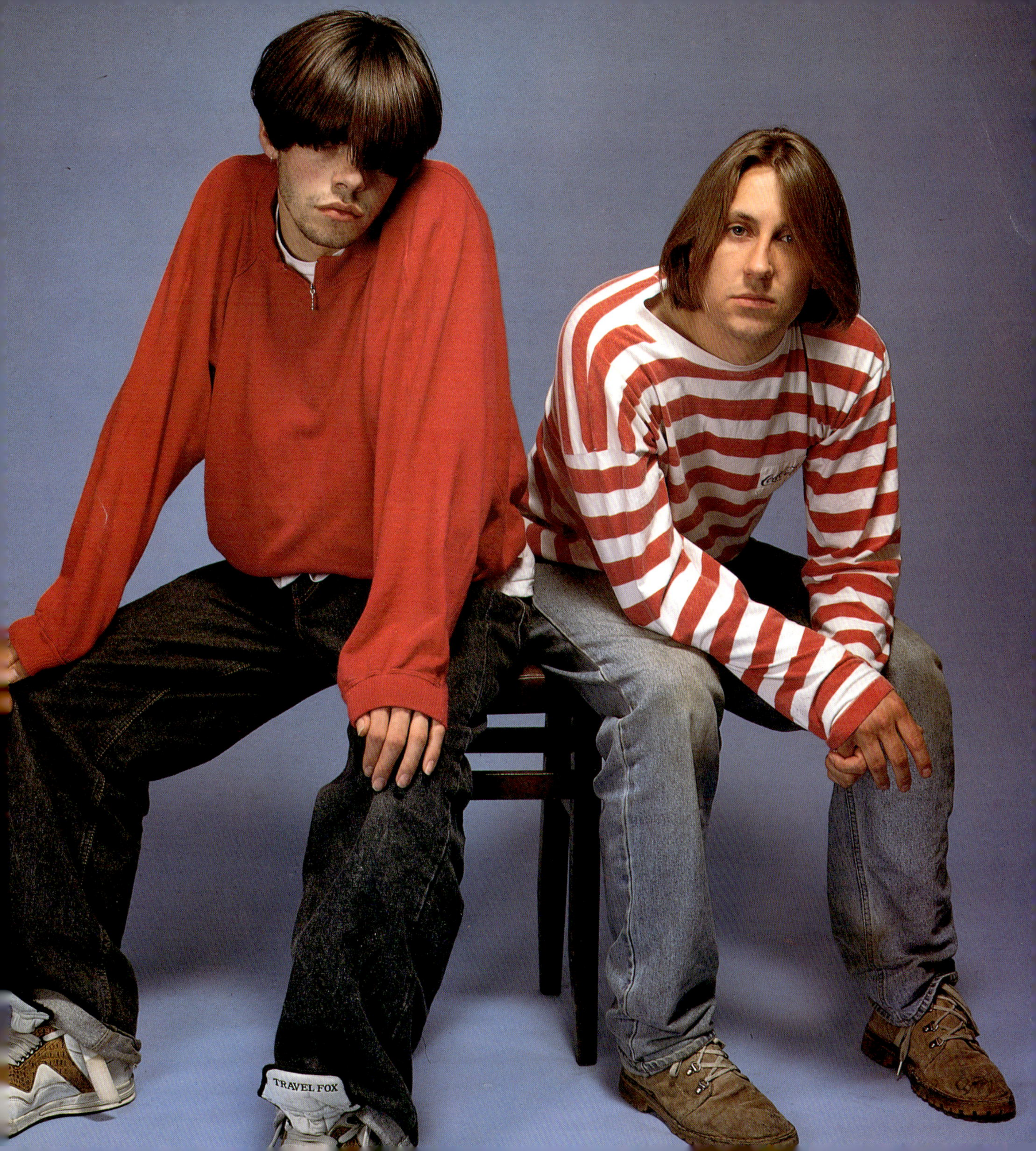
TRAVEL FOX

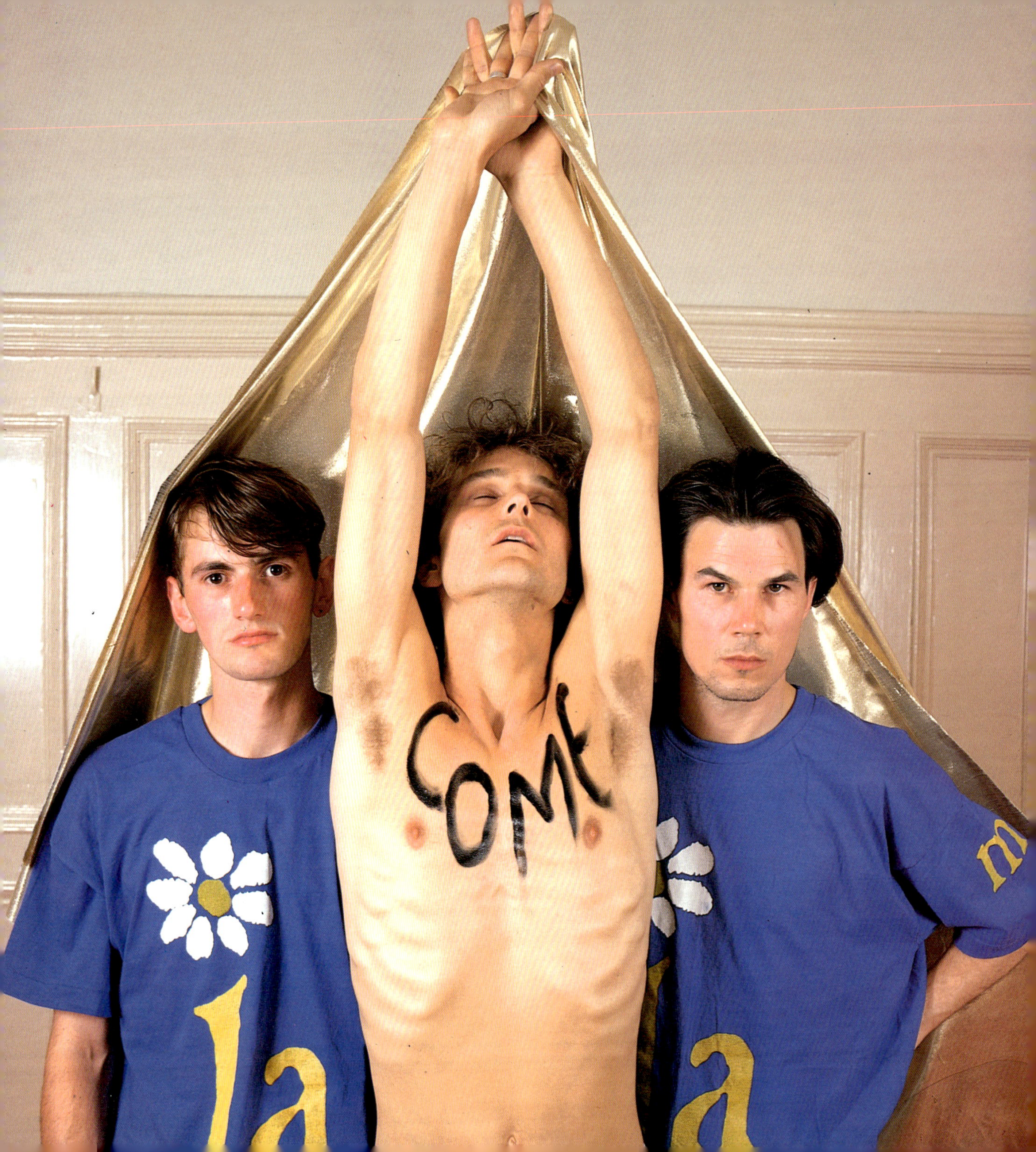
COME

An everyday tale of hedonism. Somewhere out there, somewhere over the rainbow, is a room hazy with tortured artistes. Ian Curtis slouched in a corner; Nick Cave spaced-out; Jim Morrison singing to himself; Van Gogh asleep on a couch; Bez shaking his maracas; Elvis playing pool with Hendrix. Then, one day, James' Tim Booth wanders in.

A VillaGe HYmn

And God Created Manchester

A woman in a white coat has just concluded a talk. "Do you understand?" she asks. Everyone nods intently. "Any questions?" She then passes round a flask of freaky-looking liquid. Tim follows the crowd, takes a swig. Later, he finds he has just swallowed the poison that allows great artistes to create ... but screws up their lives.

Dream, nightmare or reality? This story bewitched *Riders* on James' second album, STRIP-MINE.

"For the first three years of James it was going to be a suicide dive. The band meant so much to us we were going to die for it," confessed Tim. "Everyone was into the idea of burning-out and burning-out fast. It was no verbally-agreed philosophy, but it was what we all wanted."

James were enraptured by hedonistic fools, wild things, rock 'n' roll crazies. Early song, *Johnny Yen*, was a tribute to rebels everywhere, prompted by the boy-junkie in William Burroughs' *The Soft Machine*. 'Watch Kinevil hit the 17th bus, you got crushed in the souvenir rush/See Houdini and his underwater tricks/See the young men, itching to burn, waiting for their own star turn/Needing danger, war would do, if they can't let it out they'll pick on you/Poor old Johnny Yen set himself on fire again ...'

Tim had a dream. "I met Nick Cave and he was showing me a video of The Birthday Party doing a version of *Dead Joe*," he told *NME* in 85. "I was going, 'God! How did you do it?' Then I looked at him and his face was covered in huge craters, turning green and falling away in huge lumps and I said, 'Ah, I see how you do it.'" The Birthday Party's extremes appealed to

Tim Booth's sense of self-destruction.

"Mine's seven tabs of ecstasy, some acid, two lines of speed, a cocaine highball, various barbituates, uppers, downers and two joints of the finest sensimilla," wrote Dele Fadele. "Maybe then, I'll be fit enough to face James, wastrels and masterful steers."

In 88, Tim admitted, "From Nick Cave to Van Gogh, most brilliant artists use some kind of artificial stimulant in creating their work and end up wrecking their lives. I have much outside James to live for, but I sometimes wonder if it really might be worth it." He lived.

James first cried for attention in the pop playpen guesting on The Smiths' Meat Is Murder Tour in 85. Morrissey adored them. Declining dosh to take other acts on tour, he chose to pay James who were still scuffing their sensible shoes in small Northern venues. Stark, excessive pop extremists. Gavan Whelan, toppest drummer in Manchester (after Reni and Bruce Mitchell!); Jim Glennie, Manc bassist; Larry Gott, guitarist with glasses. And right out front, in a wash-baggied green T-shirt, Tim Booth himself. Shuddering like a tower block in an earthquake, he did an epileptic war dance. His trademark to this day. Iggy Pop outrage vs Ian Curtis having a fit. Like David Byrne dancing as if his pants were alight. What next, a Bernie Clifton ostrich walk?

Drugs? Hedonism? Chance would be a fine thing. James' public image circa 85 was of wimpy vegans, purists, even Bhuddists. Reinforced by an *NME* cover wheeze by Don Watson, where the band wore seriously-dodgy sweaters. "In their van, they're tucking into a celebratory post-gig mixture of baked beans, beansprouts and brown rice," he wrote. "They have to be back early at their bed and breakfast abode. This ain't rock 'n' roll ..."

People called James 'weirdos'. Weird! Think about it. Natural hair, sensible shoes, Aran sweaters? It was the Morrissey anti-rebel syndrome again. James' temperance romance was furthered by a series of cut-out-and-keep gigs where alcohol was prohibited and veggie-feed served. "Because we'd been so deeply involved in drugs and drink, the reaction had to be as equally extreme ... just like any revolution in life or in country," Larry explained.

'Defects we're born with/But poisons we choose/He's not there/Just a gap in the air,' teased *STRIP-MINE*'s *Not There*, cousin of *Riders*. About a loved friend spiralling downwards, romanticising junkidom/death perhaps too much, like *Sid And Nancy*. "Seeing a friend shot down like a plane, we realised the reality of burning-out. A depressing experience because we knew it could so easily have been one of us," said Tim. "It was at that point that we decided we were going to make music so good it would make us so high that we wouldn't need drugs."

This they did. Their career had been ignited in 83, with *Jimone*, a Factory 7". Boss-track, *Folklore*, was an anthem of the 'new man' fighting the current of macho traditions passed down from father to son. "Everyone plays roles," Tim told *Debris*. "If you think that you're born, you go to school, you get a job, you drink a lot and get married, then you retire and die, then you're missing out on something crucial."

After *Jimone*, appeared *James II*, neatly shredding C&A-bland pop songs on the crucial *Hymn From A Village*. 'This song's made up with second-rate cosmetic music/ powder-puff popcorn forced rhymes or lightweight bluffs/second-hand, no soul, no hate/ This language used is all worn-out/a walking corpse that won't play-dead ...' *Jimone* and *James II* were re-packaged as *VILLAGE FIRE*, for those who'd missed out first time round.

James danced through Factory like a string of cartoon characters on a Kia-ora ad. Their quirky *up* tunes did a conga across Factory's habit of too-much-grey, too-much-doom, too many primal-funksters and serious raincoats. But, before Fac caught their breath, James were away up the street, signed to US-based major, Sire, home to Madonna and Talking Heads. Unfortunately, it stopped the groove dead. "The head of Sire collects bands like they're bits of art, probably as much to make sure other people don't get hold of them, as to use them himself," said Tim.

When *STUTTER*, their debut LP, cake-walked onto the pop scene in the summer of 86, James discovered they had a record considered a flop because it wasn't Top Ten. 'Too English!' They were disqualified from indie placings, yet far too esoteric be in the 'proper' charts. Sire cut the cash-flow.

"One cynical lesson we've learnt, is that the amount of money a record company offer you is the amount of commitment they'll make. If they put money in,

OPPOSITE
James, July 1986.

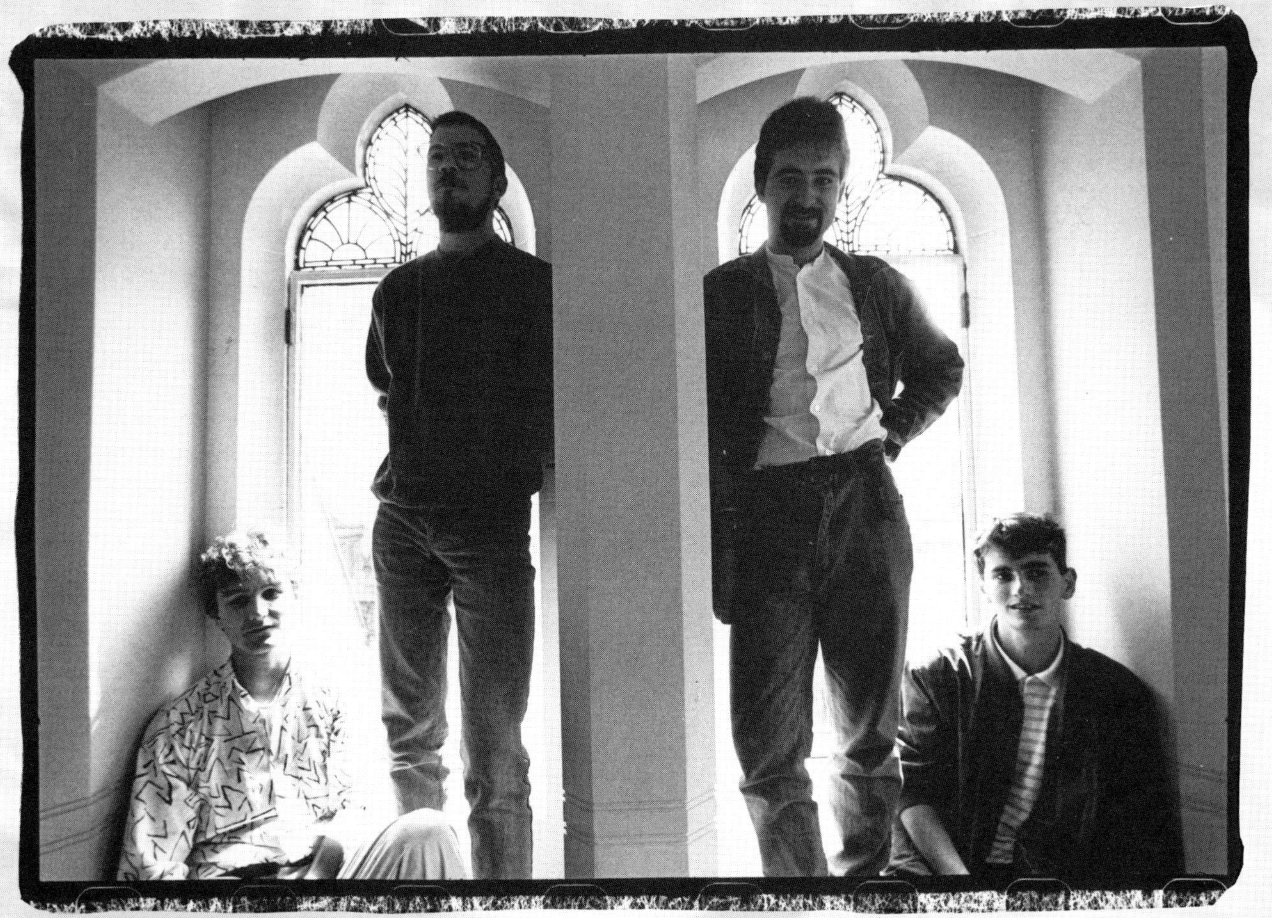

they'll want it back and so work hard to get it. We accepted a lower total from Sire thinking they were more genuine. They offered us total artistic control, only for us to learn that it meant nothing. Unless we did what they wanted, they would say it was rubbish and refuse to promote it."

STUTTER was not rubbish, just a little too *good* for Americans to make sense of. Produced by Lenny Kaye, founder of the Patti Smith Group, it was obliviously odd. Tracks like *Fire So Close* about nuclear irresponsibility, *Scarecrow* about Patti Smith, *Johnny Yen* the rebel song ...

STUTTER's commercial car-crash was trailed by an 18-month ordeal surrounding their second album. A farce even a disaster-prone Frank Spencer would find hard to equal! It started when the release date for STRIP-MINE was set for May 87. "Every time the release date was put back, we kept thinking, 'It's *got* to happen this time!' Once it even got as close as two weeks to the day before the thing was pulled!"

Managers resigned; managers were sacked; money was tight; Sire were not behind the band; the time wasn't right. Through eight different release dates, the album was re-called; Hugh Jones' mixes causing the greatest delay.

"He was mad. He didn't sleep. He'd do 24 hours, then sleep a couple, then start again," said Jim. "We had five days to do three mixes, but after five 24-hour days, through which we had to stay up, he'd only come up with one ... and a sub-standard one at that!" A fisticuffs over cash for more re-mixes ensued, after which Steve Power, producer of Sam Fox and re-mixer of Billy Ocean's *When The Going Gets Tough*, was recruited. The only remaining delay was the band's attention to detail; it took four days just to select the running order.

"Steve Powers gave us a cassette of seven or eight versions of each song to choose from. For *What For* we had 15! The differences were as minute as an increase in volume on the snare or a bit more middle on the bass!"

The result? A symmetrical album of ace songs, but without the raw feel of STUTTER. Released in October 88, only 525 days late. "We took STRIP-MINE very seriously," said Tim. "Every drum-beat, word and note has been concentrated upon."

In the indie kingdom governed by peroxide fairy princesses like The Primitives, James were a band of *Jackanory* story-tellers plugging two albums full of *Aesop's Fables*. Every song on STUTTER and STRIP-MINE had a moral, every line a metaphor.

Tim was the king of the fairy tales. At dusk he stood in Manchester's Piccadilly Gardens singing to the skies, huge flocks of pigeons circling above. "In a city of all grey, cars and pollution, you don't get many uplifting, natural sights ... It's beautiful!" he smiled. Far out. Outasite. Crazy, man.

Piccadilly pigeons inspired the single *What For*, unleashed pre-STRIP-MINE in April 88. "*What For* is our *Born To Run*," Tim told *Cut*. James tumbled into a roly-poly series of singles with anthem-like choruses, soaring hooklines. Quirkily, each had a snappy two-syllable title. *What For* was superseded by *Ya Ho*.

More morals from *Ya Ho*. Tim Booth ought to publish an anthology to be read aloud by headteachers in school assemblies. "I had the visual image of a tribe of people living on a beach, believing it was a sin to go in the water. One day someone walked in and everyone was completely freaked-out. He swam away, but no-one else would take the risk and follow. They thought swimming was the danger, not realising the danger was the quicksand sucking them in ..." A metaphor for life. Do you play or do you pass? *Gulliver's Travels* for the indie-pop generation.

Yet, 'agony aunts', James, were in deep themselves, sinking fast. Freed from Sire, but bankrupt, they had to dust themselves down, bandage their cuts and begin again.

Once more James pulled out of a bellyflop and into a stylish dive. They formed their own label, One Man Records, funded by Rough Trade. In 89 at Bath's Moles Club, a neutral zone, they archived a live album, *ONE MAN CLAPPING*. Jumbling folk-rock with freakiness, it got most anatomical on *Leaking*. 'I'm leaking down the left side, my gall bladder's burst and so has my spleen/I'm so wound-up my bowels just want to flow ...' One match of buzzer-board game, *Operation*, too many. Probably some surreal vision of spontaneous combustion or radiation sickness! Edward Lear eat your heart out. Tim Booth, the Ralph McTell of his generation, master of lyrical nonsensities. Influenced by sea-shanties and TV themes?

This was the new James. The pressure was too much. Gavan Whelan left, arranging a less stressful role with Liverpool folksters, Gone To Earth. *ONE MAN CLAPPING* was more of a last testament to James Part One than a fresh statement, for it was recorded with the old line-up. Out with the old: in with the new! Gavan was replaced by David Baynton-Power, double-barrelled session man.

James began to acquire members at such a rate that, by the year 2000, they'll be as big as the Hallé and need a tour bus the length of Oldham Street. Having widely advertised for instrumentalists, they found violinist Saul Davies by accident. He was travelling from the South to a job interview in Hull when he stopped off at a Band On The Wall workshop. The band spotted him and he was in! He was also 'out', into Pink Floyd and so cultured he had a flat in Brussels and could name eight different soft cheeses and their corresponding biscuits!

This new line-up peformed in March 89 at the Free Trade Hall, a sell-out. Tim was no longer a tortured artiste, but a mature singer with a white hat, crumpled-silk shirt and classic-cut trousers. That's what paternity does to you! For one night they sailed their ship somewhere between Genesis and Fairport Convention. The new James? Stadium folk for *Q* age-zone? In the wings, Morrissey nodded approval like a car-windscreen doll. Idiotic kids danced on stage. Whoops-a-daisy, don't trip that wire!

Sit Down, the next single in June 89, was back on the right motorway. James as adult-orientated folk was just a momentary mirage. Tim sang for all the weary, lonely, bored, bruised to sit down next to him. Who did he think he was? Jesus? Legend has it that, when James played *Sit Down* at the Apollo at the end of 89, exuberant fans invading the stage to do just that were screamed at to get off!

Sit Down's disgusting Central Station sleeve was possibly a drawing of Tim, while follow-up *Come Home* looked like a Mothercare catalogue with a baby on the cover. James' earthy phase, as Tim entered into fatherhood with his first son, Ben, was a contrast to his surreal story-telling of the past. Lyrics like, 'My girlfriend told me she was pregnant/I'm on top of the world ...'

Come Home, was another *Ya Ho/Sit Down/What For* hymn. A pop lifetime away from *Hymn From A Village*. Put it in this context. *Come Home* is the next stitch in an intellectual, acoustic-pop seam that had Lloyd Cole's *Perfect Skin* and The Lilac Time's *American Eyes* sewn-up.

Mental! Mental! Mental! Scallydelia fans streamed into Manchester, eagerly consuming Roses/Mondays/Inspirals, but also hooked on James, brainy words amidst all this dimbo hedonism. James were respected by all three. After The Smiths gave James a leg-up, they pursued a similar policy ... opened for by The Delmontes in 87, Mondays in 88, Inspirals and New Fads in 89.

"Happy Mondays used to come to all our gigs. We know them as these nutters who went wild down the front at our concerts."

Confused *Sounds* writer, Rockford, checked all his exits in May 90, "James are the Madchester missing link. Official! Not only can we now accredit them with bridging the gap between Freddie And The Dreamers and Joy Division, but also between Smiths and the current crop of dancefloor ravers." Phew!

Re-released *Come Home*, failed to make the Top 40. They re-signed to a major, Phonogram off-shoot Fontana, berth of The Lilac Time and The Adult Net and House Of Love's *Beatles And The Stones*, the 90s' most beautiful indie single.

How Was It For You, a song of sexual-ecstasy (snigger) scooped their debut 'real' hit in the singles charts. Sixth-form truancy figures soared when they rocked live at Manchester's Our Price Records. Like the Stone Roses a year earlier, they sold out Blackpool Empire Ballrooms ... twice over! Animated rag-doll Tim Booth was now a 'real' pop star?

James *are* heroes, bragging a T-shirt empire even greater than rivals, the Inspirals. Hundreds of designs on thousands of bodies seen anywhere and everywhere, even worn without bribery by one of Beats International on *TOTP*. *Come* became the *Relax* of the 90s; 'JA-M-ES' the 'Frankie Says'.

"Our singles have had a cumulative effect," Tim told *Sounds*. "*Sit Down* didn't chart, but it did a lot of work for us, the same with *Come Home*. So when *How Was It For You* came out, everyone began to think, hang on, this is brilliant!"

In a spring of procreation, James' family was now

even more extended. Joined by Andy Diagram, dreadie trumpeter with a pedigree fine enough to enter him in Crufts. In 80 the Diagram Brothers' single, *We Are All Animals*, was described as Britain's answer to Devo. Later he joined The Pale Fountains, and started freaky free-jazzers The Honkies and Spaceheads.

Well-educated, clever lyrics, sophisticated tastes, refined, sensitive, serious ... Call James vegans and they'll cut you up with violent stares; call them 'middle-class', watch the hairs on their neck rise! If there's no-such thing as 'middle-class', then there's just low-paid, well-off and a cluster of 'ordinary' inbetweens. James are the '*concerned* class.' Most people are so preoccupied with mere survival, day-to-day living, that they have no time to be 'concerned' beyond their own situation.

As a concerned band, James came-of-age on their third album, *GOLD MOTHER*, released in June 90, charting at No 9. They were 'concerned' about everything from the Secret Service Act to MPs visiting disaster zones. Until then, James' politics had been concealed in cryptic-crossword lyrics. Now they were right to the point with songs like *Government Walls*. "It's about the Secret Service Act the Government are trying to introduce to stop people talking about Peter Wright and so on. I mean, we're supposed to be living in a democracy. Basically, agents are recruited from Oxford and Cambridge, from right-wing undergraduates."

On the trail of everything sinister from spies to politicians, *GOLD MOTHER* also addresses the US God Squad, specifically TV evangelist, Jimmy Swaggart, a tradition of born-again fervour that had escalated since Billy Graham saved the 60s.

Here to save the 90s, Tim Booth and his seven disciples, anti-religion to brainwash the pop world, steal away sons and daughters, corrupt the nation.

"The intensity with which I love my own work means that if I couldn't create anything without fucking myself up, I don't know that I wouldn't just go ahead and do it," Tim once declared.

Don't do it son. The future is yours.

OPPOSITE
James, Summer 1990.

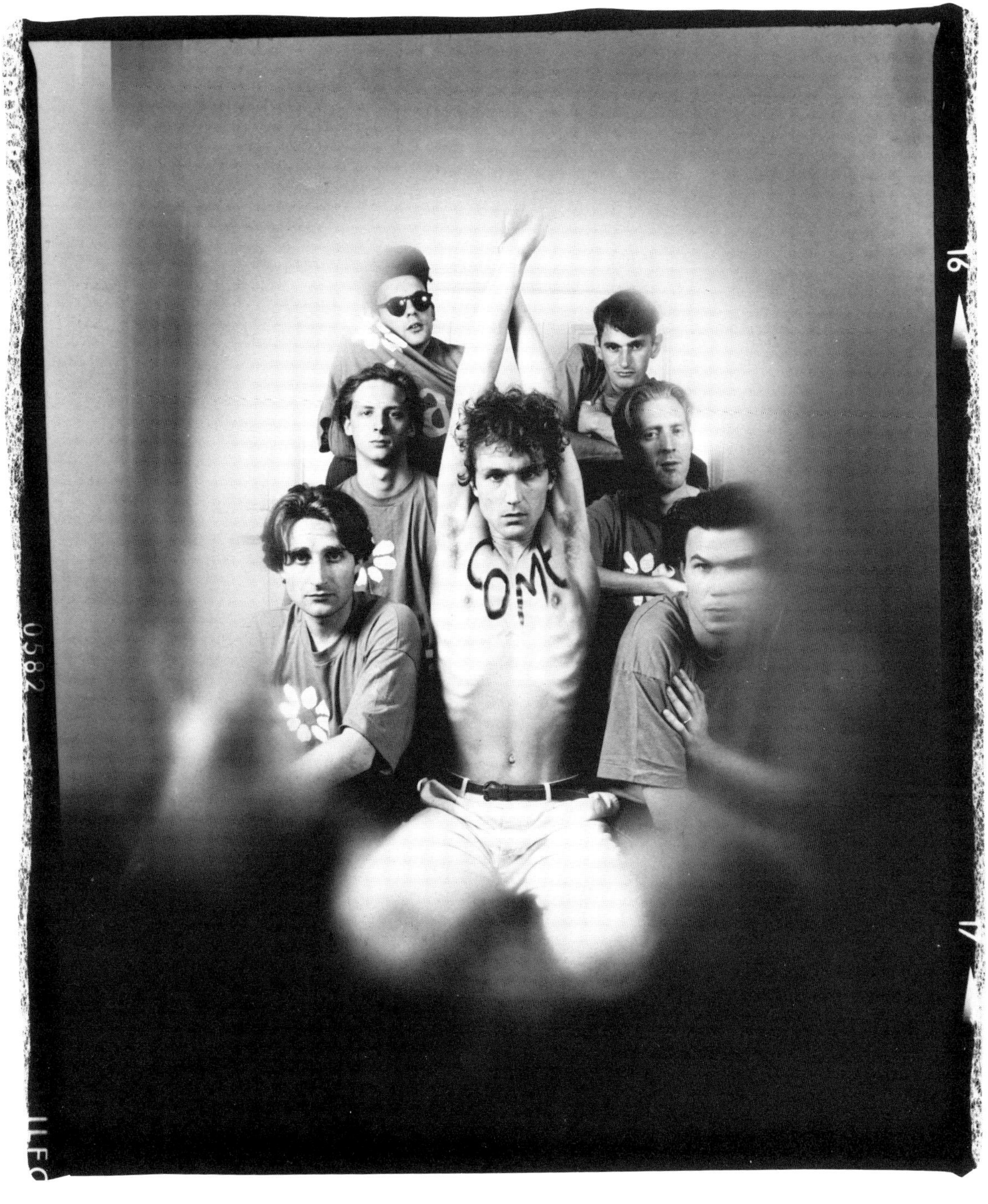

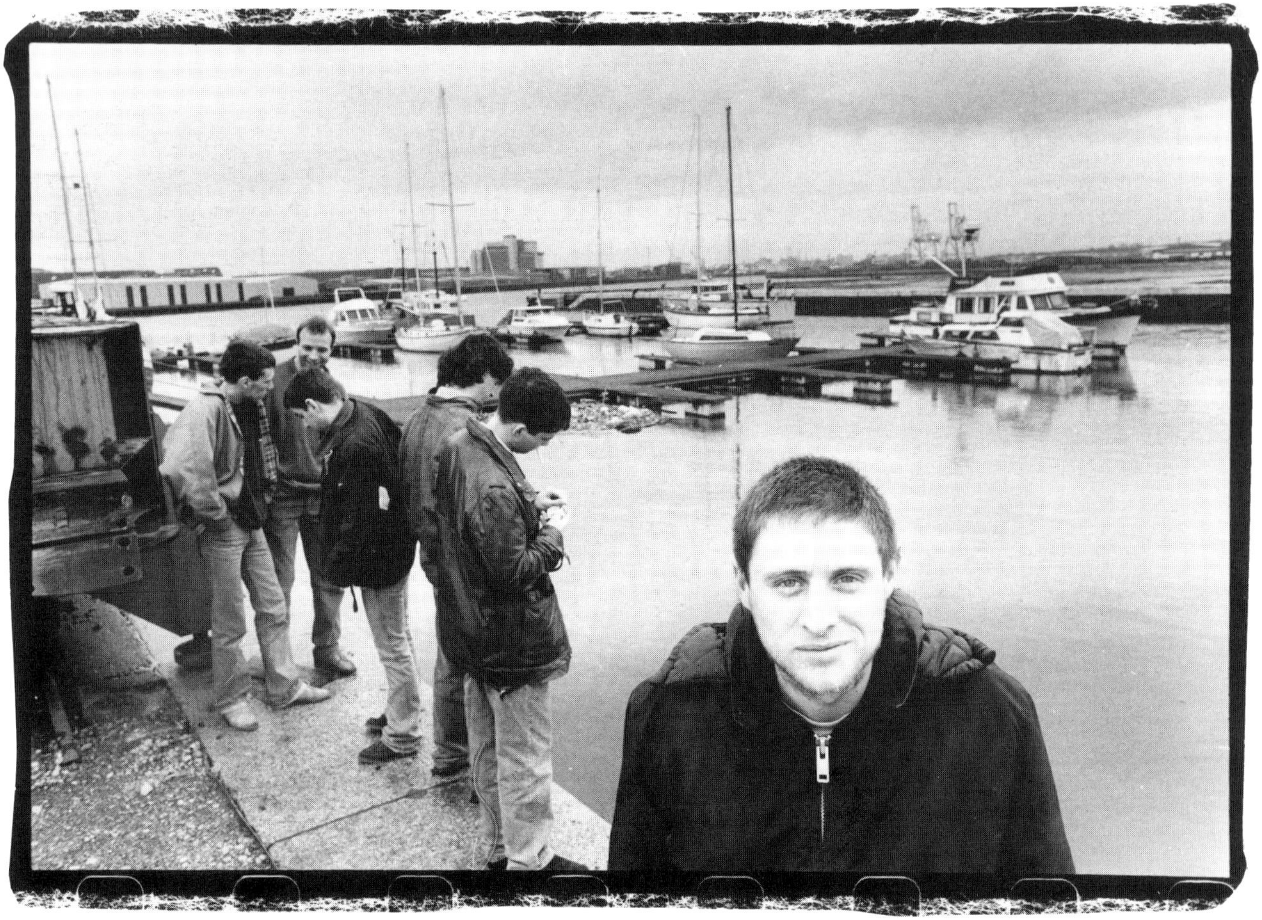

How could the clean world of pop ever make sense of Happy Mondays? A bunch of drug casualties. A gang of North Manchester headcases. A valley of bones, strung-out as shamelessly as knickers on a washing line. So animated they could be cartoon characters. Shaun Ryder as Shaggy and Bez as Scooby Doo. Batman & Robin. Dangermouse & Penfold. Just how did they go from foolish Factory's mental weirdos to international scally superstars?

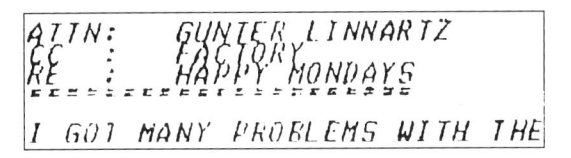

PartY PeoPle

```
ATTN:    GUNTER LINNARTZ
CC  :    FACTORY
RE  :    HAPPY MONDAYS
========================
I GOT MANY PROBLEMS WITH THE
```

13 And God Created Manchester

The arrogant, obnoxious, self-confessed 'ugly cunts' called Happy Mondays come from Little Hulton, an outskirts estate they sniggeringly call 'Little Arndale'. What the hell do European record buyers make of 'streetspeak' like 'double top', 'top geezer', 'boss man', punctuating Mondays' tunes, crude as porno shots in the middle of *Postman Pat*.

Maybe they think it's quaint.

"I live in a semi-detached potato bag. Manchester is shit," sneered Shaun Ryder (aka X, aka meatslab) back in 88. A hunch-backed, hook-nosed mid-20s guy who took to wearing DJ-like fashion glasses which made him look like Simon Bates. Or even worse, an affluent South Mancunian! "These are me respectable spectacles," he said, "so I can get into posh nightclubs!" Things changed. Now he's famous he has no trouble getting on the guest-lists.

By night and day, Happy Mondays terrorised Manchester for years before they 'made it'. When their debut EP, *DELIGHTFUL*, was released in 85, it caused a lot of talk. No-one quite knew who this bunch were, where they were from or what they were aiming for. Least of all the band!

Many, assuming Happy Mondays to be a parody of *Blue Monday* (which it probably was), expected New Order copyists. Said Shaun in May 87, "We're not trailing around in the shadow of New Order 'cos when we go out with them, we get fucking food, booze and treated right." Ok, so maybe it's more the day after Billie Holliday's *Gloomy Monday*.

OPPOSITE
Happy Mondays, Salford Quays, February, 1986.

With the release of their legendary, aptly-titled *Freaky Dancing* single (coupled with *The Egg*, all-time-Manc-fave) and later the classic *Tart Tart*, things became clearer. This lot were just a bunch of dragged-up, drug-taking nutters, badly dressed in trainers and T-shirts. A band who couldn't play, fronted by a man who couldn't sing.

"In them days, I didn't really give a toss," Shaun himself admitted to Mandi James, "Nothing took more than two minutes. I never liked the first album, I wasn't interested in working at it. The music was second, even third. It was more like us lot having a good time which counted. It was all just a big game."

And then there was Bez, their on-stage 'dancer'. Music wasn't even fourth or fifth to him. A wild-eyed shadow of a kid, cheeks drawn in and crumpled body bowing, jerking and tugging with itself on the spot. A maraca-clutching 'junkie' to the Happy Mondays' addictive, taunting noise-dance-groove, Bez always had what you might call 'casualty chic'. Looks like he's been taking drugs since he was five: probably has! Although not if you believe the perverse rumours that his dad is a high-up member of the Manc police force! Bastard son of Jim Anderton?

In January 89 Mondays played London's Dingwalls. Writing in *NME*, Jack Barron captured Bez, like a perfect Polaroid."Bez, pupils dilated wide enough to drive a stretch limo through, dances as if he's swimming in glue. Shaking his maracas like a cocktail maker with the DTs, he's that far up over the other side of the clouds one half-expects rain to come out of his eyes ..."

Meanwhile, Shaun and his bassist brother, Horse, have a family who leave nothing to the imagination. "You ought to see my Granny. When we were 13 years old we used to sit there watching her roll a joint saying, 'fuckin' hell, what are you doing, you cunt'." Did their mother encourage a life of crime too? "Yeah. When I was two she bought me a Rolling Stones record, a Beatles record, a shot gun, a balaclava and some drugs." Or so goes the legend!

As for Shaun's father, Derek, he was heavily involved with the band's early tours. "He wanted to get on the road, so we let him drive the van. He'd be away from Mum for months. Should have seen him when we went to New York. He was 'cained out of his shed, walking round 'acquiring' things. That's where most of our equipment came from."

As sales of Happy Mondays records escalated, Factory could put them up in snazzy hotels. Great for groupies and parties and flying tellies and the rock 'n' roll image of their manager, Nathan McGough, Manc music veteran and offspring of Scouse poet, Roger McGough. Remember The Scaffold's *Lily The Pink...*? He doesn't like to! He once stormed out of The Venue when 808 DJs put it on for a snigger.

Nathan got Mondays legally-signed to Factory. "Tony Wilson's a shit ... a wanker ... he wants me dead," alleged Shaun, "He must have thought we'd do a runner or he wouldn't have offered us all that money!" Money, Happy Mondays admitted back in 88, was a major aim. They claimed only to write songs when totally necessary. *Moving In With* on *BUMMED* was just a translation of the kiddies' tale *Chicken Licken*! And the rest of the time? They could be found slobbing out at The Haçienda (where, years back, they met their original manager, Phil Saxe, the man who also discovered Northside) trance-dancing to various forms of house.

Happy Mondays put the 'E' in ManchEstEr. For better or worse, the drug altered people's lives. It revolutionised the club scene. The Mondays were perversely responsible. Rumour has it that Nathan asked their accountant if they could write off their 'drug bills' against tax.

Shaun in May 90, "I've stopped taking E. Last time I did, I was the last one out of the warehouse. Didn't know where I was. I had a load of E in my pockets 'cos I was selling them then. I put about ten in my mouth to get out and they all melted. Sent me potty and I ended up having a heart attack on Oxford Road, collapsing and ending up in BUPA. Took me three weeks to recover. I couldn't even move one side of my body. Totally cabbaged." Let that be a warning, kids! Strange how all Mondays' subversive elements were lost when they got on *TOTP*. They always had a young appeal, I guess. The video for November 88's *Wrote For Luck* was filmed in Legends by movie-makers, Bailey Brothers. All those juveniles dancing like acid-heads, fuelled by crisps and coke and bubble gum and Care Bear bars. Perverse, voyeuristic as *Mini Pops*, that pervy pop series where pre-pubescent

OPPOSITE
Clockwise from top left
Shaun, Bez, Mark, Paul,
Paul, Gary, March 1990.

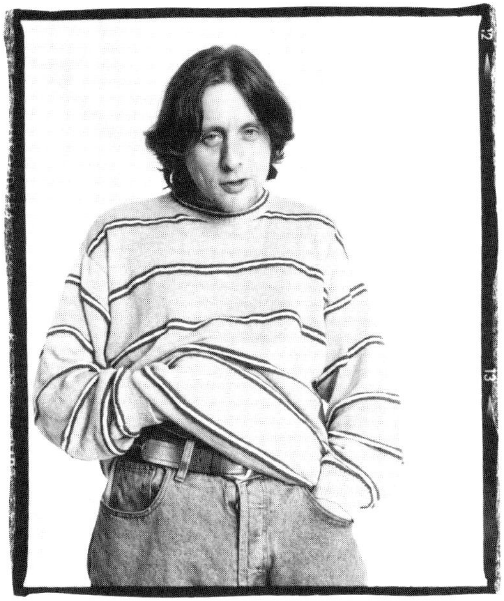
12
13

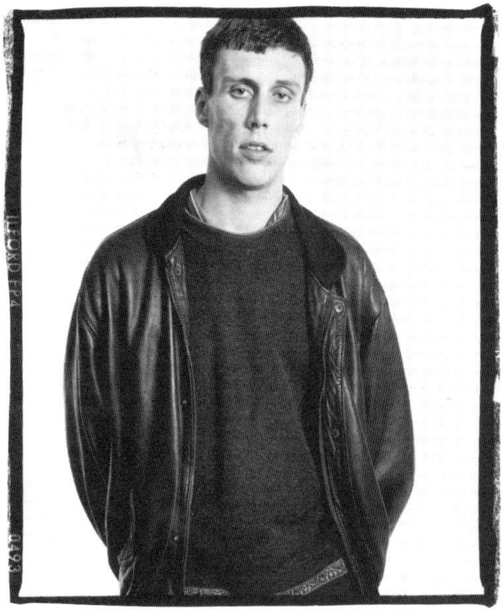
ILFORD FP4
0493

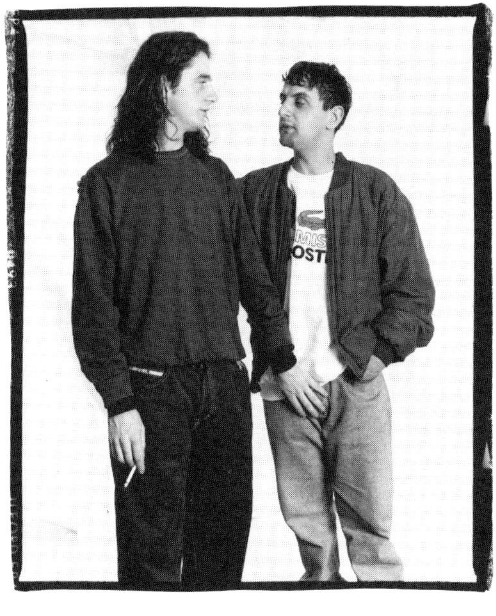

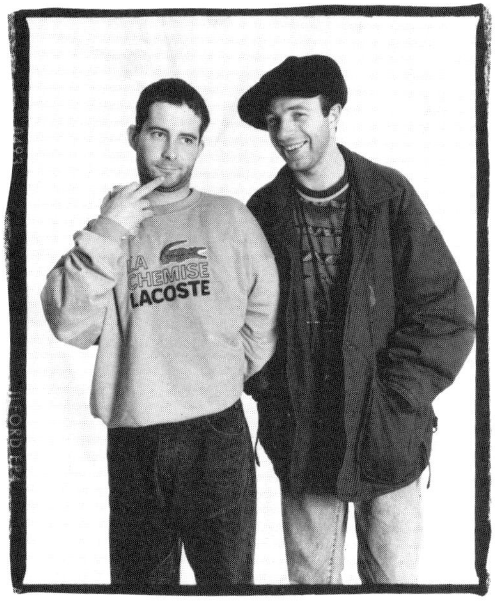
LA
CHEMISE
LACOSTE
ILFORD FP4

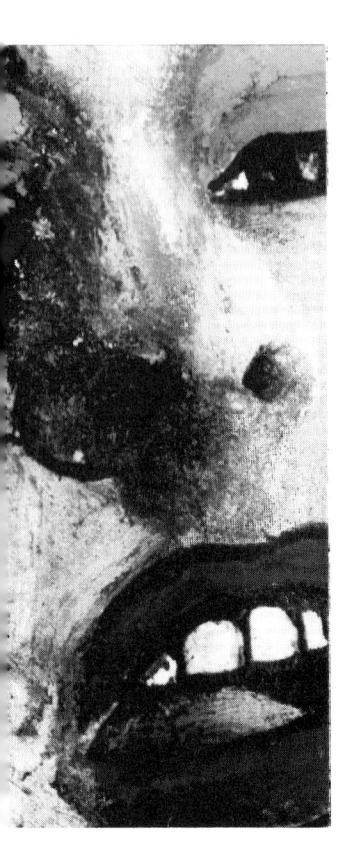

models would dress up as Adam Ant or Debbie Harry and mime their hits ... taken off air for soaring in the paedophile ratings!

Pity Nathan. Imagine being in charge of Bez! The band played at Granada TV without him ... he was in a police cell in the south of France having burgled a caravan! He also had to miss their Irish tour in 89 ... he was arrested at the airport for failing to appear at Manchester Magistrates Court for, 'charges concerning a car.' And what about when they played Blackburn ... a fight broke out and the bouncers dragged Bez off thinking he was invading the stage. Bez materialised in Ibiza in May 88, where New Order were recording *TECHNIQUE*. Barney told *M62* fanzine. "I got up one day, looked out my bedroom window and Bez was stood there. I couldn't believe it, I thought I was dreaming. He turned up because he wanted to borrow my driving licence to hire a car. It was six o'clock. About one o'clock Geoff The Cheff (ex-Corbieres) came walking up the lane saying that he'd crashed the car. He'd crashed four cars before coming out there."

Car-crashing-crazies! Speed-freaks! The Mad Fuckers! Tony Wilson sought backing for The Big Movie he'd always dreamed about ... yet, somehow, the Mondays' real-life movie is even more exciting. "Bez wrote three cars off in three weeks," Shaun told Liverpool 'zine, *Get Out*. "We keep lending him cars, man, and he keeps writing them off. Honda Prelude, Golf GTI ... and he's not even passed his test!"

Bez pipes up, "I keep going too fast, like, I keep getting in it and I drive like dead normal and I just start getting dead bored, you know what I mean? I'm burning down the road at 120 miles-an-hour, wooooaaarrggghhh! In and out of traffic, ha, ha. Can't even stop at traffic lights man, they bore me stupid ..."

Colin and Sue from The Boardwalk once rescued Bez, "Found him out of his head in the street, so we brought him in the office, gave him coffee, tried to figure out where he was meant to be. He was supposed to be gigging in Newcastle. Tracey at Factory had to arrange to fly him there!"

At the same Newcastle gig, Shaun went AWOL. "I knew I was late," he said, "When I got there, there's all these security guys giving me hassle so I said, 'let me through, I'm the singer and I'm late'. So they all start clearing the way. I ran through, got on stage and thought, 'This is a big place' and 'What's with all these posh seats?' and it turned out I was at the Simply Red gig down the road."

Mondays even managed to screw-up their New York 88 showcase at The Limelight. "Just got double, double wrecked."

Imagine the chaos when Mondays took over France in March 89. The following fax, from a French promoter, circulated, "... I got many problems with the band. First, they destroy the hotel in Grenoble. Second, they didn't want to play the night of Monday 20th in Paris. I never received a cancellation for this night. Third, they got into trouble in a club, Le Palace, in Paris. Fourth, very big fighting during the concert of Rennes between the band, the local promoter and my tour manager Antoine.

"Two members of band and crew stayed at the police station. One of the security went to the hospital (broken shoulder). I saw many bands (crazy or drug addicts) but never dangerous as they were. I can't continue to promote them in France if they have an attitude like this ..."

Pity even more Tony Wilson. Would *you* stand bail for this band?! It nearly cost him £5000 in May 89 when Bez was late for his dope trial at Eccles Magistrates Court (which had been postponed four times already). He was fined £700. Two weeks later, Shaun, on a promotion trip for *Lazyitis*, was arrested on arrival at Jersey's St Helier airport for possession of seven milligrams of cocaine. He pleaded innocent, saying he had no idea where the plastic sachet had come from! Shaun was allowed bail only because he was playing The Haçienda's Hillsborough Benefit a few days later. It was Factory who again stood bail.

Arrogant bastards! Who else could call their debut album *SQUIRREL AND G-MAN, 24 HOUR PARTY PEOPLE PLASTIC FACE CARN'T SMILE (WHITE OUT)* on a whim? Especially when there was no such track included on the original cut. Slogan of a generation, proving so popular that the Mondays ended up writing the song *24 Hour Party People* as a follow-up single. Anything to please the masses. It was produced by Velvet Underground head, John Cale, whom half the band had never even heard of! "He was double straight for a start. He'd sacked everything, so all he did was eat hundreds of tangerines. Us lot was all off our boxes. So he had patience with us, he knew what we was up to."

Whereas SQUIRREL AND G-MAN was considered wacky just for its title, BUMMED was *meant* to be offensive. "It's just a sick, stupid, sick name, man. And loads of people will get the wrong idea about it," sniggered Shaun in M62 fanzine. Just to wind everyone up more, they put a picture of a naked woman on the inner sleeve. "We get some smart groupies, where they used to be all fairly scum-bags," sneered Bez.

Vicious pop-hack Penny Anderson, manager of Dub Sex, seethed in *City Life*."I'm annoyed: not outraged, just irritated. Not at the sight of nudity, no, not at that, but I don't need to gratuitously observe anyone else's. Look here little boys - and I mean all of you - if you want to build up your wrist muscles do it in the privacy of your own home, not your design offices ..."

Fellow *NME* journo, Mandi James, agrees. "There's no point being dewy-eyed. Shaun Ryder can't sing, they're a sloppy unit, and their attitude towards women sucks. They're sexist wankers! The thing I resent most about the whole Manchester scene is that it's very male. Not like punk where women came to the front with Slits, Siouxsie ..."

Karl Denver, long-forgotten 60s star, was resurrected to sing on *Lazyitis*, released in May 89 and Single Of The Week in all the papers. "The lunatics have taken over The Haçienda!" said *Melody Maker*, while *NME*'s Helen Mead confessed, "This is what happens when the man waiting outside the school-gates says 'Try one of these, little girl!'"

Borrowing from the Beatles' *Ticket To Ride*, David Essex' *We're Gonna Make You A Star* and Sly And The Family Stones' *Family People*, it's four different tunes all being sung at once ... like a radio tuned to two stations. Or a speedy-acid trip. Quite crazy!

"It's just a shit song with shit words," said Shaun dismissively, "Every melody in it's stolen, really."

Following up *Wrote For Luck*'s Bugsy Malone affair, the *Lazyitis* video was stunning. Denver and the Mondays a-playing prison-yard football in the rain and wearing authentic Strangeways uniform!

Weird to think this crazy, lawless band were turned down by London because they 'didn't have an image'!

Time passes ... supporting Salford Jets in some pub, The Weeds at Corbieres, Flag Of Convenience at International ... playing at the Temperance Club to a half-empty Haçienda ... appearing at Platt Fields in the wet, tenth down the bill ... Happy Mondays finally made it.

The *real* thing. The biggie for the 90s. When they played G-Mex it was Manchester's biggest ever legal rave. 808 State became stadium synth-rockers every bit as pomp as Pink Floyd, while MC Buzz B was lost before ten thousand. It was The Cup Final, The Big Fight, the trippiest trip and the greatest light-show on earth, all rolled into one.

You never could pin Happy Mondays down. They were too clever ... and scallies aren't allowed to be clever. I mean, what was BUMMED all about? Was it funk? Was it country? Was it psychedelic? Was it indie-pop? Fuck knows! God knows, Jesus knows, Tony Wilson knows ... but me? I haven't got a clue. It was simply 'them'.

Happy Mondays were always 'rock music for dance people' or 'dance music for rock people' or just 'accidental genius' or simply 'fuckin' top'. The Paul Oakenfold re-mixes of *Wrote For Luck*, the delirious dance 12", *RAVE ON*, and their new tunes of the 90s have seen them finally capture their clubbing lifestyles on record.

As they say we say in Manchester, 'it's mega'.

When it comes down to it, Roses are just a trad four-man rock band; but Happy Mondays, with their madcap image and chaotic lifestyles, are the stuff *real* rock 'n' roll myths are made of.

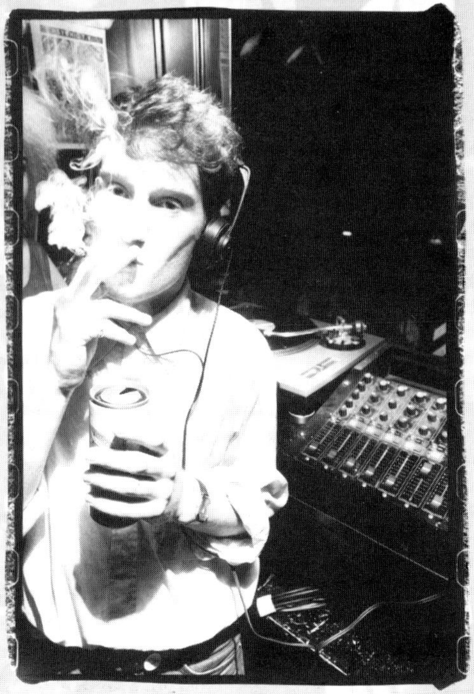

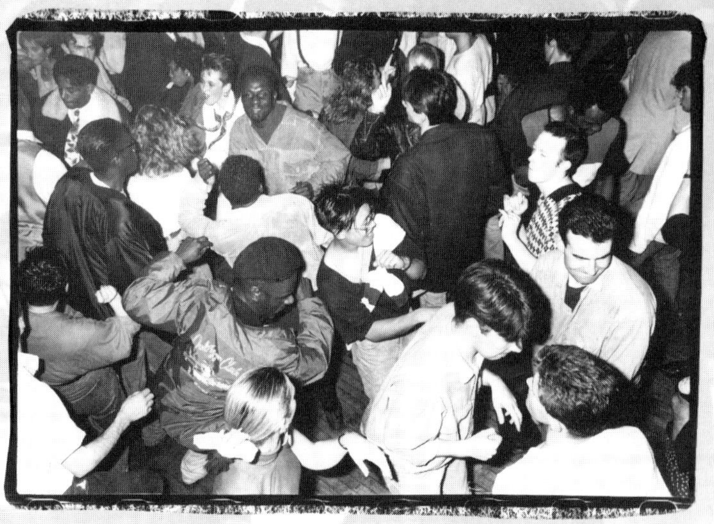

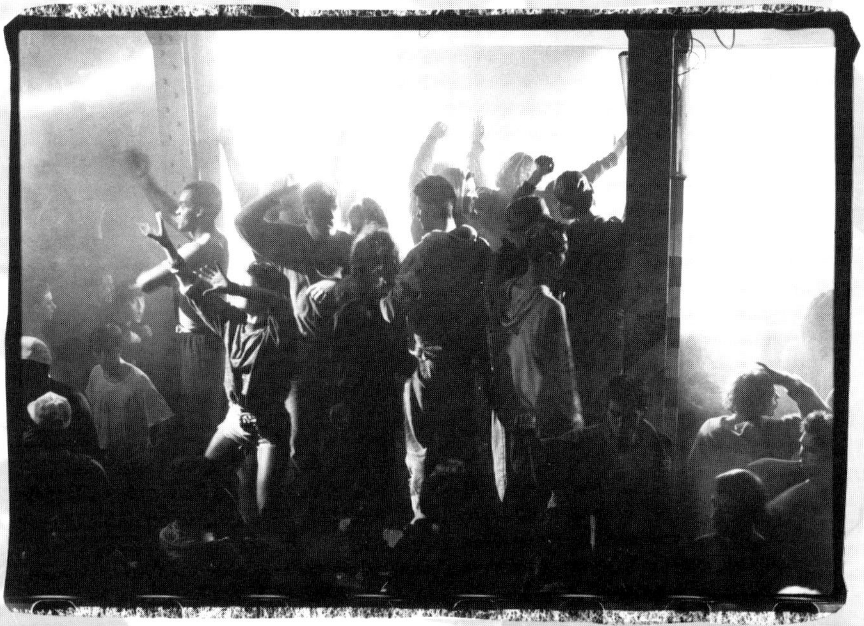

'There's a club if you'd like to go/So you go on your own/And you leave on your own/And you go home/ And you want to die ...'

Acid to EcstacY

RAVE NIGHTS

14   And God Created Manchester

Morrissey went for a night out, had a bad time, then wrote a song to depress the rest of us. Old Manchester. Raincoats. Gloom. Misery. Except things changed somewhere down the line. Electro at Legends, rap in the charts, house in the clubs.

On the most superficial level, the Manchester club revolution took just three weeks. In less than a month, The Haçienda was transformed from a 'cool' fridge that 'chilled' in too many ways, to a crazy party zone. The Summer Of Love 88 was possibly the most blissful few weeks in The Haç's history. Overnight, the Wednesday cabaret, Zumbar, became Hot with its swimming pool and free ice-pops; Stetsasonic, Phuture, Ten City, MDM, Mister Lee, Susi And The Cubans ... Mike Pickering house mixes came to life. Then one day Mondays' Shaun and Bez motored back from London with a boot full of peace 'n' love. Mondays' had always been off their heads, but this was something new. Bez was the first E-kid, up there on the stage. And Manchester discovered *drugs*; the students were away; pupils dilated, 2000 batty clubbers danced like flowerpot men; podiums were scaled and bubbles blown ...

"It was a pure fucking amazing sight. Took me a year to get to grips with it. Wished I was 18 again," says pop-hack Andy Spinoza, who tripped out on the scene. Writing in *City Life*, he called it, "... a Mancunian generation hellbent on hedonism and hooked on a lifestyle as self-assured and self-possessed as it is anti-liberal ... White working-class terrace sub-culture indulging in casual drug-taking on a scale not seen since their parents did it 20 years before ..."

To translate that. The city partyed, one nation under a groove. Looking back, it all seems so simple, so perfect, so naive. It was the very beginning. The beginning of something which would soon sweep the

OPPOSITE
Andrew Berry, The Haçienda, 1985;
The Haçienda, Summer 1988 and February 1990.

dj guest frankie knuckles
the godfather of house from chicago

fac 51 the hacienda
saturday 4th november
£3.50
9-2

country. Something already taking hold in London. It was like the very first Acid Tests in the 60s. No-one really knew what they were dealing with. In this pure, wonderful state it could not last.

"Ecstasy changed the country like Acid in the 60s. When you take it, it changes your whole life," said John Robb, punky Membranes' acid-head.

Rap Assassins' manager, Greg Wilson, observes, "The 80s was about career-minded, Thatcherite mentality. A lot of people took Ecstasy for the first time, looked around themselves and started to feel compassion for their fellow human beings. It's totally tied in with the scene."

The new drug may have been the catalyst, but the soundtrack was well-established. House music had been eating up Northern dancefloors as far back as 85 and JM Silk. Throughout the early 80s, Manchester had been ahead of its time; DJs like Chad Jackson and Greg Wilson pioneering electro, while soul-boys Colin Curtis and Mike Shaft were upfront in their jazz-funk playlists.

"Manchester's soul-jazz scene grew out of Blackpool Mecca disco scene," explains Dean, soul veteran and ex-Haç jock, "It really started happening on Wednesdays at Berlin with Colin Curtis. The idea was that the jazz tracks were difficult to dance to, so they appealed to the flash dancers. As the jazz scene died off, house music was beginning to reach Britain and Colin started playing it as a replacement at Playpen and Legends.

"House music was essentially fast music for cool black dancers. None of this arm-waving. Like all sub-cultures, when the media got involved, it was ruined."

By 86 house nights began to expand ... Graeme Park playing Sheffield's Leadmill and Nottingham's Garage; Mike Pickering's Nude Night at The Haç. House grew out of the black clubs and into the mainstream.

In 88, on the sleeve of NORTH, a Manc house compilation, Graeme Park wrote,"It was summer 1986 and clubs in London were rocking to the sounds of East Coast hip-hop and Washington go-go. Meanwhile dance floors 'North Of Watford' (especially Nottingham, Sheffield and Manchester) were crammed with people jacking to a new sound from Chicago called 'house'. And for two years, a North/South divide of a very different kind was established ..."

Since the days of Northern Soul, club culture had always been underground, word-of-mouth, either gay clubs or black soul nights. Yet, by the end of 87, house (like electro) was entering the white-fad-machine.

"To me, clubs have always been R&B-based, from Twisted Wheel in 60s, right up to 80s, when *ID* made clubs middle-class. Now most house clubs, are almost entirely white, are playing music from Germany and Belgium instead of America," says Dean who, throughout the acid house hype, stayed true to his soul roots playing The Groover's Convention at The Gallery with John Tracey (original Haç DJ). Here Dean embraced 70s soul-disco without the gimmicks of rare groove.

"Not naming any names, but you talk to DJs one year and they say they're into rare groove, next hip-hop, next house. They're always into the latest big thing. You should never ignore the past."

Just to prove Dean's point, a 87 holiday in Ibiza had inspired London DJs Paul Oakenfold, Nicky Holloway and Danny Rampling to dump rare groove and go Balaeric. Balaeric Beats opened up ears, ideas and possibilities until then taboo in clubland. It was about adding disparate styles to the mix, everything from The Plastic Ono Band and U2, to indies The Woodentops and The Thrashing Doves, anything with a good beat. The earliest hint of the indie-dance crossover of the 90s.

"I don't think the Esctasy/Acid thing came from Ibiza," said Barney of New Order, who spent the Summer Of Love 88 over there recording *TECHNIQUE*. "I found the Ibizan DJs pretty appalling. Balaeric Beats as far as I'm concerned is DJs playing 20 seconds of one track and then 20 seconds of another."

By the time New Order got home they found house music had gone mainstream. The term 'acid house' was coined. There's a disease. It spreads death and destruction. Infectious. Frightening. Unpredictable. Deadly. No, not AIDS, but *hype*. Acid house hype. Soon came the press, the money-makers, the pushers, the students. It grew and grew!

Smiley culture exploded. At first bright, colourful, funny, happy, silly, it took just a matter of weeks for it to become a moronic style for fashion wallies, dickheads, beer boys. All those horrid gipsy bandanas, headscarves, T-shirts with lurid yellow Smileys.

Throughout October and November 88, the tabloids carried out a ridiculous acid house hate campaign, although only weeks earlier, *The Sun*'s Bizarre column had been marketing its own Smiley shirts, "to keep you way ahead of Britain's latest dance craze ..." In just a fortnight they ran articles under all the following headings: 'Evil of Ecstasy', 'The Acid House Horror', 'Girl 21 Drops Dead at Acid Disco Party' 'Mr Big of Acid Parties', 'Acid Party Army of Baseball Brutes', 'Hell of Acid Kids: Pushers laugh as teenagers see terror of bad trip boy ...'

Matt Goss of Bros told *The Sun*, "I've never been to an acid house club, but my mate went to one and everyone in the place was out of their heads on drugs." In response, *The Sun* then unveiled their 'Say No To Drugs' badge, "like the Smiley badge, but with a sad face."

By this point, house music had been hijacked by the hype machine. The inspirational and hypnotic qualities of American-style house were being stolen by British acts pumping out novelty tracks: *Pump Up The Bitter*, D Mob with the chant of 'Acieed! Acieed Acieed!' Cringe.

"Some of the worst records of the year have called themselves 'acid'," jibed *Debris*' Dave Haslam "The industry has jumped on the bandwagon and crashed it. The media has written ineptly, obscenely about the 'Acid House Scene'. People who should have known better, panicked and suddenly started twittering on about how much they've always liked house. Acid house brought out the worst in people. Boys and girls forgot to follow their instincts and followed *ID* instead: the 'scene' suffocated even the most wonderfully alive record. The saddest thing was the involvement of the style fascists: the ones who tell you that you can only like one thing and one thing only ... "

"As a fad, it had the four wheels every bandwagon needs: a sound, a new drug, a fashion and controversy. Punk too had all four (The Beastie Boys had everything but the drug) and presumably that's why cloth-ears called acid house 'the new punk', when the style, content and meaning of these particular big new things were so obviously completely different ... "

Punk vs house? A daft irrelevant argument, I guess. Punk sought to destroy, believing it was the be-all to end-alls. It choose to reject all past genres. Style fascism was nothing new. Punk was angry, political, where house was just about the politics of dancing. Punk denied the past, where ravers would soon revel in stealing from it. Punk was only like house in the sense it was an energetic rising of youth culture ... Yawn. Yeah, house was soon discussed by *World At One*, *News At Ten*, *The Observer* ...

"Punk was too much like rock 'n' roll and they knew how to deal with it," Mike Pickering commented to Andy Spinoza. "They don't know how to handle this. It's gone underground again ... it appears to be very easy to make, but if you've not got a feeling - soul, for the want of a better word - you fall flat on your face." Paranoia! Fear! Snobbery! Pickering was spot on. Many, and not just the tabloids, fought house 'culture' like it was the devil herself knocking on their door. As 'real musicians' once condemned the supposedly talentless, destructive 'fad' of punk, it frightened them. Just as, theoretically, anybody could have made *Anarchy In The UK*, anybody could have created Todd Terry's *Black Riot*. The point being: not that anybody could do it, but that somebody did.

In October 88, Tim Booth of James was (mis)quoted as saying, "Rap and house may have a big following, but so did Hitler." He later clarified his position in a rant to *NME*' letters page: "*NME* is trying to give house fans the status of valiant revolutionaries surrounded by the conservative forces of oppression. Well, I'm sorry, but this state only exists in the heads of a few far out minds. It sounds like some punks I knew who enjoyed the feeling of persecution, because it made them feel important. Why on earth should they? We have seen so many fashions in music over the past few years, we should be used to it by now.

"I am not impressed by any movement that seems to be based squarely on a drug. God knows, we've seen it before. It's nothing new, just a repeated cycle. We've seen acid casualties in the 60s, amphetamine burn-outs from the 70s, and no doubt we will see the full effects of Ecstasy on another generation. I believe, one day you will regret your advice to the non-believers in the church of house ..."

Tim Booth was right in many ways. A scene fuelled entirely by a drug, a Summer Of Love based on drug dealers' greed, could *never* be anything more than a fleeting altered state. But, as naive a belief as it may be, the drug Ecstasy unleashed visions, dreams, ideas and energies which became such an *exciting* rollercoaster on their own, that the drugs themselves became of secondary importance. Soon, acid house became rave scene. By 89, it was here to stay.

Dance-philosopher, Greg Wilson: "House is not just the music, it's a state of mind."

We danced till revolution; danced ourselves to death; danced to the 'end of a decade'. The slogans were many, their sentiments sincere. It was the End Of The Century Party ... and we hadn't even finished the 80s. People no longer wanted to sit and pontificate. They wanted to move and be moved. Shag, shag, shag. Dance, dance, dance.

The End Of The Century Party. Literally the chance of a lifetime. The ultimate trip. Your one and only chance to party to the end. Be good and start planning your suicide pacts *now*. The ultimate rave is in heaven where the ghosts of dead idols socialise. You could go driving with James Dean; trip-out with Jimi Hendrix; get 'down' with Ian Curtis; make love with Marilyn Monroe or art with Andy Warhol. Take your pick! Only one fatal overdose and a decade, or less, to go. Such was the hedonism of raving.

Where once we were living for the weekend, now we were '24-Hour Party People'. In November 89 Mandi James observed, "The Friday/Saturday night flirtation with club culture has become a full-time, total commitment. What was once a brief encounter, an occasional messy, one night stand, has become a deep and meaningful relationship, a way of life. The proliferation of dance music is spreading like a virus, infecting every nook and cranny."

E-culture was no-longer confined to a few city centre clubs. It swept suburban pubs, council estates, bedrooms, anywhere you could plug in a system.

"Miles Platting, Manchester, 1989," wrote Andy Spinoza in *City Life*, "A pub called The Angel has had all the letters ... ripped off, bar one. It is now called 'e'. In a housing estate of lawless tower blocks, one regular visitor to Mike Pickering's club nights at his local, The Thunderdome, and the famous Haçienda, has fixed up a strobe light in his top floor flat."

Eight miles away, on the posher side of town, The Midland pub had become an equally looney rave-zone, taken over by Didsbury mafia, Manchester Vibe In The Area. Patriotic, vibrant, house-dominator, DJ Alfonzo, Cess and family, had this ordinary local partying throughout 89. They signed to Cut Deep Records, but the label went under before their Manc-techno 12" reached the shops. Cess ran notorious Manchester Vibe coach trips to experience Roses and Mondays in Europe, while MVITA finally hit the big time when they were invited to DJ at Spike Island. The police succeeded in ending The Midland's impromptu raves in June 90. It closed till further notice. Apart from raves, The Haçienda's biggest rival was Oldham Road's The Thunderdome on the Northern edge of the city centre. Having failed as an Irish club, punk venue, roller rink and rock club, it found its market in 89 when it became Hypnosis house rave. The Dome was a legal warehouse party of sorts, crammed with some of the roughest, nastiest North Manchester nutters. Mike Pickering took Thursdays while The Jam MCs, 808 State and Steve Williams brought a hardcore beat to the city, specialising in techno, stomping new-beat and import storm-troopers from Germany and Belgium. Thunderdome had a life-span even shorter than The Midland. Closed after being struck by a wave of drug shootings and stabbings as brutal as anything out of *Last Exit To Brooklyn*.

Steve Williams was also responsible for two of the summer's other crucial nights. Frenzy took new-beat and house to a tacky club called Sequines opposite Central Pier, Blackpool. Beach drug parties and summer fun took over. Arranged by Paul Cons, this night and Steve's night at Legends on a Monday were given the hip-Haç seal-of-approval. Blackpool was the ideal alternative for those who couldn't afford the air fare to Ibiza 89 for its third year as a Balaeric Beat holiday resort.

Acid House, aka Rave Culture or whatever, changed people's lives. A network of illegal raves kept the country moving. In Manchester, the roots were in Northern Soul and all-nighters which happened from time to time throughout the 70s and 80s. Once the hub of the world's textile industry, the Victorian warehouses and mills of central Manchester found new life. As early as 88, soul/house all-nighters were kicking off successfully around Ancoats and Piccadilly Station. With the city centre warehouses suffering constant raids, the emphasis switched to out-of-town venues.

OPPOSITE
Foot Patrol Dancers, July 1988;
Clubbing, July 1988.

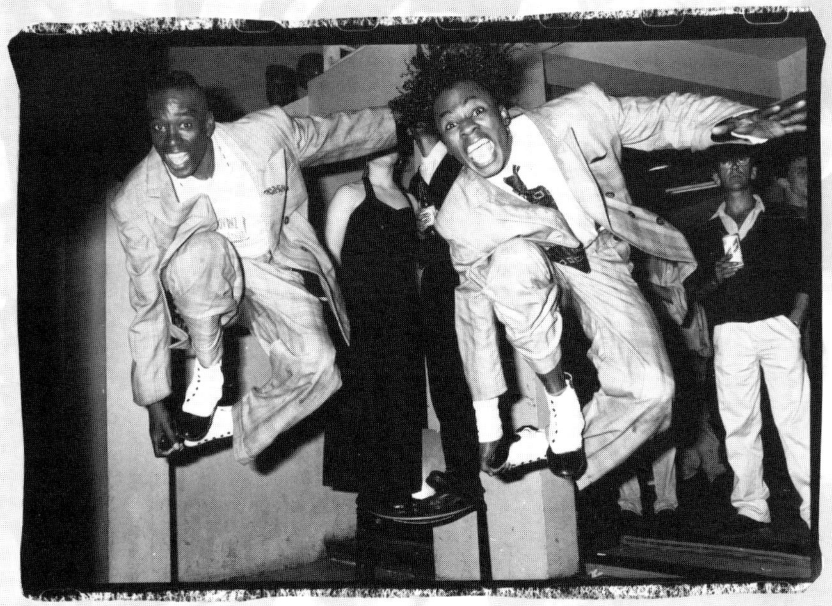
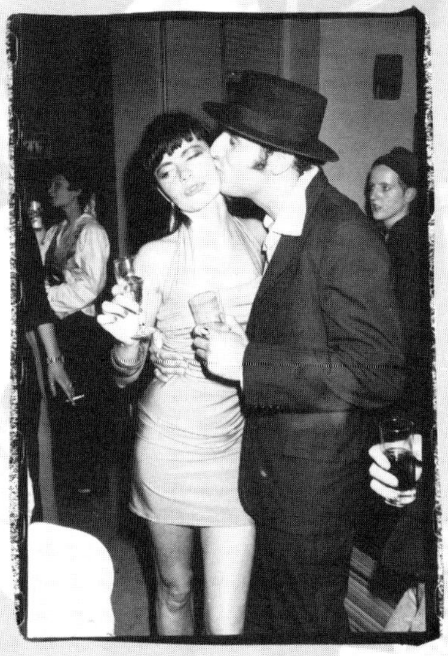
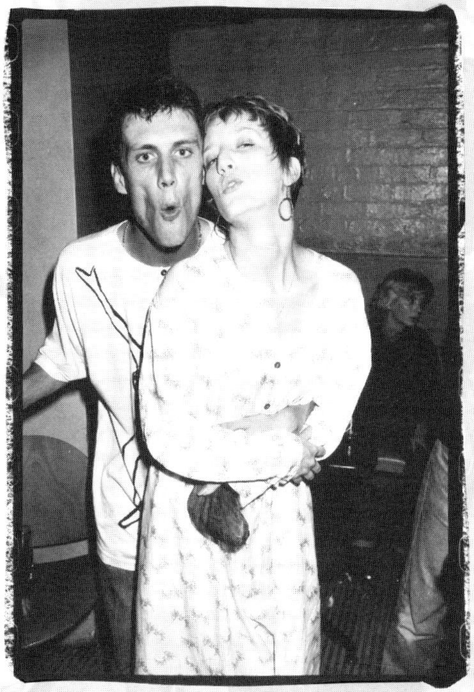

The ultimate cultural role reversal. The end of the 80s saw the (turn)tables reversed on city kids. Suddenly it was not their haunts being invaded by out-of-townies, so much as them travelling out to the sticks to party. Blackpool, Huddersfield, Preston ... Blackburn!!!

Rochdale was one venue for Joy, one of the North's best-organised, most frequent big outdoor raves. Funfair! Lasers! Chill-out tents! Hot-dogs! "Joy was my first big rave," says *NME* journo, Mandi James, "It was so exciting. I haven't felt so excited in years."

Mandi was one of the few music-hacks to actually live the rave dream. At *NME* there was only really her, Helen Mead, giggly, pig-tailed, live editor and Jack Barron, a rock visionary with his crazy Yorks drawl, shades, shaved-head and oh-so-beatnik assumed name. The other titles were even less switched on, leaving it to the likes of *Soul Underground* and *Rave* to try and catalogue the scene.

Mandi continues, "We had a car full of people, driving round all these horrendous country lanes, thinking we were nearly there, getting lost. We picked up a convoy of about 20 cars behind us. There was a real buzz. As we got nearer and nearer the place, we kept thinking, 'This isn't gonna come off. Gonna be in bed by two'.

"We got to the top of this hill and suddenly there was a massive bolt of light across the sky. It was a massive searchlight from the party. I thought I was gonna wet myself, I was so excited. Like when you're a kid and you're looking for the sea and you catch your first glimpse of blue. Then we got over the hill and saw blue lights. In five seconds we'd gone from intense euphoria to a complete downer, 'Shit! The police!'"

The Biggest Thrill in the Universe. For Graham Massey, studio wizard of 808 State, it was not his second 'teen'age, but his first (at 30!). His fave rave was in a vast Blackpool show-jumping arena.

"By the time we got there it was getting light," he smiles with faraway eyes. "The sunrise was lighting up all these people. Weird atmosphere. Wasn't off me 'ead. Half the thrill was going off in a convoy of 20 cars. It was like the kind of feeling you only get in a war: everyone pulling together!"

One anecdote typifies just how seriously underground this out-of-town scene was during 89. Two lads would drive up to The Haçienda every Friday, queue for an hour, dance till two, then get in their car and drive back to London. Every week at chuck-out-time they'd be approached by people saying 'Are you going to Blackburn?' begging for a lift. They just thought it was people scrounging a ride home and said 'Nah mate, we're off back to London'. Six months later, when it started to filter through the media, they realised they'd missed out on a whole scene!

Blackburn and surrounding area made a perfect rave venue. Blackburn, a sprawling, hilly ghost-town 25 miles north of Manchester, named in The Beatles' *A Day In The Life* for having 4000 holes in its roads. It had its very own CD factory ... but no pop stars to record on to them. The most famous person in town was probably Tommy Ball, a market-stall millionaire who revolutionised shoe-shopping with his chain of superstores. Its population had been starved of partying for one year too long.

"Blackburn was wild, incredible," says Mandi James. "You look back and think 'Did I really do that?' There was this dead old industrial building like an abattoir with a door just a few feet wide. It was surrounded by police, with people hiding in the bushes waiting for a chance to storm past, 100 at a time, through this tiny gap. Once you were inside ... vrrrooom! Music! Dry ice! So intense you could throw up!"

Party culture was not all big money-making raves. There was an element of spontaneity which made it so vibrant. Graham Massey again, "One night, after The Haçienda, we thought 'Let's do it' and started a rave in the basement under Eastern Bloc. One light bulb, one ultra-violet light, and Gerald's terrible PA. Such an atmosphere, really underground. It felt dangerous and, sure enough, at 5am the police came in and turfed us out."

It *was* dangerous. The rave scene *was* a risky thing. Fire, overdose, car-crashes.

"Call me old-fashioned, but raves are illegal so they shouldn't happen," said founder of Sunset Radio, Mike Shaft, reactionary in some of his tastes and well into law 'n' order. "If there was a massive fire at one of these places, 1000 people would die. You cannot allow that number of people to be at risk."

Mike Shaft reflected the opinions of 'grown-ups'

everywhere, but we all know rebellion is essential, so the 'kids' raved on regardless.

"It was such a fleeting thing," says Graham Massey. "Spent most of the summer of 89 in service stations. Few decent parties actually got off the ground. Went to one in a primary school in Ancoats. Just 40 people and a Dansette in the middle of the floor. Some snide geezer had heard about all these warehouse parties and decided he was gonna have one ... we'd been there four minutes and the police arrived ..."

"When the Eastern Bloc party got raided, I just wanted to cry, but I'm not one of these people who shouts 'Freedom To Party'. It's just freedom to make money!" says Mandi. "It's multi-racial and non-violent, but it's apolitical in the sense that people only organised themselves to have a good time."

Beyond raves, Manchester had one last great club adventure before the 90s clamp-down. Konspiracy. Both heaven and hell. It took over where The Thunderdome left off. In addition to the student-cum-media element, it attracted the seediest North Manchester criminal headcases and their 'Sharon' girlfriends. It was the best of all worlds: dance and indie, black and white, jazz and scally, new-beat and soul. Some regulars were old enough to remember it as early-80s Pips sporting Bowie and Roxy rooms! Other ravers were so new to the scene they hadn't even been around the day Dry 201 opened.

Konspiracy's craziest night was when they hosted the *ID* World Tour with Candyflip playing their novelty version of *Strawberry Fields* live. It was the most, probably *the* most, packed any Manc club has been since Big Black played The Boardwalk. Excessive. Konspiracy, the ultimate clubbers fantasy; 'civilised' society's worst nightmare! Seven rooms, endless dancefloors, day-glo acid murals. You could lose your mates on the way in and not find them again till 2am chuck-out time ...

But it couldn't last. At the beginning of the 90s, it felt like the End Of The Century Party had already happened. By mid-90 the rave was over. The music had stopped. We were left sweeping up the broken glass, Hoovering the carpet and re-decorating the walls before mummy and daddy arrived home.

Even the highest, most positive thinkers knew it couldn't continue. Not Konspiracy. Not The Haç. Not the rave scene in general. That was inevitable. And the Government was out to prove it with their anti-drug campaigns. 'You can only come down', they said, wagging a righteous finger, wrinkling a knowing frown. The ads read, 'Heart jumping every time you see the police. Paranoid psychosis. Your mother finding stuff. Having to find someone to score off. Never being exactly sure what you're getting. Overdose. Getting ripped off by dealers. Having to steal to cover the expense. Suppressing your immune system. Septicaemia. Jaundice. Abscesses. AIDS. Ending up in casualty on a Saturday night. Spending all your time with drug users. Losing your job ... '

Yeah. We've all been there. Bootle Street Police Station. Casualty at Manchester Royal Infirmary. Withington Hospital's psychiatric ward. Not nice places to end up when the rave goes wrong. It happens. It's the risk you take. There's more to life than drugs and it's not always worth it. An ambulance speeds away from The Haçienda ... the E generation's first casualty. The *Death Of A Disco Dancer* that Morrissey predicted. In 89, Claire Leyton from Stoke died on a night-out at The Haçienda. She was only 16. She didn't die for a cause or for her art or for a generation. She probably never even realised what she was doing could be dangerous. She took some E and her body packed up. It could just as easily have been alcohol poisoning from too much vodka, but that is hardly any consolation to her family. Her name was soon in all the tabloids.

"The death of the girl was unfortunate and unnecessary," said Tim Chambers, Haç booking-agent, "It was particularly unfortunate for the mother who'd forged her daughter's ID. The thing is, if you're going to do a drug, alcohol, cigarettes, Ecstasy, you do it to its full. You don't smoke one cigarette a day, you smoke a packet. You don't drink a mouthful, but a pint. You find out the hard way."

"Drugs do fuck you up! If you take lots of Ecstasy when you're 17, you either give up before you're 21 or you go crazy. You do get 30-year-olds walking round Whitworth Park thinking they're Jesus!" says Jon Ronson who ran away from home and got sucked up into London's squatter/drug scene when *he* was just 16.

As time went on, driving in from satellite towns to 'indulge' in 'acid house' became a totally sheep-like activity. If it was not true when the press first wrote scandals about it, it was by the time they'd finished hyping it out of all proportion. Check the sleeve of The Farm's version of *Stepping Stone*. A photo of a stuffed-sheep in scally clothing, flares, Kickers, sun-hat and all. The kids had progressed way beyond Ecstasy into speed and LSD, familiar with all the different kinds of acid from Strawberries and Purple Haze to Mind Body And Soul.

"Ecstasy's one thing, but clubs are the wrong environment to take acid. When someone's tripping they're ultra-sensitive. Back in the 60s, they preached setting, being with people you trust, in your own environment. In a club, you can't control that," warns Greg Wilson.

The Government was getting serious too. This was the 90s. Hedonism was no longer allowed. Even the slogans became illegal. Like partying in a field, the very act of gyrating your body became punishable by imprisonment. Anyone seen publicly having a 'good time' was certified insane, while anyone caught smiling in the street was automatically committed to a drug rehabilitation unit ...

The clamp-down was extreme. In 84 Tory backbencher, Graham Bright, pushed through an anti-video-nasty bill. In 90 he returned to the spotlight, introducing The Entertainments (Increased Penalty) Bill 89/90. It was as over-the-top as ID Cards, as prejudiced as Clause 28 and as evil as the Poll Tax. Said Manc Polytechnic law expert and author of pop manual *End Of The Century Party*, Steve Redhead. "The Bill will criminalise a whole section of youth culture. They're jumping on the anti-acid house bandwagon because it's hedonism. Why should young people have a good time, when the country has hit hard times, when the economy is on the decline and everyone else is in trouble?"

By the beginning of the 90s, not only had most illegal raves been wiped out, but Chief Constable Anderton was threatening to close The Haçienda, Konspiracy and a whole string of Manchester clubs by revoking their alcohol licences. Imagine the feeling in Wilson's stomach when he opened that letter! A bit like waking up to find your house, family and life have blown away in a storm.

"There has never been a clamp-down on clubs on this scale before. The next stage is not closing them down, but not letting them open, refusing licences," said Mike Shaft who, before Sunset, had DJ-ed Manchester since the 70s.

"If anyone thinks drug culture is limited to one or two clubs in Manchester, they're very wrong. It's in every up-to-date office block where people snort cocaine in the loos. Are they going to close them down?"

Manc clubland scurried to clean up and it soon became easier to leave the country than go for a night out. To enter The Haç, a passport and full body/bag search was required. Tony Wilson appeared in all the local papers being nice, respectable and middle-class and advocated a Pub/Club ID Card scheme to halt under-age drinking. The company employed George Carman, the lawyer who defended Ken Dodd against the Inland Revenue and Townsend Thoresen in the Zeebrugge ferry disaster.

"We believe we have almost completely eradicated drug use from The Haçienda with the assistance of the clientele. We've got video surveillance equipment, we have ten-minute bouncer swoops, we've got notices, we've got body-searches, we've got the whole lot," Tony Wilson told *NME*. "Most people are intelligent enough to know The Haçienda is too important to close, everybody has appreciated that. Even dear old Happy Mondays."

The Haçienda's 'licence' hearing was to have taken place in July 90, but was postponed until 91. Thus, a mighty 'Save The Haç' campaign began. Drugs suddenly became a taboo subject even in hip-circles. It was like the late 60s' San Francisco psychedelia boom where, after years of helping create/inspire the music/acid scene, its figurehead, Ken Kesey, wormed his way out of a jail sentence by announcing in public that all the kids should stop taking LSD.

In the 90s *NME*'s James Brown politely pushed Tony Wilson on the fact that he'd promoted Happy Mondays' drug image, yet now he was condemning the very same drug culture. "How does Wilson come to terms with presenting a clean club when he operates within a culture where artistic creativity is frequently inspired by going beyond the law?"

"I've said for years that, as far as running the club goes, we have to exist within the law. I think people get confused. It's very hard to sit down at three in the morning and get Bez to tell a journalist from *The LA Times* what this culture is about. Hardly any great artists have any idea about what's going on in their art, it's only the second-rate creative people, the journalists like me, who are able to talk about it.

"I'm able to talk about a culture which is in many ways stronger than punk. That it's wonderful. It doesn't necessarily mean that I advocate drug use."

Does Tony really know more about North Manchester estates (where drugs help pass the time of year), as an outsider, a grown-up, a Cambridge graduate, than Bez who actually *lives* the scally myth? Probably it was a good job Mondays spent the summer of 90 in Los Angeles recording their third album and were unavailable for comment!

Tony has pulled off many scams in his time, but this must be the greatest. Suddenly, the tide of public/press opinion was changing. Backed by Manchester City Council, the Lord Mayor's Office, and The Olympic Bid Committee, The Haçienda was talked about with all the reverence of Buckingham Palace ... as if someone had suggested bulldozing the Town Hall. Instead of calling for acid house to be outlawed, people were backing it entirely! Even *The Sun*, who started the whole anti-house hype in the first place way back in 88, had now changed sides!

In an editorial on July 26, 1990, Richard Littlejohn wrote. "The police are out of control. Most of these kids are just out to have a good time. Mob-handed prohibition tactics are no substitute for proper detective work aimed at putting the real villains out of business." It went on to support both warehouse parties and The Haçienda. Completely absurd. Remember *The Sun*'s 'Say No To Drugs' Smiley campaign?

The Haç was now fighting for its life. So what's new? If they could close The Twisted Wheel and Wigan Casino, how can its 80s equivalents be immortal?

"Why did people have to knock Wigan Casino down?" asks a nostalgic Baby Ford who, when just 13, went there with his big brother, fixed on Sherbet Dips and danced all night.

"It was the first club I went to. I used to watch the groups like Pink Fairies and Medicine Head before the all-nighter. Then the ballroom would fill up with all the guys with Adidas bags ..."

Wigan. Wigan. Wigan. Ford pays tribute to it on his album. 'All the signs lead to Wigan. All the people lead to Wigan. Holding hands. Discotheques. Wigan Pier. Mini Cabs. Selnec Bus. Idle chat. Mothers' skirts. Planet love. Cadillac. Fix your face ...'

Homeland of an itinerant hardcore. Northern Soul freaks would drive miles in search of all-nighters, like rave kids blocking ring roads in 88 to 90. The constant, over-the-top 'crackdown' on all-night events over the last 20 years is typical of this out-of-date land.

Manchester was not without its problems. A NY-style drugs war, between Moss Side and Cheetham Hill dealers, culminated in a shoot-out at an International 2 reggae gig in April 90. With no sniff of an arrest, the police just continued to take it out on the public. Having already closed down Moss Side's Reno, The Gallery and other Manc black clubs, they scored an 'own goal' as more shebeens and illegal blues clubs sprang up in Hulme and Moss Side. Where are the people supposed to go?

And if they closed every house club in Manchester, where would the kids go then? The authorities could have a riot on their hands. Even if The Haç wins its case, a string of other clubs (unable to afford top solicitors?) may already have been shut down.

This may be 'one nation under a groove', but where's all this revolution getting us when there's not a club in town allowed open after 2am; where it's treasonable to stick stamps on upside-down; where it's illegal to dance on a Sunday. Crazy, isn't it?

Even Mike Shaft, who disagrees with raves, believes you should be allowed to party 24 hours-a-day *legally*. "Manchester should be a 24-hour city, yet everywhere shuts down at 2am. If you want to party at five in the morning you should be able to. This is the 20th century, 1990. It's wrong."

1992 is nearing. Europe will soon be one big happy family. Instead of shutting things down, isn't it time Britain caught up with continental licensing laws? From Acid to Ecstasy and out the other side. Rave culture has only really made one demand ... freedom to party.

Someone said, "The Haçienda must be built." And it was. Now it must *never* close.

---

haçienda licence u

GOOD NEWS!
The Haçienda licence hearing on 23rd July re-adjourned until 3rd January 1991.
This means that the Haçienda **will remain o**
FAC 51 the Haçienda now intends to redouble open. This must involve the complete eliminat the premises
In this we continue to rely upon your help and **do not**, repeat, **NOT**, buy or take drugs in the drugs onto the premises
Please make sure everyone understands how
Thank you for your support.

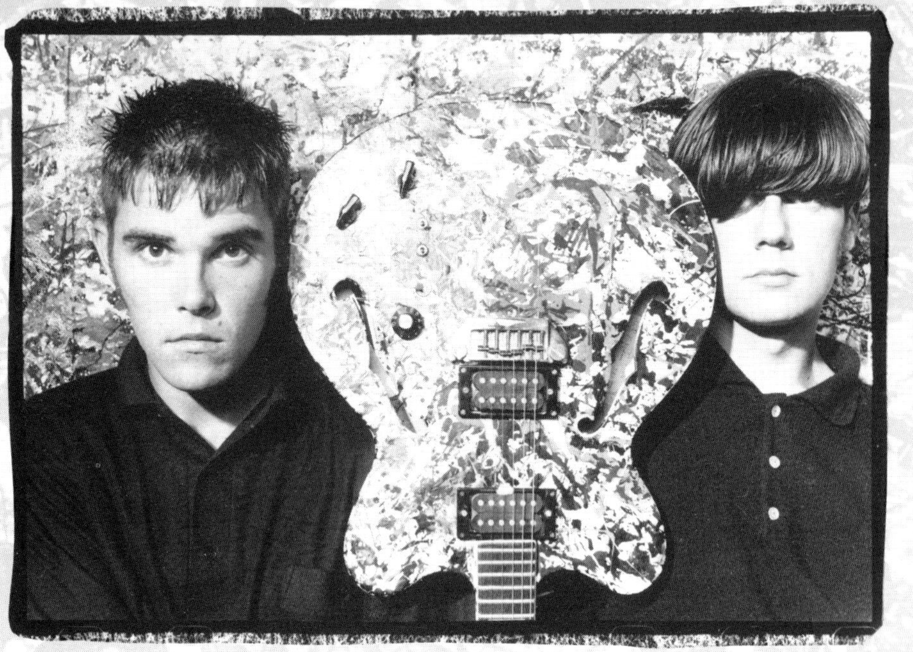

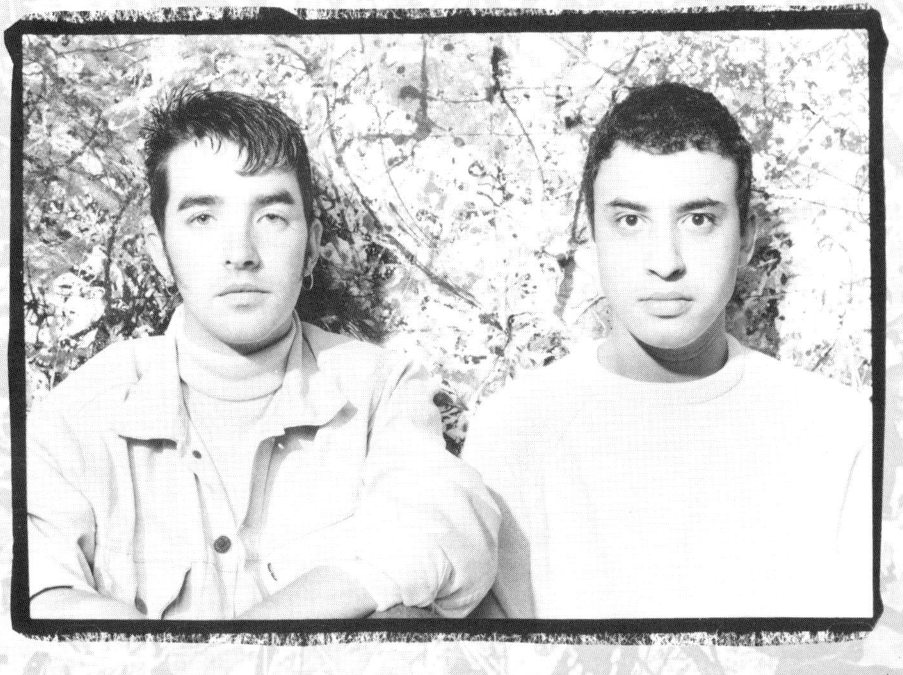

"There's going to be no in between for this band," spat Ian Brown. "We just want to do it, do it big and once it's done, it's done."

SomethinG's BurninG

And God Created Manchester

The Stone Roses were bold as brass. Right from day one. They had a vision. A craving. They thought *big*. They wanted to be the greatest rock 'n' roll group on earth. Not once have they compromised. They're for *real*. What you see is what you get.

Sleepy business bosses, early-rising shop-keepers, office cleaners. Morning commuters grasped it first. It was shocking. Outrageous. Scandalous. Disgraceful. Shame on them. Like snow silently blanketing the city, it had taken just one evening. Like a war-time blitz destroying entire towns overnight, it would be years before it was forgotten.

Manchester city centre had been vandalised. From Albert Square to Piccadilly, from Queen Victoria's statue to Central Library, spray-can terrorists had scrawled their propaganda. A foot or more high, it simply read 'Stone Roses'. Local papers claimed it was a yobbo pop band, desperate for publicity. From then on, Manc music media boycotted them.

"They blanked us. *City Life* wouldn't write about us for two years. All it is, is a bit of paint. You can rub it off. It's dead funny. It was done by some mates. We know who they are, but we're never gonna tell," explained Ian Brown.

July 85. The Stone Roses had just done their first Manchester shows. A clandestine gig at The Gallery, some warehouse parties, a Haçienda A&R showcase. "We're either going to be massive or fizzle out totally. No-one excited us, so we decided to do it ourselves." Ian told Paula Greenwood of *Muze*, in his first press interview.

A Kevin Cummins photo session captured a naive fivesome, yet to figure out their visual identity. Ian Brown, hair greased-back, clutched a walking stick; Reni and bassist Pete in raincoats; guitarist Andy Couzens with flat-top; John Squire wore a paisley

OPPOSITE
Ian and John, Pete and Reni, September 1987.

shirt, waistcoat, camp hat. "I'd like to be as big as Duran Duran," Reni told Paula.

Stone Roses. Strange name. Stone as in cold, hard, tough. Gothic almost. Dusty churches? Gravestones? Dreary cemeteries? Fountains? Carved headstones? Elaborate archways? Stone. Stone as in rock or as in The Stones or getting 'stoned'? Roses. Red roses like on Valentine's Day? Rose of Lancashire? The Roses as in cricket? Red rose of the Labour Party? Flower power, 60s, love and peace. The more you thought about it, the more mysterious it got.

"The name was a contradiction. Something hard and something pretty; something noisy but tuneful," John Squire explained.

"It was meant to be happy, not gothy," asserted Ian. Fact! The Stone Roses were *not* a goth band! Early demos *Tragic Roundabout*, *Mission Impossible*, *Trust A Fox* and *Nowhere Fast* were pure punk, poppy like Buzzcocks. Rough Trade's Geoff Travis would later describe them as looking like Pistols, while sounding like Herman's Hermits, as they progressed into psychedelia with *Heart On The Staves*, *Gettin' Plenty*, *All I Want*.

'In the misery dictionary, page after page after page,' an acapella opening to their debut, *So Young*, a fave on a session for Piccadilly's *Last Radio Show* .

"*So Young* was a piss-take of the Manchester scene and its miserable image. It was saying, 'Get out of bed and stop fucking moaning.'" said Ian, hugely over-confident even then.

So Young was backed with *Tell Me*, one of the most arrogant, self-centred, egotistical songs ever written: 'I love only me/I love only me/You can't tell me anything.' Manic, magical, majestic rock, caught between The Chameleons' *In Shreds* and Public Image Limited's *Rise*. Ian's admiration for John Lydon was creeping through.

'I am a garage flower', he sang, as guitars, bass and drums cascaded around him like a dustbin blown over in the wind. Rumoured to be worth £250 as this book goes to press!

Two years later, Inspiral Carpets released *Garage Full Of Flowers* on a *Debris* flexi, allegedly a tribute to the Roses. "'I am a garage flower' is like 'Stone Roses'...something worthwhile coming out of a mess; something noisy and something pretty," said John.

The *So Young/Tell Me* 12", was released on Thin Line, own label of their first manager Howard Jones (one-time Haç boss) on August 19, 85.

"It was alright at the time, but you've got to remember we were all fresh kids then, it was the first time we'd been in a studio," Ian apologised.

Cropped hair. Leather trousers. Railway lines. Two mis-spent years after *So Young*, The Roses' ever-evolving vision took them to rock label FM Revolver. The single *Sally Cinnamon* was a charming love song, written in 86 when cute Scots pop bands Primal Scream and Pastels entwined the indie scene. The sleeve pictured a bubble-gum machine, perfect for a band besotted by sweeties, penny-trays, ice lollies. "We used to get the train to Hazel Grove, just to go to this newsagents where they've got the biggest, best penny-tray in the world," Ian confided. His local newsagent on Barlow Moor Road, Chorlton, reveals he also loves Funny Feet lollies. So much for drug-crazed scallydelia!

'I'd rather be no-one with someone/than someone with no-one ...' Ian sang on *Sally Cinnamon*'s flipside. It was *Adored Part One*, positive pop. Where Smiths' followers would hide at home under a blanket of self-pity, hatred and misery, Roses' fans would soon be streaming down the streets fuelled by enormous self-belief, courage, arrogance.

Still in 87. The Roses met Paul Fletcher from Stockport free-sheet *Buzzin'* in an Italian restaurant. By this time, they'd joined manager Gareth Evans, who proudly claimed *So Young* was a collector's item, selling for as *much* as £4.50! "*So Young* wasn't good enough, in fact it was a pile of shit ... seriously," said Ian, as the restaurant erupted into a crazed, rock 'n' roll spaghetti fight.

Food fights, ice pops, a splash of graffiti? The Roses were a laddish bunch, but never real scallies. While North Manchester lads like Happy Mondays were well-deep in the council-estate smack-scene, the Roses were getting bevvied in bedsit-land.

May 87. In the furthest alcove of The International Club, two ropey blokes were chatting.

"Men's nipples ..." slurred one, turning to the girls at the next table, "... don't you find them attractive? Sexy?" A mad glint in his eye, he persisted, "Men's nipples, don't you find them erotic?"

The girls stared back, speechless at this novel chat-up line. The other guy smirked. "What do you think of the Stone Roses?" he drawled, giving his mate a poke in the ribs.

"Errrm ... well, they're better than that band Inspiral Carpets." Laughter.

"Don't you know *who* we are?" Blank stares. "*We're the Stone Roses!*"

"Oh ..."

"Look!" says one of the guys, producing a paper from his pocket. "See!" (*Buzzin'* had just been published. On the cover, a gawky Ian Brown in a Frank Spencer beret.) "That's me!" It was.

The nipple-obsessed one was Reni, a minor-league Keith Moon. The girls were Manc plugger Alison Martin and yours truly!

Reni's pervy sense of humour was confirmed when he was spotted stepping out of a car wearing suspenders ... he was working as a kissagram for Livewires in Chorlton!

The Roses weren't familiar faces ... yet. Notorious only in name. They didn't have a proper deal. They'd had no media attention. No-one south of Stoke had even heard of them. Yet soon Gareth would book them a series of Friday night dates at The International (which he owned). Each would pull 800 people!

It was The Chameleons syndrome. Like those Middleton pomp-rock heroes, the Roses had gained a laddish, often violent, following without media hype. The Chameleons pulled in 2000 at the Free Trade Hall in 85, seats collapsing in a frenzy of hero-worship. In 87, the Roses were following the same route.

November 88. One Sunday afternoon, John Squire and Ian Brown meet me at the cemetery gates. That's *the* cemetery gates. Southern Cemetery where Morrissey would take strolls with Linda of Ludus. It was once the biggest graveyard in Europe, acres of it, but Ian and John refused to go in and read the stones. "Can't be doing with death," muttered John. Then why choose here ...? "*Us*!" they exclaimed. "Gareth said *you* wanted to meet us here!" Mmmmm. Another Gareth Evans piss-take. Settled instead for a picnic table on Hough End Fields, a mile or so walk from their Burton Road flat.

Ian and John were monosyllabic, difficult interviewees, giving one-line answers to standard questions. No great long-winded quotes, just an indestructible belief that they were the best band in the world and sooner or later the world would recognise this!

"If I thought we were going to remain selling 2000 records, I'd give in now," said Ian. "But I seriously think we're gonna be huge. You can't keep a good band down."

88. And the Roses were taking off. On May 30 at International 2, they played a benefit with James for the North West Campaign for Lesbian and Gay Equality, an anti-Clause 28 event.

Following a false start with Rough Trade, they then signed to Jive/Zhomba's off-shoot, Silvertone. *Elephant Stone* was their first single, a shimmering, spacey pop song produced by Peter Hook and coupled with *Full Fathom Five* ... the same track backwards! Heaven. Captured the essence of a new magical, transformed Stone Roses (Mark III). Santana. Monkees. Yardbirds. Stones. Byrds. Beatles ...

"The most obvious thing about the Stone Roses, is that they've got 'special' stamped all over them," wrote perceptive fan, Andy McQueen, in *M62* fanzine at end of 88. "Not since The Smiths' hey-day, have I seen such an ecstatic audience reaction. There's a buzz and an 'attitude' round them that's so exciting. How can you deny it?"

The Roses ended 88 with gigs at International 2 and Central London Poly. March 89 took them to Warrington's Legends and The Haçienda's Monday club, closely followed by an awesome sell-out at International 2. The Roses at The Haç, as historic as The Smiths' gig six years earlier. *Snub TV* filmed it, Ian Brown, gurning his 'yooou-knooow' goldfish-look, singing out-of-key, Cressa wriggling on the spot.

"Bollocks to Morrissey at Wolverhampton, to The Sundays at The Falcon, to PWEI at Brixton ... I'm already drafting a letter to my grandchildren telling them that I saw the Stone Roses at The Haçienda ..." raved *NME* pop-kid, Andrew Collins.

Once they scrawled their name across our city in aerosol. Now the Stone Roses etched it across our hearts with *Made Of Stone*, their second Silvertone single. Images of dusty inner-cities. Cars burn and tin-twisted grills grin back at you.

Enemies called them plagiarists. Yet there were so many wheels on the Roses' caravan of love, the

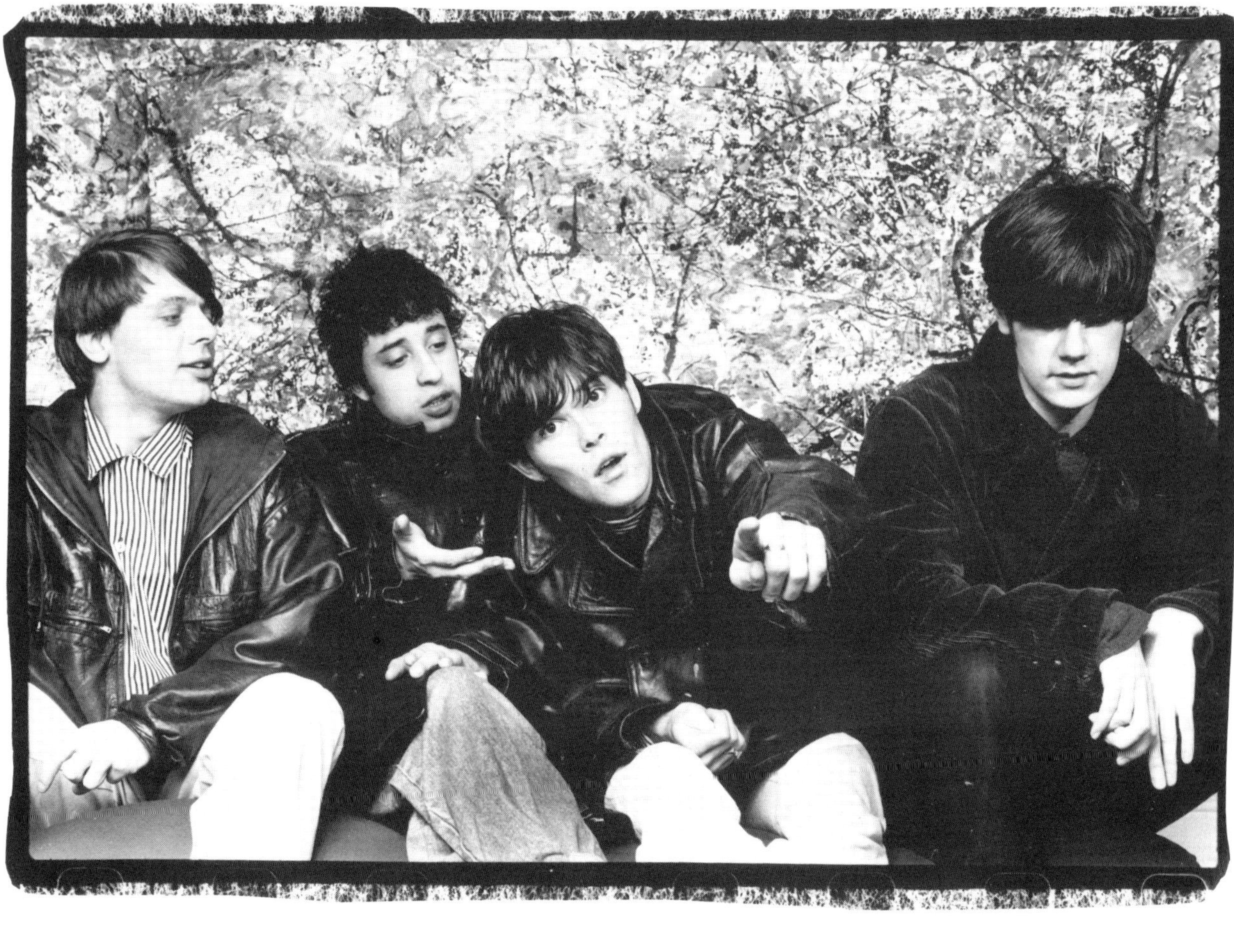

music press couldn't make their minds up. Check these comparisons. 'Durutti Column in overdrive'. 'Wired intensity of Dukes Of Stratosphere's *25 O'Clock*'. 'Spear Of Destiny sound-a-likes a few years back'. 'Languor not seen since Edwyn Collins and Orange Juice'. 'A more mature Primal Scream'. 'An untogether Bunnymen'. 'Pilfered Status Quo ...' April 89 ... *the* album. It needed no title. The music said it all, fading in with *Adored*. "It leads into this house of delights," gushed *Melody Maker*'s Bob Stanley. "Gently at first, as it fades in with a throbbing bass-line, through corridors of harmonics. Then suddenly you're in the main hall. Vast, oak-panelled, chandeliers hanging from the ceiling and right in the centre there's something dazzling, blinding, loud and intense and it's dragging you closer. You're in. It's a drug and you're hooked ..."

The Roses are not a 60s rip-off. Nothing is that easy. John Thomas Squire, Alan John Wren (Reni), Gary Michael Mountfield (Mani) and Ian George Brown, pulled together strands of genius from 30 years of youth culture. Full of contradictions!

Ian Brown, born in 63, son of Jean and George. The mod who scootered round seaside resorts. Ian Brown, the beatnik who hitchhiked Europe Jack Kerouac-style. Ian Brown, the hippie who said, "It's not where you're from, it's where you're at." Ian Brown, the punk, anarcho mischief-maker, situationalist. Johnny Rotten sang, 'God save the Queen/She ain't no human being.' Ian Brown called for *Elizabeth My Dear* to be boiled alive. Same song: different tune. See what I mean? "I believe in anarchy as a state of mind. Trying to be free," said Ian.

Ian Brown, the guru? Every year another Jesus walks on water, breaks the bread, drinks the wine. Jesus was the first hippie, acid-head, house guru and psychedelic star, selling capsules of love, peace and miracles (didn't have an 'E' in his name for nothing!) 'I am the resurrection and I am the light', sang Ian Brown, a line borrowed from a city centre church hoarding.

Self-taught artist, John, formulated the band's familiar paint-splash style in his bedroom. "I've never tried to pass my paintings off as my own," he said. "We wanted to put Jackson Pollock's paintings on the covers, but they cost three quarters of a million each!" May 89. The Roses had refused to support New Order in US; Pixies in Britain. "They've never supported anyone in their life and see no reason why they should start doing so now," said a spokesperson. Rumours spread that they'd also turned down Stones supports in Canada. "Fucking hell, we're not opening up for them. They should open up for us! It's obscene that they're even touring. Mick Jagger? I want to punch him out!" ranted Ian.

"Two years ago I was booking all the bands at Town And Country," said promoter, Phil Jones. "Gareth would call all the time and beg me to give them a support, *any* support! I refused, because I knew they couldn't even pull a hundred people in London."

May 89. The Stone Roses got their London show, at the ICA. It clinched their media hype. *NME*'s Steve Lamacq was rather reserved, seeing them not as the future of rock 'n' roll, just another big indie, another Sundays, another Mega City Four. "They are what favourite bands are all about," he wrote, unsensationally.

Favourite band? Favourite band? We're talking The Greatest Group On Earth here.

August 12, 1989. The fourth stage of the Roses' career began. It was this day that they became a 'phenomenon'. "New age droogs who've skipped The Clockwork Orange in favour of paint-splattered lemon ..." James Brown, *NME*.

The aliens had landed. The invasion of the Mancunoids. Flares. The widest, scruffiest, daftest flares in the universe, strolled along Blackpool's promenade. First just one or two, then in handfuls, then armies of them walking six-abreast clogging up the pavements like cowboys in a Wild West movie. Flares. Old flares, new flares, wide not just at the ankle but all the way up. Legs heavy with denim, sucking up sea-spray.

The invasion of the Mancunoids. Imposters from outer-somewhere. Arm-in-arm, row-on-row of saggy T-shirts. Not just any old saggy T-shirts, but long-sleeved, cheap rubbish. Stretchily mass-produced, awesomely badly-fitting. Sleeves three or four inches longer than arms, so they could be pulled over hands and gripped in clenched fistfuls, like the baggy pullovers of shivering street urchins.

"We wanted to play Blackpool to give people a day out

OPPOSITE
Stone Roses, March 1988.

to finish their summer. When you've got no money and you live in Manchester and you're a kid, there's nowhere to go," Ian told *NME*.

"Make sure you get this right. With flares coming back, people have got to realise, that you can't wear anything wider than 21" bottoms. Anything more looks ridiculous,"

John explained, "Trousers look better if they're long. You've got to have lots of crumples on the way down to your shoes."

Blackpool was also the perfect place to buy a white Reni sun-hat! The Roses sold-out 4000 tickets to Empress Ballrooms. Ian had acquired a yo-yo on the prom, a whizzing, whirling, curling, dizzy, dizzy red-blue acid yo-yo, dancing tripping colours in front of the fans' eyes.

Promoter Phil Jones, dropped in favour of rival, Simon Moran, revealed. "I had a whole tour lined up. All the seaside resorts. Southend. Brighton. Weston-Super-Mare. We were going to book buses and take everyone round on a magical mystery tour." At the backstage party, Reni slumped at a table, really down. "So we've got a hit album, so we've done this gig? So what? We're nothing. It's not real. We're nothing to The Rolling Stones. Got too far to go ..." he ranted. An odd ending to a day-out at the seaside.

The invasion of the Mancunoids. At each Roses 'happening' from then on, the scenes would get crazier. By October, it even crossed the channel to Europe. Flapping, slithering, dragging its way through Paris. Drunk, drugged, loud, obnoxious Mancs spewing up over their Kickers. As blindly 'patriotic' as football faithfuls, singing 'Manchester, la, la, la'. They were to see the Stone Roses play (and win) away. Culmination of a riotous European tour.

"Patriotism is the last refuge of the scoundrel and the same goes for regionalism," an embarrassed John Squire later told Stuart Maconie.

The Roses were heading La Cigale above Felt, The Chills and The La's, at Les Inrockuptibles Festival. Mancunians out-numbered smart, cravat-wearing locals by at least two to one!

The invasion of the Mancunoids. The Roses opened many minds. Paris, Pigalle's red-light district. Pimps, loud body-vendors selling their junk; tempting lads into strip joints. The glow of red lights illuminating jostling hoards of pervy Parisians, pissed-up tourists, down-and-outs, she-men, he-women. Kind of crazy non-stop action.

Manc yobs headed for the bar, pestering the distraught bar staff, shouting, "'Ere love, 'ow 'bout a pint," like they were back home in some scummy Salford pub. In the heart of Paris, a Manchester band was playing Manc music to Manc kids. It had exported a convoy of T-shirt traders, ticket touts and even drug dealers. How much money had the band lost due to bootlegging? The band didn't care. "Touts have to earn a living. How much money do I need? If you're getting bootlegged, you're gonna be earning enough money anyway aren't you?"

"Acieed, Acieed, Acieed," one shifty guy muttered under his breath, twitchy as a dormouse, pacing round and round, ducking, diving, looking behind him like a man on the run, paranoia personified. Meanwhile, a blubber-faced, sweat-drenched boy was experiencing the traumas of a debut acid trip, scribbling words like 'Wow', 'Love' and 'Yeah!' all over his skin in crimson felt-tip.

Cess Buller, of Didsbury's MVITA gang, transported over on his luxury coach, The Cess-X-Press."The Manchester vibe is taking over the area of Europe," he exhorted. "Manchester! Manchester! Manchester!" they jeered when the band appeared. "Paris! Paris! Paris!" retorted Ian Brown, later to coin the phrase, "It's not where you're from, it's where you're at."

Four weeks later, Manc troops swarmed out of Wood Green tube station. Walking, walking, walking in convoy through North London to Alexandra Palace, up, up, up the hill to this tower in the sky. By lunchtime a security guy, like the villain in a Bond movie (bald head, seven foot tall, gold-plated teeth), was fending off kids promised free tickets by the band.

Alexandra Palace, November 18, 89. The same night Happy Mondays played the Free Trade Hall. On top of the world. A big fuck-off oblong exhibition hall with a roof that reached to heaven ... but no soul. More like a school assembly hall. The Roses opened with *Adored* and ended with *I Am The Resurrection*, just like their album. But their set was fraught with problems. "Honestly, the sound-check was superb," said promoter, Phil Jones. "Then the audience came in and somebody cocked it up."

OPPOSITE
Spike Island, May 1990; John, Glasgow Green, June 1990.

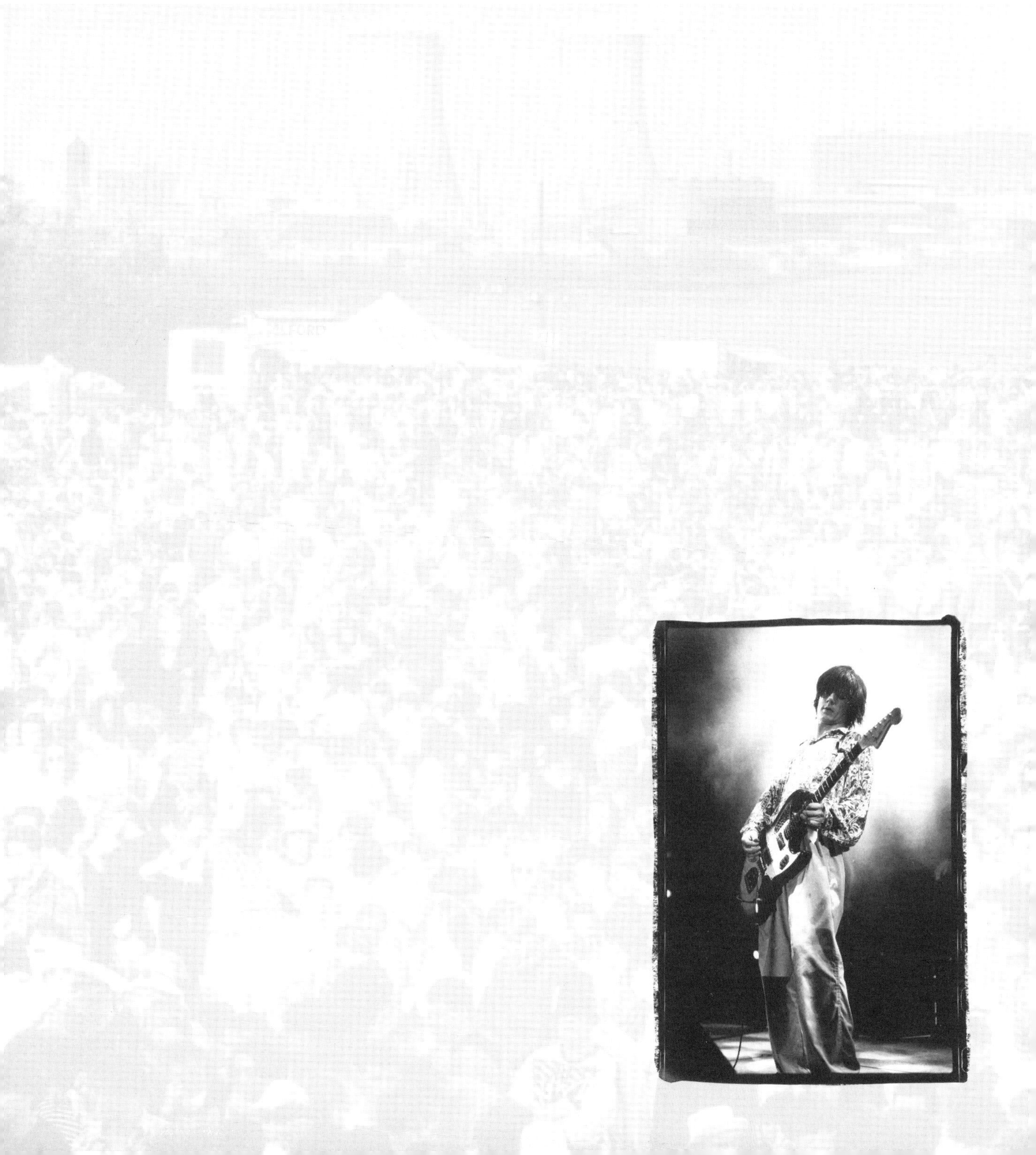

"This show belonged somewhere in 1975," wrote *Melody Maker*'s unsussed John Wilde in a 2000-word Roses slag-off. "Never mind flares. It symbolised everything sluggist, stagnant, worn-out and obsolete." Yet, as the Ally Pally buzz echoed, *Fool's Gold/What The World Is Waiting For* hit the Top 40 at No 13 that very week. Thursday's *Top Of The Pops* was about Manc domination with 808 State at No 12; Mondays' *Rave On* at 30, and Inspiral Carpets just outside the 40. Manchester entered the 90s top-of-the-class.

"The most impressive, exciting pop band in the world," said Bob Stanley of *Melody Maker*, having flown out to see them play Copenhagen, Lund and Stockholm in a warm-up for Spike Island.

90s media spectacles. The ruins of the Berlin Wall; pop stars playing support act to the freed Nelson Mandela; a bunch of no-good lifers over-running Strangeways Gaol ... and four ordinary Mancs holding the world's press at seige at the top of the Piccadilly Embassy Hotel on 26 May, 90. The Roses had already been sued by FM Revolver for criminal damage, having daubed (shock! horror!) their office with paint. They lapped up the press hype, driving away with a sign 'The Manchester Four Are Innocent!' Now was the time for another scam.

The night before Spike Island, the world's press was summoned to a live Roses' trial. An élite bunch of 50 or so news-hounds took part in this ridiculous farce. The foursome took a table at the far end of the room. Edgy, insecure, defensive, chain-smoking, drinking Perrier. The press conference was a joke. A waste of time. An hour of embarrassed silences as the band gave (reasonable) one-word answers and the press struggled to think of anything to ask. Such probing questions as "Do you get many groupies?", "Where will you play after Spike Island?"

"Are you the new Rolling Stones?" asked a hack who'd flown in from the US. "It's 1990 innit?" sneered Ian. "So I say to you ... the Rolling who?"
Silence.
"What will you be doing in five years?" asked Linda Duff of *The Daily Star*?" "Let me look into my crystal ball ..." sniggered Reni. "What a stupid question," finished Ian.
Silence.
"Do you go to acid house parties?" asked another hack. Ian coolly, "Yeah, I've been to parties where there's been acid."
Silence.
It went on like this til a Moss Side ex-pat, now a New York journo, freaked out and ranted how the press had travelled all this way just to be treated like shit. A fight broke out. Pandemonium! Typical Roses' humour. Gareth grinned on.

Spike Island May 27, 1990? Very nearly 21 years since Woodstock. A coming of age. In the 90s, dancing, having fun, not-giving-a-fuck was the biggest act of rebellion kids dared. Car-crashing-crazies playing tag with motorway police patrols, jamming up ring roads in the dead of night, holding hostage rural homelands.

Woodstock 69: Spike Island 90? Bar two World Wars and the Queen's Silver Jubilee, Spike Island was *the* Event Of The Century. Or so it seemed! Overground celebration of an underground feeling. The second Summer Of Love 88 was about taking E in steamy clubs; at the third everyone dropped acid at outdoor raves; the fourth was about breathing *life*, sharing *love* at Spike Island and Glastonbury 90.

Woodstock 69: Spike Island 90? The word spread. Fast. Exciting every comprehensive, club and factory in Britain. Spike Island, a country park between Manchester and Liverpool, that *no-one* had ever heard of, was going to be the North's biggest legal rave, greater even than Mondays' at G-Mex. *Everyone* was there. Doors opened at 2 pm, sounds started at 3pm. "We want people to come back to gigs. We want to make every show an event, most of all, we want people to talk about it," said Reni in 85. Five years on, his dream was reality.

Woodstock 69: Spike Island 90? Though Central and Granada telly pulled out of filming, Spike Island was well-documented. The audience got more coverage than the band. Flower children in a 20-year time-warp. Pissed-up beer boys in Northside sacks. Scallies with World Cup footie-tops. Acid-goons sporting dungarees. Cool-kids in circular shades. Heads in Hendrix shirts talking revivalism. Clone scallydelics slithering in the mud. Rock 'n' roll bimbos with bleach-blonde hair. Teeny-boppers in tour T-shirts.
Strange times indeed.
Widnes had *not* wanted these crazies in *their* town. A

petition was signed, river-barges tried to knock down bridges, born-again Christians protested against Sunday partying. Yet, when this myriad bunch hit town, they were harmless.

Spike Island had a guest-list of 1000, penned into an exclusive backstage area where Nigel Pivaro, ex-*Street* star, chatted to Ian McCulloch of Bunnymen and 808 State, the Mondays and all of Manc pop mingled. Free beer! Free food! Both were guaranteed in the Silvertone hospitality tent. Too good to be true! One beer tap for 1000 people. A free-for-all free-fall. "Spike Island was beautiful," said one reveller. "I sat in the media enclosure. It felt very idyllic, like I was sat in the garden of Eden ..."

Outside, in the 'real' world, there was just one beer tent for another 30,000 scallydelics. Kinda groovy mayhem. No cigarettes on site either. And everyone's carefully-packed crates of beer, orangeade and picnic hampers were cruelly confiscated at the main gates and dumped into skips. From the start people were unhappy, squatting down, bored. Entertainment came from DJs Paul Oakenfold, Dave Haslam, MVITA, Frankie Bones. Plus African pop from Thomas Mapfumo and new-beat from Gary Clail.

"The DJs we wanted to play weren't given long enough," a miffed Ian Brown told *The Face*. "We thought it was in our hands till the actual day. The promoters could have done more for people."

Just hours before the kick-off, Ian Brown had the term 'VIP' Tippexed off all security passes. "Everyone's equal ... there are no VIPs in this world," he murmured enigmatically.

Right on baby. Outasite. Crazy, man. In Ian Brown's opinion, everyone's a star. He slouched backstage in an old T-shirt, carrier bag over his shoulder, like some school-kid with his PE kit. Cooler than Jesus, saintly almost.

"I was 100% relaxed," he told Simon Dudfield of *The Face*. "If all these people had come to see us, they wanted it. So why should I have been nervous?"

By the time the band came on, the crowd was restless, bad-tempered, impatient. The mood had dulled after seven hours standing in a field; 30,000 faces waiting for a revolution that never happened. Out at the fringes of this huge rave-zone, on the edge of the Mersey Estuary, tired, bored, detached, bewildered beings stumbled over Coke cans, beer glasses, chip wrappers.

"We've been waiting, waiting since three o'clock for 'something' to happen. It still hasn't happened yet," said one guy as the clock of the world ticked ten. The band had been on 40 minutes.

It 'happened' right at the end of Roses' set, just as we'd all given up hope. The haunting acoustics of *Elizabeth My Dear* followed by an awesome version of *I Am The Resurrection*. Spacey guitar riffs, spiralling into the sunset, out over the mudbanks of the Mersey, lit up by the glow of a crescent moon. A Pink Floyd-scale lighting rig, cart-wheeling, beams criss-crossing the sky like Berlin border lights. The finale? A bonfire-night extravaganza of fireworks.

Only 10.30pm and time for bed. Strange really. Even Jesus returned for an encore. The Roses *just* resurrected themselves before they'd died.

Woodstock 69: Spike Island 90? Flower children, beaten-up hippie buses painted day-glo, acid freaks, revolutionaries? Spike Island's children of the revolution were the sons and daughters of these original hippies, brought up in the Thatcherite 80s. Love, peace and unity? Nah, ultimately, Spike Island was more to do with designer tour T-shirts. The children of the revolution came, saw and went home again ... filing back to reality.

The revolution never came after Woodstock. How could Spike Island have been any different?

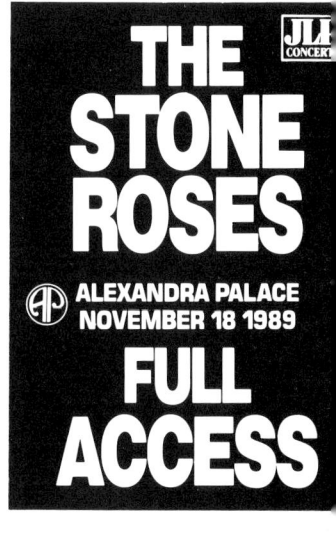

The Roses' summer-of-love 90 single, *One Love*, was hyped to be No 1. It reached No 4. No matter. As the man said, "We just want to do it, do it big and once it's done, it's done."

THE STONE ROSES

ALEXANDRA PALACE
NOVEMBER 18 1989

FULL ACCESS

Identity

Scallydelia. A fashion concept that grew up from the underground. The Manc kids were as scruffy-as-hell. They wore tops and jeans as baggy-as-sacks. They shopped on Oldham Street, went to clubs, bought indie records from Eastern Bloc and took drugs that made them as crazy-as-asylums.

ScallYdelia

And God Created Manchester

The rise and rise of scally culture. Jumbo cords, thick-wedges, Scouse football teams, The Farm, Merseyside scruffies, Manc Perry Boys, Midlands Mods, Penquin parkas, Scooter lads, Reni sun-hats, North Manchester council estates, Mondays' mates, the Baldricks *ID* 88. Yeah ... forget Morrissey-esque quiffs and James Dean-styled 501s, scallydelia (or whatever you must call it) was the one youth cult that was purely working- class. Its origins can be traced back through Liverpool and Manchester folklore.

All those pastel wallabies, primary Kickers and psychedelic hues and downwardly-mobile guitar bands were where the scene began. As Roses and Mondays and the beats of the dance underground finally hit the mainstream at the end of the 80s, so too did these fashions. Tie-dye, floral baggy shirts, flares and pussy-packers stormed the chainstores in time for their Spring/Summer 90 collections. Even Dorothy Perkins, Miss Selfridge and other ladylike fashion boutiques were at-the-ready with rails of purple hooded-tops.

Styles and music, 'flowering' underground for months and years, were now utterly acceptable. In 84 the teenies worshipped Wham, wore day-glo green and ra-ra skirts. By 88 the kids were Brosettes sporting bomber-jackets/Doc shoes/CCCP watches, all styles stolen from the 80s student/gay chic. By 90, no 13-year-old could play-out without a purple hooded-top, lilac Kickers and a copy of Happy Mondays' *Hallelujah*. Weird.

All the 'happening' Manchester acts became part of the scallydelic style. The Charlatans, Roses, Mondays, Inspirals, James ... all either wore the gear or made

OPPOSITE
Leo of Identity, September 1990;
The Baldricks, February 1988.

fortunes from it, marketing their own scally T-shirts. Tim Burgess of The Charlatans said he wore flares, "'cos me old man wears straights," ... while the very week The Charlees signed to Beggars Banquet, manager Steve Harrison was spotted in Affleck's spending £1000 of the advance on new gear for The Ladz. Really rare thing to see stars of *Top Of The Pops* wearing the same clothes as yourself!

Inevitably, the chainstore gear was fairly trashy. Like Funki Junki, a new line of mass-produced club-wear designed by a precocious business-school chappie with a well-heeled daddy. Horrid. Horrid. Horrid. And then Joe Bloggs ... more Manc scally-gear, aimed at the chainstore network.

The expansive showrooms of The Legendary Joe Bloggs Inc sit boldly in the heart of Salford's cash-and-carry quarter, in the shadow of the even more legendary Strangeways Gaol. As scally-looking characters bustle to-and-fro stacking crates for worldwide export, you can hear the cash tills ringing. The annual turnover is £25,000,000.

"The only difference between being rich and poor, is that now I've got more to lose and you've got more to gain," says managing director, Shami Ahmed, on the defensive. He's an eligible 27 and potentially a multi-millionaire.

Imagine the possibilities! Champagne! A Ferrari! A big fuck-off Bentley with a personalised number-plate! A fistful of fifties to wave at those you've left behind! A Park Lane apartment with your own personal lift! Such is Shami's world. He greets you wearing his cool Italian-style suit. Mr Sophisticated, or what?

"How can a man like that, surrounded by so much wealth, be creative?" asks Leo of rival, Identity.

The origins of Joe Bloggs and its spin-off label, Orange Juice, lie in the Ahmed family's wholesale business, Pennywise. Just one of a stronghold of Asian/Mancunian clothing companies north of the city centre. Quick fashion tip here ... why not try some bulk buying, the cash-and-carrys are at least 30% below shop prices.

By comparison with, say, Wranglers, Joe Bloggs are a toy-town business. But who's complaining when you've sold half a million pairs of flares in two years and been part of a genuine fashion revolution? First they introduced 25" bottoms, the widest in Britain; then 30", the widest in Europe. They were also one of the first to cash-in on the hooded-top at the chainstore level. Cultural foresight or pure fluke?

Shami does not hide his lack of street-knowledge. "It was an accident. It wasn't a design brainwave. The idea behind the flares was just common sense. It occurred to me the new generation hadn't worn flares, so I brought them back."

This is an over-exaggerated claim. Shami was certainly not the first to re-introduce flares, just the first chainstore company.

During 88 Joe Bloggs sponsored Happy Mondays. Shaun told *M62* fanzine. "The jeans are mega jeans, aren't they? Top jeans. Good jeans. Some good gear with JB on. I've bundled loads of gear, man, that I wouldn't go out and buy, but I'd wear it. It's a joke innit? I mean, I need the clothes."

Though months behind the real Manchester fashion designers, Joe Bloggs clothing was a huge working-class phenomenon. Once an Arthur Daley joke, the flares revival was now a reality. Likewise, the humorous, well-naff concept of an anti-designer brand, 'Joe Bloggs', has managed to capture the aspirations of a generation turning away from American and European influences and looking closer to home.

"Joe Bloggs is to Britain what Gucci is to Italy," quipped Shami.

Cheap and scruffy, somehow Joe Bloggs captured the very soul of what it meant to be young-Northern-white-male and working class. Barry Grant on *Brookside* and The Lads on *Coronation Street* never wore anything else on screen in 90. Meanwhile, Inspiral Carpets, 808 State, Rig all received some form of sponsorship. Bloggs was involved in Bop Cassettes' Manc compilation *HIT THE NORTH* and even began targetting the laddish market with hoardings at soccer grounds!

"Of course it's a uniform," said Maria Cairney in *City Life*, April 89, when scally really started kicking, "But it is, by designer standards, an inexpensive one. Try some Joe Bloggs mega-baggy jeans with 20" bottoms. Put them on and try hard not to assume a John Wayne 'big-bow-leggy' stance."

Yet, by the time Joe Bloggs started printing their totally naff 'Happy Stoned Carpets, We Celebrate You ...' T-shirts, Manchester was utterly embarrassed!

No hip kid would be seen dead in Joe Bloggs gear once it had been bought up by tourists, teeny-boppers, department stores and second-generation 'scallies'. Scallydelia!!! Forget Joe Bloggs.

The real street-wise scally shop has always been Identity. It was launched in 84 by unemployed 27 year-old ex-mobile-disco DJ, Leo Stanley. Since falling in love with Joy Division in 80 and winning a Manchester Sounds slot at The Venue (then an indie hang-out), he's had a passion for Manc music culture. His small clothes stall, Identity, hurtled though every daft phase in youth culture, starting with army surplus, the tail end of punk, then goth, overcoats and hippie nonsense. It even tried out Next-style smart clothes and chinos!

Then, in the Summer Of Love 88, Leo really found his true 'identity' with acid house and Smiley culture. It was at this point that he began to start fashions rather than just mimic them. Flares, hooded-tops, Manchester pride T-shirts followed and Identity became the perfect outlet for Inspirals and James T-shirts.

The slogans on the 'Pride' T-shirts soon became the slogans of a generation, a fashion trend, a whole wave of youth culture even. 'Manchester North Of England' was the first, then 'Born In The North, Return To The North, Die In The North', 'This is Not Manchester ... This Is A Trip' and, inevitably, 'Woodstock 69: Manchester 89'.

"It was a tourist idea. Like 'London, Tower Bridge' shirts. Someone said to me, 'But we don't get tourists in Manchester.' I said, 'We will do one day, when *it* happens.' I didn't know what *it* was, I was just being hopeful. Now they're bought up by tourists, students, Manchester music fans, ex-pats ..."

Selling 500 a week, 1000 at Christmas 'Manchester North Of England' is now an historic piece of clothing. It has helped ensure Leo a turnover of £1million. It was also the title of a compilation album, released in June 88 by Bop, which featured James' *Sky Is Falling*, Inspiral Carpets' original *Joe, The Man From Delmonte's Australia Fair*, Johnny Dangerously with *Subway Life,* Bradford's *Lust Roulette*, a Railway Children oldie ... plus a number of forgettable and embarrassing moments from Jean Go Solo, Pepplekade 14, Penny Priest ...

From 'Manchester North Of England' onwards, Leo's T-shirt creativity has diversified. He negotiated for six months to ensure official merchandising rights with the Reverend Martin Luther King's family, because he doesn't believe in bootlegging. Now he has an official licence to produce 'I Had A Dream' shirts worldwide! Then there's 'On The Sixth Day God Created MANchester' and 'On The Seventh Day The Clubs Closed And God Stayed Cool' ... inspiration for a book title!

"One night I was tripping out of my head, coming out of The Venue ... and the acid was making me very spiritual. That's when I came up with the idea," says Leo, a Catholic who knows the Bible inside out.

"On the back it said 'Jesus likes to party too.' Jesus was the original James Dean. He had a posse of 12 men, pulled crowds every town he went to and was crucified because the authorities didn't like him. Nowadays, a DJ has a posse, does warehouse parties and the authorities don't like it either!

"Jesus was a raver. He preached love, peace and let's everybody get it together. You only read about him up till he was 13, then nothing until he was 30. Two years later he was crucifed! What did he do in those hidden years? Have girlfriends? Go out drinking? Just 'cos you're having a good time and doing drugs doesn't make you the anti-Christ."

Yeah, Jesus was a raver too and, if he'd been from Manchester, it's almost certain he would have been a scally!

As scallydelia became the newest international language since Esperanto (but, hopefully, not as big a folly), Manchester was beseiged. Americans, Germans, Italians, French ... even a Soviet film crew turned up.

Working with BBC 2's *Reportage* team, they filmed a Manchester music documentary, to be beamed right across the Soviet Union. If any trendy elements of Moscow youth could defect, they would head for Manchester! Suddenly, it was not just Manc music, but Manc fashions conquering the world.

In 1992 Europeans will unite. Not long away is a time when we'll all share the same currency ... the E! Aka the Ecu! Spooky. If the politicians and the multinationals had their way, every city would look the same. Same department stores. Same fast-food joints. Same fun-pubs. Same diesel-smelling bus stations. Same ...

And Manchester? Yeah, it's no different.

Check The Arndale, the biggest covered shopping area in the Universe. Artificial light, artificial flowers, artificial shop assistants for consumers who live artificial lives. Only opened in 77, it feels like it's been there for ever.

This is light years from the heart of Manchester. Manchester and its music are special because they are independent, off-the-wall, individual. Thus, Manchester has its 'alternative' shopping centres, fast becoming a Manc-pop paradise. And at the heart of it all, Oldham Street.

Oldham Street is on the wrong side of Piccadilly. The domain of major stores like C&A and British Home Stores, until they fled to the Arndale, and haunted still by ghosts of the Woolworth fire in 79. After a period of dereliction, it hit boomtime again in 89 with the rise of scally culture.

At its heart, Affleck's Palace. A shopping wonderland with Identity and Eastern Bloc having prime positions on the ground floor. Affleck's is Manchester's Kensington Market ... except ten times better and far, far, far more imaginative, wonderful and exciting: student-wear, flat-top hair-dressers, designer 'cult' posters and postcards, soul records, joss-sticks, tarot-reading, café ...

Affleck's Palace has grown and grown since the early 80s. In the beginning it was a dirt-cheap punk flea-market, filled with spruced-up jumble clothes. Now there are designer items for every youth cliché to wear: goths, hippies, club-goers, Brosettes, pop-kids, scallies, James Dean.

Choose your cult and take your pick! In just a few yards you'll come across every item of trend-wear you could desire.

This part of town is a haven of youth culture. For skate-kids there's 50/60 Split, premier northern skate-shop; while The Bike Shed is full of mountain bike clobber. For beatniks there's Exit and, below, Howl, a trendy, poster-plastered, veggie café where there's no natural light and ceiling fans strobe.

Eastern Bloc Records is internationally hip. A Mecca. Best record shop in the UK, for sure. They started in 85 as a co-op, Earwig, with nothing but a tiny stall in Affleck's. Now they have two shops, their own label, and a ridiculous turnover. Rarely has anyone pulled off such success without selling out.

Their retail policy was revolutionary. They would stock no products on major labels, no products they didn't like and specialise, not just in British guitar bands, but also heavy dance imports and obscure hardcore releases.

Eastern Bloc has remained at the front-line ever since. In 88 they were taken to court for displaying the cover of A Flux Of Pink Indians' *The Fucking Cunts Treat Us Like Pricks* in the window; in 89 they were reprimanded for selling rave tickets; their Into-the-90s New Year 'do' was raided by dozens of police ... with their new toy ... a fuck-off helicopter, making its debut rave raid like something out of *Miami Vice!*

Eastern Bloc has always been a meeting place for bands, kids, DJs; with sussed staff, either fans or DJs themselves, to help you make your choice. Justin, Nipper, Mike, John ... not forgetting Mr Indie Pop himself, Andy McQueen.

A Guy Called Gerald, 808 State, MC Tunes all began hanging round Eastern Bloc and later appeared on Creed Records, the shop's own label. Inspiral Carpets received backing from here, while Mad Jacks' crazy-tripping-Hendrix single, *Weeping Wind*, was released on Creed in early 90. Then came the inevitable, FRO Records, aka Fuck Right Off Records ... no name could be more appropriate to the arrogant, upfront attitude of Eastern Bloc.

As the only sorted importer of the heavier European house/new-beat sounds à la Bizz Nizz, Eastern Bloc has hugely influenced northern dance floors in the past couple of years. Fuck Right Off is the logical conclusion. The label managed to licence Rhythm Section's *Laser Nation*, Rhythm Device's *Acid Rock*, Louis Vega's *House of Vega* and other European tracks that had been import hits for months. Not forgetting Wrexham's K-Klass, produced by Steve 'Dome' Williams.

Eastern Bloc is not the only record shop in town. Just across the street is Vinyl Exchange, a second-hand shop so cool that certain members of the national music press mail their freebies North to get a better price! Decent competition being Kingbee in the suburbs, where you get the best deal in Manchester.

Elsewhere in town are Expansions, Piccadilly and Spin Inn, all documented elsewhere in this book.

Eastern Bloc and Identity are joined by Dry 201 as Manchester's hippest, coolest, most-photographed musical landmark *ever*. Dry 201, also on Oldham Street, was opened in July 89. The concept? Somewhere for Haçienda ravers to go during the day. It wasn't quite what anybody expected ... not even the planners.

On the opening night trendy guests were suspicious. They decided it looked like either a school canteen, a University Hall, a shower room, a toilet, a DHSS waiting room or a Yates' Wine Lodge. All, including manager Leroy Richards, seemed to agree it was, in some ways, 'unfinished'!

Dry seemed to be about natural materials. Great expanses of wood, marble, stainless steel. A bar that stretched the length of the block, from the entrance on Oldham Street to the fire door on Spear Street. For seating, rows of neat wooden tables and chairs and, at the far end, a chill-out sofa-zone with enough corners for the more famous to hide in. You name them, they've been here.

Yet Dry was not a place for hiding. Dry 201 was (and is) essentially a place to meet a few mates, but also be *seen*. A little slice of London snobbery here in Manchester. Not quite the Soho Brasserie, but very nearly. People had very quickly decided Dry 201 was the coolest bar in town, though Greens, Polars and Cornerhouse were still in the running.

Conceived by Ben Kelly Design, Dry was first publicised in wacky Haç-style by copies of the blueprints sent out to the media.

There's a great story about a local newspaper, who naively phoned up to tell them, "err ... I think you've sent us your plans by mistake. Do you want us to post them back?"

"Dry is for everybody, not just people who go to The Haçienda," Leroy told *City Life*'s style columnist, Marian Buckley, the week it opened. Yet, with huge Haç-style bouncers on the door, it was not always that simple.

Dry, Affleck's, Eastern Bloc, Oldham Street. This is where the Manchester musical revolution *really* took place.

Here, where the Saturday-afternoon consumers spend their wages and pocket money to keep the rest of us in jobs. Like Carnaby Street's early days in the 60s. A golden quarter of a mile. A corridor of hipness. Birthplace of scallydelia.

Scallydelia. A fashion concept that grew up from the underground. The Manc kids were as scruffy-as-hell. They wore tops and jeans as baggy-as-sacks. They shopped on Oldham Street, went to clubs, bought indie records from Eastern Bloc and took drugs that made them as crazy-as-asylums. Should soon be a dictionary definition.

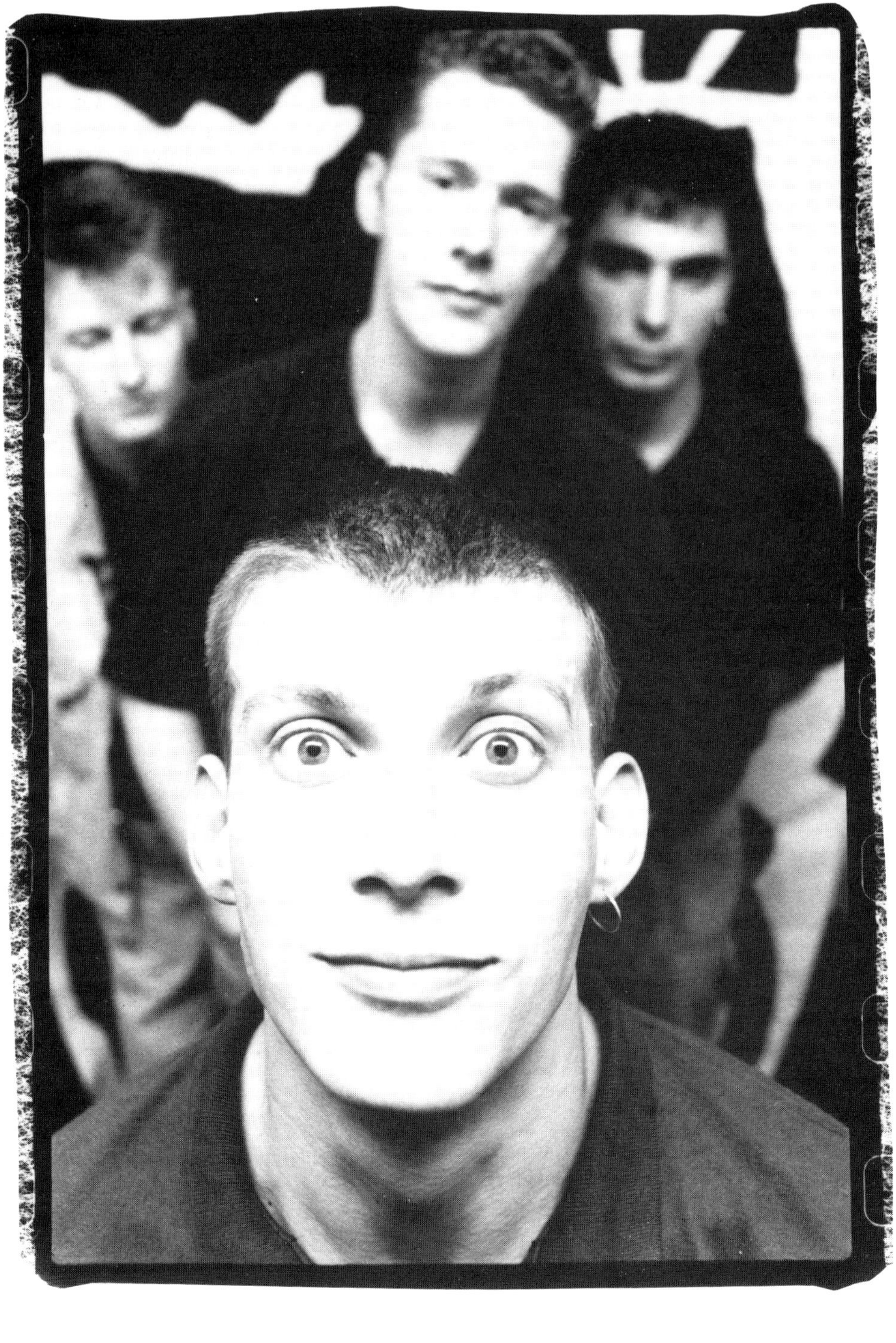

Life in the 80s. Thatcher as Queen; greed as king; fame was everything. Ask the man who smashed every window in the High Street thinking he was on *Game For A Laugh*. It was the matt-black, high-tech designer era the 60s' movie-makers fantasised about ... videos, computers, satellite telly, synths, samplers, drum-machines ... pull-out, pop-up, E-free, free E, colourful, full-colour, sensational, unique, unmissable consumer boom. The slogan? 'Buy now: worry later'. Leaving the 20th century in hedonistic style.

and GOD created MaNChESTeR Into the 90s

17 *And God Created Manchester*

Exit the 80s. Enter the 90s. Decade of revolution. Decade to the end of the century. Decade to recover from the decadent 80s. Decade to save the planet. All aboard the love-mobile. A new attitude, vibe, feeling, lifestyle, dream. From Glasgow to Cornwall, London to Liverpool, youth culture chilled-out, Manchester leading the way. Raves, house, indie-dance, scallydelia, Ecstasy and ecological hype, had radically changed people's perception of the world. For *real*. Candyflip bubbled, "In the 90s people are developing a hippy attitude. Things had to move away from that whole 80s thing of me, myself and I. Now it's just us, us, us. Not just people, but the whole planet. People are striving for harmony."

All aboard the love-mobile. "Religion's too small a word for what I have," Reni of the Roses told *Smash Hits*, July 90. "I don't believe in religion. I believe in man and woman, the planet, the people, everyone pulling together before it's too late." Man.

All aboard the love-mobile. Manchester Vibe was echoed nationwide. Scots The Soup Dragons & Junior Reed snatched a Top 40 hit with a cover of the Stones' *I'm Free* (Heavenly Records).

"I was at UFO, this hardcore house club in Glasgow," front-man Sean told *Melody Maker*. "All of a sudden the *My Bloody Valentine* remix came on, then a Sly and The Family Stone track, then Hendrix and everybody kept dancing. It's all to do with spirit ..."

London 'discovered' Manchester, soon My Jealous

OPPOSITE
New Fast Automatic
Daffodils, July 1989.

God, Eusbesio, Five Thirty and Flowered Up were being hyped. Flowered Up, a slice of Manc scallydelia in the centre of The South. Kids from Regents Park Estate, a council-zone as scummy as Wythenshawe, Gorton or Little Hulton.

"Home to chronic alcoholics, Vietnamese boat-people, the unemployed, the unemployable, mental defectives, single-parent families, robbers and whores," wrote Jack Barron in *NME*.

Before their debut, *It's On*, was even released, they'd been on every music-paper cover. Unfortunately, the record was like The Tweets doing *Step On*, tales of a Cockney E-dealer. Flowered Up were to scally what John Otway was to punk. A kind of Ian Dury and The Blockheads of E-culture. "You know those flowers in urban areas and on wasteland, the ones that grow out of the cracks in the city pavements and flower up. That's us!" they said. Hit me with your rhythm stick.

"Yeah, course we know Mondays, we stayed at Bez's gaff," they told *Melody Maker*. "We used to go partying in Manchester before the whole scene started. We heard it was kickin' up there in The Haç and that the Mondays had got onto a good buzz, so we went up. And now they're mates, same as Roses, we're on good terms with them all." Some of my best friends are Mancunians ...

"What do we get up to when we're together? We get shit-faced and have a laugh." Sex, drugs, rock 'n' roll. All aboard the love-mobile. 'Flowered up', a good adjective. Flowered up like Candyflip. Ric Peete and Dizzie Dee, a duo into incense sticks, beads, Aqua Libra, kaftans. Friday ravers from Stoke who'd motor to The Haç. Driving home one night, *Strawberry Fields Forever* came on the radio. They braked ... and it became their second single, after *Love Is Life* with its corny, "Mental! Mental! Mental!" chant. The Chairman of the Beatles Appreciation Society sneered in disgust while Paul McCartney admitted he liked it.

Bop City observed, "Candy Flip were even bestowed the dubious honour of being the only group invited to appear live on *Blue Peter*. Poor Biddy Baxter, if only she knew how close she came to corrupting the nation's youth. *Strawberry Fields*, the anthem of a pop-eyed, spaced-out beatnik generation. What were they singing about? *Drugs! Drugs! Drugs!*"

"Ecstasy," said *NME* southerner, Danny Kelly, on Granada TV in 1990, "has this amazing quality. It enables white men to dance." Why he appeared on a Manchester music documentary was never explained. Nevertheless, he was spot on.

"Let's hope acid house will finally kill off all them guitar bands for good," said Dave Rofe, owner of soul label, DFM, in 88.

In fact, the opposite came true. The Stoned Happy Carpet crews bloomed in an age as turned-on to club tunes as guitar-based pop. White men put down guitars and picked up the groove. Indie bands released dance 12"s; clubs spun rock tunes. The doors of perception were opened. The Smiths asked *How Soon Is Now? This* was *now*! Dance music diversified. Anything went. Happy Mondays' *Hallelujah*; the Stone Roses' *Fools Gold* pumped house dancefloors.

"Rock and dance have come together and it's the end of musical snobbery," said Wilson in the *Manchester Evening News*. "It's the start of the 21st century."

Classics and novelty cash-ins were just molecules apart ... Flowered Up's *It's On,* for example! Soulsters The Chimes covered U2's *I Still Haven't Found What I'm Looking For*. Glasgow jangle-darlings Primal Scream transformed the Stones' *Sympathy For The Devil* into *Loaded*. Liverpool's original scallies, The Farm, used *Stepping Stone* as a house groove. Bristol's Shut Up and Dance made Suzanne Vega into a club-artiste.

Primal's Bobby Gillespie told *ID*, "I hope a lot of kids, 15 or 16, whose first cultural thing was house music, can come and watch our band, and really get off on that, and see how good rock music can be."

The dance/indie mix started in student discos, but crossed into serious Manc clubs. DJ Hedd, Dave Haslam, is the grandfather of indie DJs. Since 86, his Temperance Club, Thursdays at The Haç, had been packed every week. He mixed Madonna, Smiths, Big Black, James, Public Enemy and ACR, soon getting into house and Roses. "It's a mixture you wouldn't hear at any other club in the world," he boasted.

Veteran Dave Booth took an indie-60s-dance fusion to every club in town. Scene With A Built-In Trip started at 42nd Street in 86 playing Beatles, Hendrix, 70s funk, hooked on classics like Steve Wonder's *Superstition*, *Sympathy For The Devil*, *Stepping Stone*. What began as a fave with the goth-alternative crowd, struck gold in 89 when these oldies infiltrated clubs across Britain.

Dave Booth is a modest celeb who has DJ-ed some of Manchester's finest indie nights. Summer of 89 was The Hangout at Isadora's, a wine-bar ignored since 82 when it was 666 Club, boasting gigs like Dead or Alive, and The Chameleons. Subtitled, Two Rooms Too Much, The Hangout combined Dave Booth playing indie/60s with Dave Haslam's hip-hop grooves. An oil-wheel projector spun psychedelic dreams over bobbing heads.

Other DJs followed. Tin Tin and Leo from The Venue, Temptation on Wednesdays at The Ritz, Stuart and Phil C at The Boardwalk. Dave Booth launched 1992, a house night at the Poly, while Friday's Freaky Dancing at 42nd Street (MC Tunes' fave club night) stayed true to Booth's culture mish-mash.

Enter children of the 70s! Conceived, born and brought-up since the original, authentic Summer Of Love 67. Enter Tim Burgess, lead singer of The Charlatans. Another of those 'flowered up' post-Moz lads, fooling with drugs, buying up hooded-tops, loving every minute. A peach-faced kid with a Jagger sneer, bobbing head and shiny new red Kickers ...

Tim was not new to the scene. He travelled Manchester on the Smiths pilgrimage in 88. More uncool still, he once got off on The Membranes, The Vibrators, Anti-Pasti, The Exploited, The Sub Humanz, Crass and The Clash. "It made a massive impact on me. It was brash, so expressive, so positive."

Melody Maker called him an "anarcho-syndicalist." Translate that to anarcho pop-kid. "I always thought anarchy was a good symbol," he pontificates. "None of the band has paid their Poll Tax. We'd rather go to jail. I caught the tail end of the Poll Tax riots in London. Came out of the tube onto Tottenham Court Road, and there it was! Cars turned over, windows smashed, everyone looting. I didn't join in. Just stood there watching, in awe of it all. The only thing I threw was a wobbler."

Poles apart from Gary Newby of The Railway Children, "If I have a threatening letter, I'll pay up. Wouldn't want to go to court over it!" Wet-as-a-puddle!

Mind you, Tim Burgess himself was a Cheshire kid; born in Salford, brought-up in Northwich. Not very scally! More like a 12-year-old Milky Bar kid, like one of those angelic schoolboys on a TV commercial. When I grow up ...

"Tim looks remarkably like Paddington Bear when he wears his brown-flared cords and duffle coat, but without the marmalade sandwich," said issue two of Charlatans-zine, *Looking For The Orange One*, released before they even had a record out!

Tim was kidnapped by The Charlatans from The Electric Crayons, a rock 'n' roll indie band who, in 89, released *Hip Shake Junkie/Happy To Be Hated* (Emergency Records). About as meaningful as *Be Bop A Lula* or *Tutti Frutti*! "You've been waiting ten years for a group like The Electric Crayons, you don't realise it yet, but you have!" ranted the press release. Oh yeah?

In October 89, The Charlatans mailed-out their first demos, printed six T-shirt designs and launched their own label, Dead Dead Good. All co-ordinated by Steve Harrison, manager of Omega Record Shops in Crewe and Northwich. Yet, they still couldn't get a gig in Manchester, rejected by both The International and The Boardwalk!

They began January promoting their debut single, *Indian Rope*, with low-profile gigs in Stoke, Aldershot and Chester. The hype had started. On January 25, they *sold out* The Boardwalk!

By March they'd filled the University; by June The Ritz was packed and their second single, *The Only One I Know* was in the Top Ten, selling 100,000. After being chased by every company in the country, they chose to stay indie and signed to Beggars Banquet. As quick as that! It took Roses six pages to get to the Top Ten; Charlatans do it in just two sentences.

Charlatans became a *Smash Hits* pin-up band, a pop act, kids' telly faves. "It wasn't intentional. It wasn't planned. It's a bit frightening. *Just Seventeen* made up an interview with me! It's worrying as well because everyone in the band went off their heroes once they got in the Top Ten."

Clone Mancs? Far from it! Sure The Charlatans, in their original line-up, played obscure dates with Roses, while Steve Harrison, aka Mr H, used to go on scooter runs with Ian Brown (so goes the legend). But musically, The Charlatans used to be Makin' Time, an early 80s mod band who ruled among the parka classes, supporting The Untouchables. Their use of

---

The Charlatans

Indian Rope 12" Single

RELEASED JANUARY 1990 ON DEAD DEAD GOOD RECORDS THRU NINE MILE / CARTEL

CATALOGUE Nº GOOD ONE (12)

CATCH THIS BLOODY MARVELLOUS BAND AT THE NORTHWICH "RAVE" FRIDAY 15TH DECEMBER.
VENUE - WINNINGTON REC TICKETS £3.00 FROM PICADILLY AND OMEGA MUSIC (NORTHWICH OR CREWE)

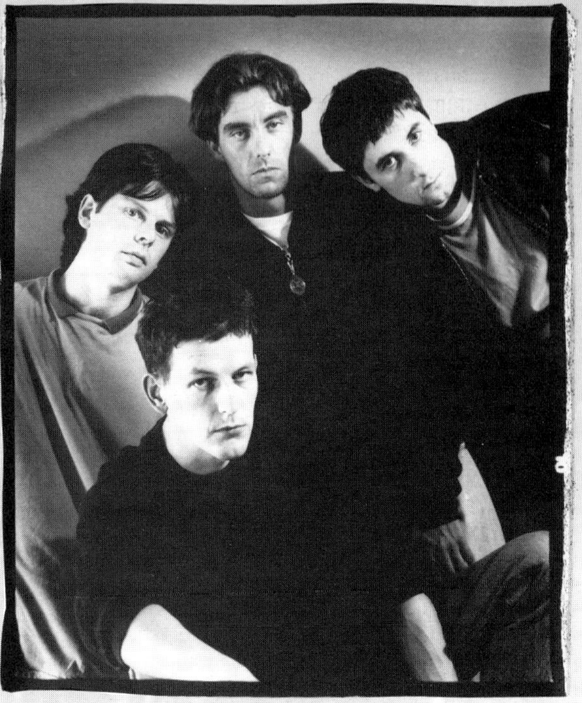
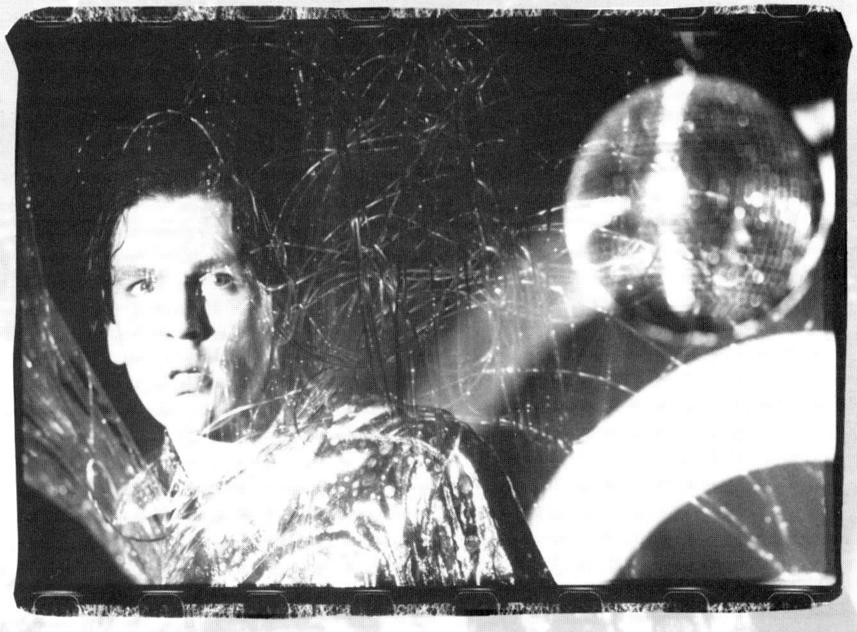

a Hammond organ connected more with mods, The Prisoners, than Inspirals.

The Charlatans were *not* a Manchester band! All but Tim were from Wolverhampton. Like The Soup Dragons, Flowered Up and Primal Scream, they'd caught the Manchester vibe. They were tagged 'scallydelic', like Paris Angels, Northside and Rig. Scallydelic was concocted by bored music journalists for a laugh. The joke went too far. None of these had heard of each other before being linked in the media! "The most-appreciated gags I do anywhere outside Manchester is where I put down the music scene," says Henry Normal, local 'poet' and *City Life* columnist. "I get onstage and say, 'Sorry we're late, but I've just been fitting flares and a hood to the VW ...'"

The 'posh' Charlatans were classes away from the 'scummy' Paris Angels and Northside. Lock-ups, set-ups, fix-ups. Daytime soaps to numb the brain and a bunch of good tunes to keep you sane.

The Boardwalk, September 3, 89: 200 lads in footie-tops, E-ed-up, flailing in flares, cheered their mates on stage. They weren't fashion victims. The hype hadn't started yet. There were no trendies, no students, no journos. Just beer-boys having a laugh. This was Paris Angels, the *East* Manchester posse, Tameside, Denton, Ashton, Guidebridge, places even *more* neglected than North Manchester. Bash Street Kids in Joe Bloggs clothes who blagged their way on to an already overcrowded bandwagon.

"All this daft scally title is just a load of bollocks," spat vox-popper, Rikky Turner. "We've just got a casual attitude and a casual image. Nothing fancy. What's a scally anyway? Something that *The Daily Mirror* mustered up. Scallies are from Liverpool, they died in 83. *Brookside* started. Scallies ended. Know what I mean?"

They preferred to call themselves 'council estate P-funk.' That means George Clinton vs Pink Floyd vs Happy Mondays. The Paris Angels were moochers. Moochers hang around tower-hamlets spliffing up. "We're heading into funkadelic. 70s funk mixed with watered-down 80s funk, added to 60s guitar music." Some mean bastard picked Paris Angels off a street corner, put them on the Manc-bandwagon. Then, just as it was gaining speed heading for the Top 40, they were pushed off, tumbling back into the gutter.

'One nation under a groove/One nation on the move/ Nothing can stop us now', drawled *Don't Fake Mine* optimistically, on compilation *HIT THE NORTH* (Bop). Paris Angels also appeared on another cash-in album *HOME* (Sheer Joy), featuring The Fall, World Of Twist, Swirl, D-Tox, Milltown Bros. Their track was a version of Bowie's *Stay*, a mixed-up musical dream. "The '76 era Bowie was in, was a good era. Especially the flares and cocaine look."

Seven angels, ministers of grace, Rikky, Simon Worral, Mark Adge, Paul Webster, Toity Blake. Not forgetting manic maraca-shaker Jane Gill, the female Bez or Betty-Boop-on-E. And Scott Carey who got sacked from Inspirals for being too rock 'n' roll. Together they produced *Perfume*, debut single on Sheer Joy, a strange choice for a band chased by every major in Britain. Multi-layered wah-wah pop verging on 70s' dross. "I'd been wearing flares for a year before it came back into fashion," Rikky confessed.

Playmates, Northside, were another dispossessed gang claiming what was theirs. A first demo, recorded at Abraham Moss College, proved they couldn't play or sing. The bass was up so loud it sounded like a jumbo take-off. Yet *Moody Places*, *Shall We Take A Trip* and *A Change Is Coming Round*, were the first songs to lyrically document the 'new' scene. Nights at The Haçienda, drugs, council estates, shopping at Eastern Bloc. For that alone, they deserved fame.

"*Moody Places* is dead optimistic. It's a fuck-off to all the snide faces and Jekyll people who try and tell us what to do. They should get out there, get on it and mooch," drawls Dermo.

They were managed by Phil Sachs, boss of an Arndale market clothes scam. "There have always been what I call 'The Boys' in Manchester," he told *MEN*. "They're usually tough boys, into a bit of blagging. I've always specialised in gear for those lads. They'd come out of the nick and straight down here."

Phil called a few local journos. "There's this new band, a scally band, somewhere between Mondays and Roses," he said, "Will you write about them?"

Having argued with Phil, Northside's mate Macca took over. By the time it got to their debut gig, they had a 'vibe'. The week before, Identity had strategically stocked-up with Northside shirts. On September 29, 89, their first gig at The Boardwalk *sold out* ... chaotic,

OPPOSITE
The High, July 1990;
World Of Twist, 1990.

crazy, completely astounding venue and band.

They played the Free Trade Hall supporting Mondays, were signed to Factory and played The Haçienda! Wilson snapped into their cloned Mondays' 'scallidom'. So what if they couldn't play? At least it would *sell*. For Factory, Northside were a marketing exercise. Their drum-kit once belonged to Mondays, and before that still, Buzzcocks, spanning a decade of Manc pop domination. Except where Pete Shelley & Co played three-chord wonders, Northside only had two!

Dermo, Cliff, Tim, Wal. Ugly? Well, you should see them close up! At The Haçienda, the band looked identical to the crowd. Exactly how it should be! Probably the first time since punk that had happened. Northside were high-rise ravers with a taste for Talking Heads, Genesis, Fleetwood Mac, Peter Gabriel ... A sign of things to come in the 90s? A second 'progressive' period?

Their debut single, *Shall We Take A Trip/Moody Places,* was wrapped in a lurid Central Station cover. If Peter Saville/Johnson & Panas/Factory's minimal-grey-typeset styles were the image of the matt-black designer 80s, Central Station are the loud, garish full-colour boom of the 90s. Once their blood-cousins, Mondays, had guaranteed them work, they began to parcel James and other Mancs in bright poster-paint pop art. Soon they even had their own exhibition at the City Art Gallery. Arthur Askey, rather than Marilyn Monroe! Fifteen minutes?

Central Station's lack of subtlety, their splash-it-on *impact* art, fitted Northside. They had no tact either! Their single (banned for its, "Sing LSD," chorus) was awkward, big-footed, but at least it was straight to the point! Unlike South Manc band, World Of Twist, Northside weren't smart enough to understand complicated hallucinogenics.

Watching World Of Twist onstage is like staring into Lewis' window at Christmas. A frivolous box of chocolates, filled with exotic centres; a voyage on the Starship Enterprise; a trip to Disneyworld; a night-out at NASA; swimming in a skip of milk-bottle tops.

World Of Twist were a Sheffield-born synth band that had been kicking around for years. When A&R reps packed Isadora's in March, their set began behind a red satin curtain emblazoned with the camp proclamation: 'Welcome To Our Show!'. Two gigs later, they'd signed to Circa Records.

Seeing World Of Twist at International 1 in August 90, was like seeing that *first* gig all over again. No-one tells you to drop out of school, form a band, have fun. No-one tells Kylie fans about 'indie' until it makes the charts. You find out by chance. Equally, you go on celebrating average Manc bands, unaware how much more is possible.

World Of Twist are not scally-sheep. *They* use their *imagination*. They are Manchester's greatest visual group. Huge rotating cigarette packets, enlargements of their own heads, oil-wheels, optic-fibre curtains, a six foot high ever-decreasing spiral. A hallucinogenic heaven of stage props straight out of an Inspector Gadget cartoon. Like Bond, World Of Twist probably carry lighters that let off tear gas, fountain pens that fire poisoned bullets and pocket-books that expand into full-size parachutes!

Not neglecting the music, World Of Twist combine so many unlikely moods. Imagine pouring Gladys Knight And The Pips, New Order, Syd Barrett, Chairman Of The Board, Phuture, 808 State into a cocktail shaker and jogging them till they all blend into one. Singing LSD without being blatant, they write about the tunnel of your mind, submarines and rainbows. Still too soon to draw any conclusions. As the last words of this book rushed to press, they were just cracking open their cocoon. We had yet to see their wings.

In 1990 there was a new Manc band every week being hyped to heaven. Sunriser, who invited A&R men to a party in their Rusholme bedroom, or Perfect Name, Woodstock-rockers who supported The Charlatans. And The High, Manc veterans, featuring Chris Goodwin and Andy Couzens, original Inspirals/ Roses. They were known as Buzzcocks Foc until they sacked Steve Diggle, releasing a single, *Tomorrow's Sunset*, in 89 (Thin Line). Their own follow-up, *Box Set Go*, was more like The Wedding Present than Happy Mondays.

Welcome to the 90s. Do your own thing, do it to extreme and get rich/happy. Enterprise culture became more than a numbers-game disguising dole figures. Instead of a nation of shop-keepers, we became a nation of T-shirt sellers and musicians. If you can't beat 'em, join 'em. One year of poverty too many. Thatcher's wicked ways worked. Apathy turned

The Perfect Name

PURE BUZZIN' TACKLE

to determination. Not to overthrow the Government, but to fight back by getting your own wedge of this 'never had it so good' prosperity myth.

Bands got sussed, labels took professional advice, suddenly the indie industry was no longer a labour of love. You didn't have to be on a major to get in the charts. Bands like Inspirals built T-shirt empires, no-good street kids like MC Tunes were *Smash Hits* pin-ups; the poorly-paid employees of Piccadilly Records got a loan, bought-out the company and opened up on their own.

"If you're on the dole and you've got nothing going for you, you'll get on to what's going on and make some money out of it," said someone who did just that. "It's a very Thatcherite thing, but that is how you have to exist. Sticking your 'Pay No Poll Tax' poster in the window isn't enough. You have to get out there and do something ... like make money for yourself!"

Welcome to the 90s. The lunatics took over the asylum. The roof-seige of HM Prison Strangeways was Manchester's finest ever rave! Inmates took over the prison, climbed to the roof, installed a sound-system and partyed to the end. Their wives cheered them on waving home-made 'Strangeways Rave On' banners. The seige entered Manchester folklore, commemorated on bootleg T-shirts sold on street-corners. The Smiths' *STRANGEWAYS HERE WE COME* had new significance!

Welcome to the 90s. Assassins' manager, Greg Wilson, "You're gonna have not just love and peace, but ultra-violence. *Clockwork Orange* is the 90s. It's a preparation for the year 2000. That's the 'future'. It's gonna freak people's heads. It's totally unique!"

Welcome to the 90s. World history in the making!
January: Berlin Wall falls.
February: Mandela released.
March-April: British earthquake; Poll Tax riots; siege at Strangeways.
May: Roses at Spike Island; Man Utd win FA Cup.
June: Mad Cow Disease brings meat industry to its knees.
July: England 'nearly' win the World Cup; peace in our time, East and West no longer at war!
August: Confrontation with Iraq ...
September: Manchester Olympic bid fails.
October: **And God Created Manchester** published.

Welcome to the 90s. "People are fed up with what's going down," said Ian Brown at the end of 89. "They've had to take all this shit from an uncaring Government for years. I can't blame them. It hasn't reached breaking point, but when it does, you'll know. They'll take to the streets and bring the bastards down. Just you wait."

Welcome to the 90s. The unthinkable has become reality. From now on, *anything* is possible. The authorities might clamp down on hedonism, but so what? The Manchester music explosion of the late 80s will continue to boom into the next century.

Welcome to the 90s. Decade of revolution. Decade to the end of the century. Decade to recover from the decadent 80s. Decade to save the planet.
The future is ours.

Sarah ChamPion

Child of the 70s. Born in South Manchester with a one-in-two chance of survival. Grew up to be energetic, anarchistic and disorganised. Hip young gunslinger. Rock 'n' Roll wild child.

Discovered John Peel show when she was 13. Launched first fanzine immediately. Saw The Fall when she was 14. Caught The Smiths and visited The Haçienda when she was 15. By the time she reached 16, she was an official write for *NME*, the youngest since Julie Birchill.

At 17, she was Pop Editor of *City Life*, Manchester's listings magazine, and declared war on everyone over 25. By 18 she had her own weekly pop page in the *Manchester Evening News*.

And God Created Manchester is Sarah Champion's first book, written at the age of 19.

Her motto? 'The future is ours.'

Ian T Tilton

Child of the 60s. Born in Blackpool and spent 18 years in his bedroom. Grew to be weird, artistic and a perfectionist; modest, quirky genius with a sick sense of humour.

Doctors and priests warned that self-abuse could cause hearing problems and at the age of 15 he was diagnosed as deaf and forced to abandon his ambition to become a marine biologist. He took up photography.

Moved to Manchester after college to launch a glamorous career as Britain's funkiest music photographer. Within six months made the cover of *Sounds* and began ligging his way round the world on major music commissions.

Photographed album covers for The Smiths and Stone Roses, exhibited *Girders and Other Machines* and *36 Hour Party People* for Granada and published *Thank You Very Glad - The Wedding Present*, and *Guns 'N' Roses*.

He is currently collecting tins of figs and working on four major exhibitions: *Rubbish*, *Backstage*, *The Dinner Party*, *And God Created Manchester*.